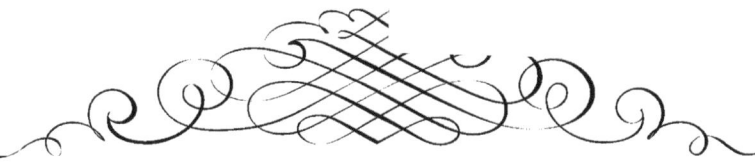

ISBN 978-1-330-37321-7
PIBN 10043198

This book is a reproduction of an important historical work. Forgotten Books uses
state-of-the-art technology to digitally reconstruct the work, preserving the original format
whilst repairing imperfections present in the aged copy. In rare cases, an imperfection in
the original, such as a blemish or missing page, may be replicated in our edition. We do,
however, repair the vast majority of imperfections successfully; any imperfections that
remain are intentionally left to preserve the state of such historical works.

English
Français
Deutsche
Italiano
Español
Português

www.forgottenbooks.com

Mythology Photography **Fiction**
Fishing Christianity **Art** Cooking
Essays Buddhism Freemasonry
Medicine **Biology** Music **Ancient
Egypt** Evolution Carpentry Physics
Dance Geology **Mathematics** Fitness
Shakespeare **Folklore** Yoga Marketing
Confidence Immortality Biographies
Poetry **Psychology** Witchcraft
Electronics Chemistry History **Law**
Accounting **Philosophy** Anthropology
Alchemy Drama Quantum Mechanics
Atheism Sexual Health **Ancient History**
Entrepreneurship Languages Sport
Paleontology Needlework Islam
Metaphysics Investment Archaeology
Parenting Statistics Criminology
Motivational

THE TUDOR
TRANSLATIONS

EDITED BY

W. E. HENLEY

XXII

///

HISTORY OF TWELVE CÆSARS

TRANSLATED INTO ENGLISH BY

PHILEMON HOLLAND

ANNO 1606

With an Introduction by

CHARLES WHIBLEY

Published by DAVID NUTT

IN THE STRAND

Edinburgh : T. and A. Constable, Printers to Her Majesty

THE TABLE

THE TABLE

THE HISTORIE OF
CAIUS CÆSAR CALIGULA

• 1

ERMANICUS father of Caius Cæsar, sonne of Drusus and Antonia ¹, no sooner was adopted by his Unkle Tiberius, but forthwith he bare the office of Questureship five yeeres before hee might by the Lawes ² ª, and after it, the Consulate ³. And being sent into Germanie to the Armie, when A.U.C. 767, 770, 771. upon newes brought of Augustus death, the Legions all throughout stoode out most stifly and refused Tiberius for their Emperour, offring unto him the absolute government of the State (whether their constant resolution or kinde affection herein were greater it is hard to say) he stikled and repressed them, yea and soon after having subdued the enemie, triumphed. After this, being created Consul the second time, and driven forth perforce ⁴ ᵇ, (before he entred into that honorable place) to compose the troubles and to quiet the State in the East parts : when hee had deposed ⁵ the King of Armenia, and brought Cappadocia A.U.C. 772. into the forme of a Province, in the 34 yeere of his age, he died of a long disease at Antiochia, not without suspition of poison. For, besides the blackish and swert spots which were to be seene all over his body, and the frothie slime that ranne forth at his mouth, his heart also (after he was burnt,)

---

¹ Daughter of Antonius the Triumvir, by Octavia, Augustus sister.
² *Annariæ.*   ³ 7 yeeres after.   ⁴ From the said armie, wherewith he was acquainted.   ⁵ *Deiecisset.*

2 : A   1

CAIUS
CÆSAR
CALIGULA
they found among the bones all sound and not consumed: the nature whereof is thought to be such, that if it bee infected with poyson, it checkes all fire and cannot possibly bee burnt.

2

But, as the opinion of the world went, his death contrived by the wicked plot of Tiberius, was effected by the ministerie and helpe of Cn. Piso : who about the same time being President of Syria, and not dissimuling that hee was to offend either father or sonne[1] (as if there were no other remedie but needes he must so doe) made no spare, but beyond all measure dealt with Germanicus (sicke as hee was) most rigorously, both in word and deede. For which, so soone as he was returned to Rome, hee had like to have beene pulled in peeces by the people : and by the Senate condemned he was to die.

3

It is for certaine knowne and confessed, that there were in Germanicus all good parts and gifts as well of body as mind : and those in such measure, as never to any man befell the like : to wit, for shew full of passing beauty, favour and feature, with strength and valour answerable thereto : and for wit excellently well seene in eloquence and learning of both kinds[2]: the very attractive object, he was of singular benevolence[3], endowed with a wonderfull grace and effectuall desire to win mens favour and deserve their love. The onely defect that he had in his making and personage, were his slender shankes : and yet the same also by little and little became replenished with continuall riding on horseback[4] after his meate[a]. Many a time wounded hee his enemie in close fight hand to hand. He pleaded causes of great importance, even as touching the Decree of Triumph[5]. And among other

---

[1] Tiberius himselfe, or Germanicus his adopted sonne. [2] Greeke and Latine. [3] The good wil and affection of men, counted among the gifts of fortune. [4] For they used then no stirrops and therefore the bloud and humours wold descend to the legges. [5] *Triumphale ;* some reade *Triumphalis,* as if he gave not over pleading when he had triumphed, or received triumphall Ornaments.

2

TWELVE CÆSARS

monuments of his studies he left behind him in Greeke, Comædies also. Both at home and abroad civile [b] he was, in so much as he would goe to free and confederate Cities without any Lictors [1]. Where ever he knew any Sepulchers of brave and worthy men to be, there his use was to offer unto their ghosts. Being purposed to enterre in one tombe the olde reliques and bones dispersed of those that were slaine in that great overthrow with Varus, he first gave the assay with his owne hand to gather and carie them together into one place. Moreover, to his slaunderers and backbiters (if he lighted upon them), of what quality so ever the persons were, or how great cause so ever they gave, so milde, so remisse and harmelesse hee was : that notwithstanding Piso reversed and canciled his Decrees, plagued and persecuted a long time his Dependants, yet could he not finde in his heart to be angry with him, before he had for certaine knowne, that hee attempted his person with poysons and sorcerous execrations : and even then verily, hee proceeded no farther against him, but, *more maiorum* to renounce all friendshippe with him, and to give his domesticall friendes in charge to bee revenged, if ought happened to himselfe otherwise than well.

4

Of these vertues hee reaped most plentifull fruite; so liked and loved of his kinsfolke and friendes, (for I let passe all other affinities and acquaintance of his) as that Augustus after hee had continued a long time in suspence, whether he should ordaine him for his Successor or no, recommended him at length unto Tiberius for to be adopted : so highly favoured of the Common people, as that many doe report and write, whensoever hee came unto a place or departed from thence, divers times by reason of the multitude flocking to meete him and to beare him companie, he endangered his owne life in the preasse. As he returned out of Germanie, after the suppressing of seditious tumults and mutinies there, all the Prætorian cohorts every one went out to encounter him upon the way : albeit warning was given before hand by

[1] Sergeants or officers.

3

proclamation, That no more than twayne of them should
goe forth. But as for the people of Rome, of all sexes, ages,
and degrees, they ran out by heapes to meet him xx miles
from Rome.

5

Howbeit, farre greater, and more assured testimonies of
mens judgement touching him appeared at, and after his
death. The very day wherein he left this life, the temples[1]
were pelted with stones[a]: the altars of the Gods cast downe:
the Domesticall *Lares*[b], by some flung out of dores into
the street; yea, and new-borne babes of wedded parents
throwne forth to be destroied[c]. And, that which more is,
the report goeth, that the very Barbarians, notwithstanding they were at variance and civill warre among themselves, yea and had taken armes against us, yet, as it were in
some domesticall and common sorrow[2], agreed all to make
truce and a cessation of armes for a time. Some of their
Princes also and Potentates, to declare their extraordinarie
mourning and regret, did cut off their owne beards and
shaved their wives heads. Yea, the very King of Kings[d]
himselfe, gave over his exercise of hunting: and dissolved
the Societie of his great Peeres and Princes at his table:
which among the Parthians is as much as a Law-steed[3][e].

6

At Rome verily, when as the Citie upon the first rumour
of his sicknesse, in amazednes and heavie chere expected the
messengers that came after; and all of a suddaine in the
evening the voice went currant, (although the Authors were
unknowne,) that now at length he was recovered: running
there was every where from all parts with lights[4] and sacrifices[5] into the Capitoll: yea the very dores of the temple
were like to have been burst open, that nothing might stand
in their way and hinder them, so desirous and earnestly bent
with joy to pay their vowes. In so much as Tiberius was

---

[1] Or, the images of the Gods within the temples.   [2] Touching them all
and every one privatly.   [3] At Rome, *i.* a stay of all Courts and Pleas, in
token of a publick sorrow.   [4] Torches, Tapers, etc.   [5] Which they had
made, *pro salute Germanici, i.* for the health and welfare of Germanicus.

4

awakened out of his sleepe with the shoutes and voices of the people rejoycing, and from every side with one accord resounding this Note,

Salva Roma, salva Patria, salvus est Germanicus.

Safe is Rome, safe is our Country, safe is Germanicus.

Also, when now at the last it was knowne abroad that he was departed this life, the publick sorrow by no comfortable words nor edicts and proclamations could be repressed, but continued still even all the festivall daies of the moneth December [a]. His glory and the misse of him thus deceased, was much augmented also by the outrages of the times ensuing: whiles all men were of opinion (and not without good reason) that the fiercenesse of Tiberius which soone after brake forth, was held in and kept downe by the reverent respect and feare that he had of him.

7

He wedded Agrippina, daughter to M. Agrippa and Julia: by whom he had nine children: of which faire issue twaine being yet Infants were taken away by untimely Death: one died when he was now waxen a jolly boy, passing full of lovely mirth and prety talke; whose counterfait in the habite of Cupid, Livia [1] dedicated in the Chappell of Venus Capitolina: and the same Augustus was wont to kisse while it stood in his bed-chamber, so often as he entred into it. The rest survived their father: three of the female sex, Agrippina, Drusilla and Livia, borne all one after another in the space of three yeeres: likewise as many male children, Nero, Drusus and Caius Cæsar. As for Nero and Drusus, the Senate upon imputations laid by Tiberius, judged them to be enemies unto the State.

8

Caius Cæsar was borne the day next preceding the Calends of September [2], when his Father and C. Ponteius Capito were Consuls. The place of his Nativitie, by the disagreement of writers, is left uncertaine. Cn. Lentulus Gætulicus writeth,

A.U.C. 765.

---

[1] Augusta.   [2] The last of August.

5

THE HISTORIE OF

that hee was borne at Tibur: Plinius Secundus, within the
Country of the Treviri, in a towne called Ambiatinum[1], upon
the very Confluents[2].   For evidence and proofe whereof hee
farther saith, that certaine Altars are there to be seene
carying this Inscription, 'For the child-birth and deliverie
of Agrippina[3].'   But these verses following, divulged soone
after that he came to be Emperour, do plainly shew, that
borne he was in the very Camp, where the Legions wintered.

In castris natus patriis nutritus in armis,
Iam designati principis, omen erat.

Borne in the Camp, in Fathers warres with souldiours rear'd was he;
A signe, that then ordain'd he was an Emp'rour for to be.

I my selfe do find among the Records, that Antium was
the place of his birth.   Plinie refelleth Getulicus, as if he
made a lie by way of flattery, because to the praise of a
young and glorious Prince, hee would fetch some argument
and matter even out of a Citie consecrated to Hercules: and
was the bolder, as he saith to abuse the said Lie, for that,
indeede, a yeere almost before, Germanicus had a sonne
borne at Tibur, named likewise Caius . Cæsar: of whose
amiable childhood and untimely death we have spoken
before.   And as to Plinie himselfe, confuted he is by the
Calculation of the times.   For, they who have recorded the
Acts of Augustus doe all agree, that Germanicus was sent
into Germanie after the time of his Consulship expired,
when as Caius was already borne.   Neither can the Inscription of the Altar one jote make good his opinion : considering that Agrippina was delivered of daughters twice in that
Country.   And what child-birth so ever it was, without
respect and difference of sex, called it is *Puerperium*: for
that in old time folk used to name little girles also *Puerœ*,
like as little boyes *Puelli*.   There is besides, an Epistle of
Augustus written, not many moneths before he died unto
Agrippina his Niece as touching this Caius, (for there was
not now living any other Infant of the like name) in these
wordes: 'I have no longer agoe than yesterday taken order

[1] Or Ambitivum.   [2] The meeting of two rivers.   [3] *Ob Agrippina*
puerperium.

6

TWELVE CÆSARS

with Talarius and Asellius, that with the leave of God they bring the boy Caius upon the 15 day before the Calends of June[1]. I send besides with him of mine owne servants a Physician whom Germanicus (as I have written unto him) may if he will retaine and keepe with him still. Farewell my Agrippina and endeavour to come well and in health to thy Germanicus.' It appeareth I suppose sufficiently that Caius could not in that place be borne, unto which he was conveied from Rome not before he was well-neere two yeares old. And as for those verses, these selfe same evidences likewise discredite them: and the rather, because they have no Author. We are to follow therefore the onely authority that remaineth, of the Records and publick Instrument: seeing especially that Caius evermore preferred Antium before all other retiring places, and loved it no otherwise than his native soile: yea, and by report, was fully minded once (upon a tedious wearinesse that he had of Rome City), to transferre thither even the very seat and habitation of the Empire.

9

He gat his surname Caligula by occasion of a merry word taken up in the Camp, because he was brought up there in the habit of an ordinarie and common souldiour among the rest[a]. With whom, how much besides he was able to doe in love and favour by meanes of his education and daily feeding with them, was most of all knowne; when after the death of Augustus, he onely (no doubt) with his very sight and presence quieted them[2], what time they were in an uprore and at the very point of furious outrage. For they ceased not to mutinie, untill they perceived that he was about to be sent out of the way for danger of the sedition, and appointed to the next City adjoyning. Then and not before, turning to repentance, they staied and held back his coach, and so by prayer averted the displeasure that was toward them.

10

He accompanied his Father also in the Expedition into

[1] 18 of May.   [2] He was then but a child, about 3 or 4 yeeres old.

7

THE HISTORIE OF

Syria: from whence being returned, first hee abode in house with his Mother: and after that shee was banished and sent away, hee remained with his great Grandmother Livia Augusta: whom deceased hee praised in a funerall Oration at the *Rostra*, when hee was as yet but a very youth in his *Prætexta*: and then removed he to his Grandmother Antonia. From her in the twentieth yeere of his age hee was sent for to Capreæ by Tiberius, and upon one and the selfe same day, he did on his virile gowne[a] and withall cut the first downe of his beard, without any honourable solemnitie, such as his brethren before him had at their Commencements. Heere, notwithstanding hee was tempted by all the deceitfull traines that they could devise, who would have drawne and forced him to quarrels, yet gave hee never any occasion, having rased out and quite forgotten the fall and calamity of his mother, brethren and neere friends, as if nothing had befallen to any of them: passing over all those abuses which himselfe had endured with incredible dissimulation: so obsequious and double diligent besides, to his Grandfather and those about him, that of him it was said and not without good cause, 'A better servant and a worse Master there never was[1].'

11

Howbeit, the cruell disposition and villainous nature of his owne, hee could not even then bridle and hold in: but both at all castigations and punishments of such as were delivered over to execution, most willing he was to be present : and also would haunt Tavernes and Brothel-houses, mens wives also suspected for adulterie, going about from place to place disguised under a peruke of false haire[a], and in a side (womans) garment : yea, and most studiously gave his minde to learne the artificiall feate of dauncing and singing upon the Stage. And verily Tiberius was well content to winke heereat and suffer all, if haply thereby his fierce and savage nature might have been mollified and become tractable. Which the old man (as he was a Prince right prudent and one most quick of sent) had foreseene well enough long

[1] Passienus was the Author of this Apophthegm.

before: in so much as divers times he gave out and said openly, That Caius lived to the destruction of him and them all: likewise, That he cherished and brought up a verie *Natrix*[1], which is a kind of Serpent, for the people of Rome, and another Phaethon[b] to the whole world.

12

Not long after, he took to wife Junia Claudilla[2], the daughter of M. Silanus a right noble gentleman. And then, being nominated to succeede Augur in the roume of his brother Drusus, before his investure and installation therein, he was advanced to the sacerdotall dignitie of a Pontifie[3]; a notable testimonie of his pietie, and towardnesse, when as the royall line and imperial Court beeing desolate and destitute of all other helpes[4], Sejanus also suspected and soone after overthrowne, he should thus by small degrees arise to the hope of succession in the Empire. Which hope, the rather to confirme, after his wife aforesaid Junia was dead in childbirth, he sollicited unto filthie wantonnesse dame Ennia the wife of Nævius Macro[5], then captaine of the guard and Pretorian cohorts: having promised her mariage also, in case he ever attained to the Empire: and for assurance hereof he bound it with an oath and a bill of his owne hand. By her meanes being insinuated once into the inward acquaintance of Macro[6], hee attempted, as some thinke, Tiberius with poison: and whiles he was yet living, but labouring for life, commanded his ring[7] to be plucked from his finger: but perceiving, that he gave some suspicion of holding it fast, hee caused a pillow to be forced upon his mouth, and so with his owne hands stifled and strangled him: yea, and when his freed-man[8] made an outcrie at this cruell and horrible act, he gave order immediatly to crucifie him. And verily this soundeth to truth, considering there bee some Authors who write, That himselfe afterwards

---

[1] Commonly taken for a water snake.   [2] For Claudia: as Livilla for Livia, after his ordinary maner, to name women *Hypokoristicos*, by their Diminutives.   [3] A Bishop.   [4] Issew Male, except himself, and Tiberius a very child the sonn of Drusus.   [5] *Enniam, Nævii Macronis.*   [6] Who wrought the fall of Sejanus.   [7] Signet.   [8] Tiberius freed-man.

THE HISTORIE OF

professed, if not the murder done, yet at lestwise his intention, one day to doe it. For, hee made his boast continually, in reporting his owne pietie, That to revenge the death of his Mother and brethren, hee entred with a dagger[1] into Tiberius bed-chamber whiles he lay asleepe; and yet upon meere pittie and commiseration bethought himselfe, flung away the weapon and so went backe againe. Neither durst Tiberius although hee had an inkling and intelligence of his designment, make anie inquisition at all of the matter or proceede to revenge.

13

Thus having obtained the Empire he procured unto the people of Rome, or (as I may so say) to all mankind their hearts desire: being a prince of all that ever were, most wished for of the greatest part of provinciall Nations and of the souldiors, because most of them had known him an infant: and generally of the whole comminalty of Rome, in remembrance of his father Germanicus, and upon compassion they took of that house in manner ruinate and extinct. As he removed therfore from Misenum, albeit he was clad in mourning weed and reverently did attend the corps of Tiberius, yet went he among the altars, sacrifices and burning torches[a] in a most thick throng and joifull traine of such as met him on the way: who beside other luckie and fortunate names called him *Sidus, i.* their starre, *Pullum, i.* their chick, *Pupum, i.* their babe, and *Alumnum, i.* their nurceling.

14

No sooner was he entred into the citie of Rome, but incontinently with consent of the senate and the multitude rushing into the *Curia*, after they had annulled the wil of Tiberius, who in his testament had adjoyned coheire unto him another of his Nephews under age[2], and as yet in his *pretexta*, permitted he was alone, to have the ful and absolute power of all, and that with such an universal joy, that in three moneths space next ensuing and those not fully

---

[1] Rapier or spud.   [2] Tiberius the son of Drusus.

TWELVE CÆSARS

expired, there were by report above 160000 Beastes slaine for sacrifice. After this, when as within some fewe dayes he passed over by the water but to the next Ilands of Campania, vowes were made for his safe returne: and no man there was who did let slip the least occasion offred, to testifie what pensive care he tooke, as touching his health and safetie. But so soone as he was once fallen sicke, they all kept watch by night about the Pallace: neither wanted some, who vowed to fight armed to the very outrance for his life thus lying sicke, yea and devoted their verie lives for him if hee recovered [1][a], professing no lesse in written bils set uppe in publike places. To this surpassing love of his owne Citizens and Countrie men, was adjoyned the notable favour also of foraine states. For, Artabanus King of the Parthians, professing alwaies his hatred and contempt of Tiberius, sought of his owne accord to him for amitie: yea he came in person to a conference with one of his legates (or Lieutenants) that had beene Consul, and passing over Euphrates, adored the Ægles [2] and other militarie ensignes of the Romaines, as also the Images of the Cæsars.

15

Himselfe also enkindled and set more on fire the affections of men by all manner of popularitie. When he had with many a teare praised Tiberius in a funerall Oration before the bodie of the people, and performed the complement of his obsequies most honorably, forthwith he hastened, to Pandataria and Pontiæ, for to translate from thence the ashes of his mother and brother, and that in foule and tempestuous wether, to the end that his pietie and kindnes might the more be seene. And being come to their reliques, very devoutly himselfe with his owne hands bestowed them in several pitchers. And with no lesse shewe in pagent wise, having wafted them first to Ostia with a flag (or streamer) pitched in the poupe or sterne of a galley guided by two rankes of Oares and so foorth to Rome up the Tiber, by the ministerie of the most worshipfull gentlemen of Rome: he conveighed

---

[1] Offred to lay down their owne lives.   [2] The maine standards.

11

THE HISTORIE OF

them within two Fercules (or frames) devised for the purpose
into the Mausoleum, even at noone day when people were
assembled there in great frequencie.   In memoriall likewise
of them he ordained yeerely dirges and sacrifices to be performed with religious devotion to their ghosts by the whole
Cittie.   And more then that, he instituted for his mother
solemn games within the Cirque; and a sacred Chariot
withal wherin her Image to the ful proportion of her bodie
should be carried in the pompe.   But in remembrance of his
father he called the moneth September, Germanicus.   These
ceremoniall duties done, by vertue of one sole Act of the
Senate, he heaped upon his grand-mother Antonia whatsoever honours Livia Augusta had received in her whole time.
His Unkle Claudius, a knight of Rome untill that time and
no better, he assumed unto him for his Colleague in the
Consulship.   His brother Tiberius[1] he adopted the verie
day that he put on his Virile gowne, and stiled him Prince
of the youth.   As touching his sisters, hee caused in all Oaths
this clause to be annexed[2], 'Neither shall I prise my selfe
and children more deere, than I do Caius and his sisters.'
Item, he ordained that in mooving and propounding of
matters by the Consuls unto the Senatours, they should
begin in this form, *Quod bonum*, etc., *i.* That which may be
to the good and happie estate of Caius Cæsar and his sisters,
etc.   In the semblable veine of popularitie, he restored all
those that had beene condemned, confined and exiled, yea he
freely dispensed with them, pardoning whatsoever crimes or
imputations remained still behinde from before time[3].   All
the bookes and registers pertaining to the causes of his
mother and brethren, because no informer or witnesse should
afterwardes neede to feare, he brought together[4] into the
Forum : where protesting before hand, and calling the Gods
to record with a lowd voice, that he had neither red ought
nor medled once therewith, he burnt them.   A certaine
pamphlet presented unto him concerning his life and safety,
he received not, but stood upon this point, That he had

---

[1] His cosin germaine, for such are called brethren.   [2] The forme of oth,
that any man tooke.   [3] As we say, from the beginning of the world to this
day.   [4] *Convectos.*

12

done nothing wherefore he should be odious to any person: saying withall, That he had no eares open for informers and Tale-bearers.

16

The Spintriæ, inventers of monstrous formes in perpetrating filthie lust, he expelled forth of Rome, being hardly and with much ado intreated not to drown them in the deepe sea. The writings of Titus Labienus, Cordus Cremutius and Cassius Severus, which had beene called in and abolished by divers Acts of the Senate, he suffered to be sought out againe, to be in mens hands extant, and usually to be red: seeing that it concerned him principally and stood him upon most, to have all actions and deedes delivered unto posteritie. The Breviarie of the Empire, that by Augustus had beene wont to bee proposed openly, but was by Tiberius intermitted, he published. Unto the Magistrates he granted free Jurisdiction, and that there might be no appealing to himselfe. The Gentrie and knighthood of Rome he reviewed with severity and great precisenesse: yet not without some moderation of his hand. Hee openly tooke from them their horses[1], in whome was found any foule reproch or ignominie: as for those, who were culpable in smaller matters, hee onely passed over their names in reading the Roll. To the ende, that the Judges might bee eased of their labour, unto the foure former decuries hee added a fifth. Hee gave the attempt likewise to bring up againe the auncient manner of Elections, and to restore unto the people their free voices. The legacies due by the last will and testament of Augustus (although the same was abolished): as also of Livia Augusta, which Tiberius had suppressed, he caused faithfully and without fraud to be tendred and fully paide. The exaction called *Ducentesima*[2a] of all bargaines and sales, he remitted throughout Italie. The losses that many a man had sustained by fire he supplied: and if to any princes he restored their kingdomes, hee adjoyned withall the fruicte and profits also of their rents, customes and imposts growing to the Crowne in the middle time between: as namely, unto Antiochus

[1] Publike horses of service.   [2] Some read *Centesimam.*

CAIUS
CÆSAR
CALIGULA
Comagenus who had been confiscate and fined in an hundred
millians of Sesterces. And that he might the rather be
reputed a favourer of all good examples, hee gave unto a
woman, (by condition a libertine) 800000 Sesterces [1], for that
she being under most grievous and dolorous torments, concealed yet and would not to die for it, utter a wicked fact
committed by her Patron. For which things, among other
honours done unto him there was decreed for him a shield of
golde [b], which upon a certaine day everie yeare, the colledges
of the Priestes shoulde bring into the Capitoll, with the
Senate accompanying them, and Noble mens children as well
boyes as girles, singing the praises of his vertues in musicall
verse tuned sweetely in meeter. Moreover, there passed a
decree, that the day on which hee beganne his Empire
should be called *Palilia* [c], imploying thereby, as it were a
second foundation of the Cittie.

17

A.U.C. 790,
791, 793, 794.
He bare foure Consulships: the first, from the Calends of
Julie for ii. monethes: the second from the Calends of Januarie, for 30 dayes: the third unto the Ides of Januarie: and
the fourth unto the seventh day before the said Ides [2]. Of
all these, the ii. last he held joyntly together. The third,
he alone entred upon at Lions [3]: not, as some deeme, upon
pride or negligence: but because, being absent, he could not
have knowledge that his Colleague died just against the very
day of the Calends. He gave a largesse [4] to the people twice,
to wit, 300 sesterces to them a peece, and a most plenteous
dinner he made as oft unto the Senate and degree of gentlemen, as also to the wives and children of them both. In the
latter dinner of the twaine, he dealt over and above, among
the men garments to be worne abroad : unto the women and
children, gardes welts [5], or laces, of purple and violet colour.
And to the ende, he might augment the publike joy of the
Cittie with perpetuitie also, hee annexed unto the feast
Saturnalia one daye more, and named the same *Juvenalis*.

[1] *Ostingenta sestertia.* Some read *Ostoginta*: *i.* 80000, and this commeth
neerer to the truth. [2] The seventh of Januarie. [3] In France. [4] *Congiarium.* [5] *Fascias:* some expound these to be ribbands, garters and gorgets.

14

TWELVE CÆSARS

18

He set foorth games of Sword-fencers, partly in the
Amphitheater of Taurus, and partly within the *Septa* in
Mars feild, into the which he inserted and brought in, certaine troupes of African and Campane Champions to skirmish
by companies : even the very best, selected out of both Countries. Neither was he alwaies himselfe president at these
solemnities and publike shewes, but otherwhiles enjoined the
Magistrates or else his freinds to take the charge of presidencie. As for stage plaies, he exhibited them continually
in diverse places and in sundrie sorts : once also in the night
season, burning lights throughout the Cittie. He skattered
likewise and flung (among the common people) missils[1], of
many and sundry kinds to skamble for : and dealt man by
man, paniers with viandes therein. At which feasting, to
a certaine gentleman of Rome who over against him plyed
his chawes full merily, and fedde right hartily with a greedie
stomacke, he sent his owne part : as also to a Senatour for
the same cause, his letters patents, wherein he declared him
extraordinarily, Prætour. He represented besides, many
Cirq-games, which held from morne to even : interposing
one while, the baiting of Panthers[2]; another while the
Troie-justing and Turnament. But some especiall sports
there were above the rest, and then the Cirq-place was laide
all over with vermillion and Borax Minerall[3] : where none
but of Senatours degree ruled and drave the Chariots. Some
also he put foorth upon a sodaine, namely when as he beheld
from out of the house Gelotiana, the preparation and furniture of the Cirque, some few from the next open galleries
jettying out[4 a], called unto him for the same.

19

Furthermore, he devised a new kind of sight, and such as
never was hearde of before. For, over the middle Space[5]
between Baiæ and the huge piles or dammes at Puteoli containing three miles and 600 paces well neere, hee made a

[1] *Missilia*, small gifts.   [2] Or Leopards.   [3] Red and greene.   [4] *Mænianis.*
[5] An arme of the sea.

15

THE HISTORIE OF

bridge: having gotten together from all parts ships of burden, and placed them in a duple course at Anchor, with a banke of earth cast thereupon, direct and straight after the fashion of the high way Appia. Uppon this bridge he passed to and fro for two dayes together: the first day mounted on a courser richly trapped, himselfe most, brave and goodly to be seene with a chaplet of Oke-brances: armed with a battaile axe, a light targuet and a sword, clad also in a cloke of gold: the morrow after he appeared in the habit of a Chariotier, ryding in a chariot drawne with two goodly steedes of an excellent race: carrying before him Darius a boye, one of the Parthian hostages with a traine of the Prætorian souldiers marching after in battaile raie: and accompanied with the Cohort of his minions in British wagons [1]. Most men I wote well, are of opinion that Caius invented such a kind of bridge, in emulation of Xerxes, who not without the wonder of the world, made a bridge of planks over Hellesponte an arme of the Sea, somewhat narrower than this: others, that by a bruite blazed abroad of some huge and monstrous peece of worke, hee might terrifie Germanie and Britaine, upon which countries hee meant to make warre. But I remember well that beeing a boy, I heard my Grandfather report and tell the cause of this worke, as it was delivered by his owne Courteours, who were more inward with him than the rest: namely, that Thrasyllus the great Astrologer assured Tiberius when hee was troubled in minde about his successour, and more enclined to his naturall and lawfull nephew [2] indeede by lineall descent, That Caius should no more become Emperour than able to runne a course to and fro on horse-backe, through the gulfe of Baiæ.

20

He set forth shewes also even in forraine parts, to wit in Sicilie at Saracose, the games called *Actiaci* [3]: likewise at Lions in Fraunce, playes of a mixt nature and argument: as also a solemne contention for the prise in Eloquence both

---

[1] *Essedis*, Belgick or French.   [2] Tiberius, the sonne of Drusus Tiberius the Emperors son.   [3] Some read *Hasticos*, as running at tilt.

16

TWELVE CÆSARS

Greeke and Latine. In which tryall of maisteries, the report
goeth, that those who were foiled and overcome, conferred
rewards upon the winners, yea and were forced to make compositions in their praise. But looke who did worst, they
were commanded to wipe out their owne writings, either
with a spunge or els with their tongues, unlesse they would
chuse rather to be chastized with ferulars or els to be ducked
over head and eares in the next river [1].

21

The buildings left halfe undone by Tiberius, namely, the
Temple of Augustus, and the Theatre of Pompeius, he
finished. He began moreover a conduict in the Tiburtine
territorie : and an Amphitheatre neere unto the Enclosure
called *Septa* : of the two works, the one [2] was ended by his
successor Claudius, the other was forlet and given over quite.
The wals at Saracose by the injurie of time decaied and fallen
downe were by him reedified : and the temples of the gods
there, repaired. Hee had fully purposed also to build anew
the palace of Polycrates at Samos : to finish Apolloes temple
called Didymeum at Miletum : as also to found and build a
Cittie upon the top of the Alpes : but before all, to dig
through the Isthmus in Achaia : and thither had he sent
alreadie one of purpose, who had beene a principall Captaine
of a Cohort in the Vaward, to take measure of the worke.

22

Thus farre forth as of a Prince : now forward, relate we
must as of a Monster. Having assumed into his Stile many
surnames, for called he was *Pius, i.* kind : *Castrorum filius,
i.* the sonne of the camp : *Pater exercituum, i.* Father of
hosts : and *Optimus Maximus Cæsar, i.* the most gracious
and mightie Cæsar [3], when he hapned to heare certaine
Kings [4] (who were come into the Cittie for to do their
duties and to salute him) contend as they sate with him at

---

[1] *Rhodanus Rhosne.* [2] The conduict. [3] Usurping the Attributes of
Jupiter. [4] Agrippa and Antiochus.

17

THE HISTÓRIE OF

supper, about the Nobilitie of their birth and parentage, hee
cryed foorth

Εἶς κοίρανος ἔστω, εἶς βασιλεὺς.
One Soveraigne Lord, one King let there be [a] :

and there lacked not much but that presently he had taken
the Diademe upon him and converted wholly the shew of
Empire, into the forme of a Kingdome [1] [b]. But being told
that he was mounted alreadie above the heigth and state
both of Emperours and also of Kings [2], thereupon from that
time forward hee began to challenge unto himselfe a divine
Majestie : and having given order and commission, that the
images of the gods, which either for devout worship done
unto them, or for curious workemanship seene upon them,
excelled the rest, (among which was that of Jupiter Olimpi-
cus) should bee brought out of Greece unto Rome, that when
their heads were taken of, he might set his owne in the
place [3]: he enlarged the *Palatium* [4] and set out one part therof
as far as to the forum. Transfiguring likewise and turning
the Temple of Castor and Pollux into a porch or entrie [5],
he stood manie times in the middle between the said two
gods, brethren, and so exhibited himselfe to be adored of all
comers. And some there were who saluted him by the name
of Jupiter Latialis. Moreover he ordained a Temple pecu-
liarly appropriate to his owne godhead, as also priests and
most exquisite Osts [6]. In his saide Temple stood his owne
image all of gold, lively portraied and expressing his full
proportion : the which was daily clad with the like vesture
as himselfe wore. The masterships of the priest-hood by
him instituted, the richest men that were, every time of
vacancie purchased : such as made greatest suite and offered
most therefore. The Osts or sacrifices aforesaid were these
foules, Phœnicopteri [c], Peacocks, Tetraones [d], Numidicæ [e],
Meleagrides [f] and Phesants [g], and those to be sorted by
their kinds ; and so every day killed. And verily, his usuall
manner was in the night to call unto the Moone when she

---

[1] Under Cæsars.   [2] *Principum,* for the Romaine Emperours were called
Principes.   [3] The portraict and proportion of his owne selfe.   [4] The
Palace in that Mount, that stood in *Forum Romanum.*   [5] To his Pallace.
[6] Sacrifices.

18

TWELVE CÆSARS

was at full and shining bright out for to come and ly with him in his armes: but in the day time, he talked secretly and apart with Jupiter Capitolinus: one while by whispering and rounding one another in the eare, otherwhiles speaking more lowde and not without chiding: for he was heard in threatning wise to utter these words, Εἰς γαῖαν Δαναῶν περάω σε, I will remove and translate thee into the lande of the Greeks: untill such time as being intreated (according as he tolde the tale himselfe) and invited first by him for to cohabite, he made a bridge over the temple of Augustus of sacred memorie, and so joyned the *Palatium* and Capitol together[1]. And soone after, to the end that he might be nearer unto him hee layed the foundation of a newe house in the voide base-court of the Capitoll.

23

Hee could in no wise abide to be either reputed or named the nephew of Agrippa by reason of his base and obscure parentage: yea and angrie hee would be, in case anie man either in Oration or Verse inserted him [2] among the images of the Cæsars. But he gave it out openly, that his owne mother[3] was begotten by incest which Augustus committed with his owne daughter Julia. And not content with this infamous imputation of Augustus, the Actiack and Sicilian [4] victories by him atchieved, hee streightly forbad to be celebrated yeerely with solemne holidaies, as beeing unluckie and hurtfull to the people of Rome. As for Livia Augusta his great Grand-mother, he called her ever and anon Ulisses in a womans habite: yea and in a certaine Epistle unto the Senate he was so bold as to lay unto her, Ignobility[5] as descended from a Decurian of Fundi[6] who was her Grandsire by the mothers side, whereas it is evident and certaine by publick records that Aufidius Lingo[7] bare honourable Offices in Rome. When his Grandame Antonia[8] requested secret conference with him, he denied her, unlesse Macro Capitaine

---

[1] From the *Palatium* to the Capitoll.   [2] Agrippa.   [3] Agrippina, supposed to be the daughter of M. Agrippa and Julia.   [4] *Siculasque*, not *Singulasque*.   [5] *i*. Basenes of birth.   [6] Aufidius Lingo, or Lurco.   [7] Or Lurco.   [8] By the father side, to wit, the mother of Germanicus.

THE HISTORIE OF

of the Guard might come in betweene to heare their talke. And so, by such indignities and discontentments as these, hee was the cause of her death : and yet, as some thinke, he gave her poison withall. Neither when shee was dead daigned hee her any honour, but out of his dining chamber beheld her funerall fire as it was burning. His brother Tiberius he surprised suddainly at unwares, sending a Tribune of Souldiours, who rushed in upon him and so slew him [a]. Likewise Silanus [1] his Father in law hee forced to death, even to cut his owne throate with a Razour, picking quarrels to them both and finding these causes : to wit, that the one [2] followed him not when hee tooke sea beeing very rough and much troubled, but staied behind in hope to seize the Citie of Rome into his owne hands, if ought hapned but well unto him by occasion of tempests : the other [3] smelled strongly of a Preservative or Antidote, as if hee had taken the same to prevent his poisons. Whereas, in very truth Silanus avoided thereby the unsufferable paine of being Seasick and the grievous trouble of sayling : and Tiberius for a continuall cough that grew still upon him used a medicine. For, his Unkle Claudius he reserved for nothing else but to make him his laughing-stock.

24

With all his sisters, hee used ordinarily to be naught : and at any great feast hee placed evermore one or other of them by turnes beneath himselfe, while his wife sat above. Of these sisters (as it is verily thought) he defloured Drusilla being a virgin, when himselfe also was yet under age and a very boy : yea, and one time above the rest hee was found in bed with her and taken in the manner by his Grandmother Antonia, in whose house they were brought up both together. Afterwards also when shee was bestowed in mariage upon Lucius Cassius Longinus, a man of Consulare degree, hee tooke her from him and kept her openly, as if shee had beene his owne lawfull wife. Also when he lay sicke, he ordained her to be both beire of all his goods

---

[1] Whose daughter hee had maried.   [2] Silanus.   [3] Tiberius.   [4] His Successour in the Empire.

and Successour also in the Empire. For the same sister deceased, hee proclaimed a generall cessation of Law [1] in all Courts. During which time, a capitall crime it was for any man to have laughed, bathed, or supped together with parents, wife or children. And being impatient of this sorrow, when hee was fled suddainly and by night out of the Citie, and had passed all over Campania, to Saracose hee went; and so from thence returned speedily againe with his beard and haire of head overgrowne. Neither at any time ever after, in making a speech before the people or to his Souldiours concerning any matters were they never so weighty would hee sweare otherwise than by the name of Drusilla [2]. The rest of his sisters, (Livia and Agrippina) hee loved neither with so tender affection nor so good respect, as whom he oftentimes prostituted and offred to be abused by his own stale catamites. So much the more easily therefore condemned he them in the case of Æmilius Lepidus, as adulteresses and privie to his treasons and waite-layings addressed against his person. And he not onely divulged the hand-writings which were sought out by guile and adulteries, but also consecrated unto Mars Revenger those three daggers prepared for his death [3], with a title over them, containing the cause of his so doing.

25

As for his mariages, a man may hardly discerne, whether hee contracted, dissolved, or held them still with more dishonesty. Livia Orestilla, what time she was wedded unto C. Piso, himselfe (being one who came in person to the Solemnization of the mariage) commaunded to be brought home unto him as his owne wife: and having within few daies cast her off, two yeeres after he banished and sent her away; because in the middle time betweene, shee was thought to have had the company [4] againe of her former husband.

---

[1] To signifie a solemne mourning.   [2] *Per nomen*, some reade *Numen, i.* the godhead or divine power: for he equalled her with Venus, and commaunded that she should be worshipped as a Goddesse; and as Dion writeth, named she was Panthea, and women were compelled to sweare by her, as by Juno.   [3] By them, to wit Lepidus and his two sisters: or by him, for their death.   [4] Or sought againe for the company, etc. *repetiisse.*

THE HISTORIE OF

Some report, that being an invited guest at the Nuptiall
supper, he charged Piso sitting over against him, in these
termes, 'Sirra, see you sit not too close unto my wife': and
so, presently had her away with him from the table: and
the next day published by Proclamation, That hee had
met with a mariage after the example of Romulus and
Augustus ᵃ. As touching Lollia Paulina maried already to
C. Memmius, a man of Consular degree and ruler of Armies:
uppon mention made of her Grandmother as the most beautifull Lady in her time, he all of a suddaine sent and called
her home out of the Province[1]: and taking her perforce
from her husband, wedded her and shortly turned her away:
forbidding her straightly for ever the use of any mans body
whatsoever. Cæsonia, for no speciall beauty and favour of
her owne above others, nor yet because she was in the flower
of her youth, (considering shee had beene the mother already
of three daughters by another man): but onely for that shee
was a most lascivious woman and of unsatiable lust he loved
with more ardent affection and constancie: in so much as
many a time he would shew her to his Souldiours in her
haire, clad in a Souldiours Cassocke[2] with a light Target
and an helmet riding close unto him: but to his friends,
starke naked also[3]. When she brought him a childe[4], hee
vouchsafed her then, the name of his wife and not before;
professing and making it knowne, that in one and the selfe
samè day, he was become both her husband and also father of
the Infant of her body borne. This babe he named Junia
Drusilla: whom hee caried about with him through the
temples of all the Goddesses, and bestowed at length in the
lap of Minerva[5], recommending it to her for to be nourished,
brought up and taught. Neither had hee any surer signe
and evidence to believe she was his owne and of his naturall
seede conceived, than her curstnesse and shrewdnesse: and
that qualitie had shee even then at the first, in such measure,
as that with her perilous fingers shee would not sticke to

---

[1] Where she was with her husband aforesaid.   [2] Shorte cloake or horse-
mans coats chlamyde.   [3] Like as Candaules King of Lydia, did to his
friend Gyges.   [4] A daughter.   [5] Goddesse of good arts and sciences.
Virgil, *operum haud ignara Minervæ.*

22

TWELVE CÆSARS

lay at the face and eyes of other small Children playing together with her.

26

Vanitie it were and meere folly, to adjoine hereunto, how he served his kinsfolke and friends, to wit Ptolemæus K. Jubaes son and his owne cousin german[1] (for hee also was the Nephew of M. Antonius by his daughter Selena[a]:) but especially Macro himselfe, yea and Ennia likewise, who were his chiefe helpers and advanced him to the Empire. All of them, in right of their neere affinity, and in consideration of their good deserts were highly rewarded, even with bloudy death. No more respective was hee one whit of the Senate, nor dealt in gentler wise with them: some, after they had borne the highest honours, hee suffred to runne by his Wagon[2] side in their gownes for certaine miles together: and as he sat at supper, to stand waiting one while at the head, another while at the foote of the table, girt with a white linnen towell about them. Others, whom hee had secretly murdred, he continued never the lesse calling for, as if they were alive: giving it out most untruly some few daies after, that they had wilfully made themselves away. The Consuls had forgot by chaunce to publish by proclamation his Birth-day; for which, hee deprived them of their magistracie: and so for three daies space the Common-wealth was without the soveraine authoritie[b]. His owne Questour, who hapned to be nominated in a conspiracie against him, hee caused to be scourged: and the cloathes out of which hee was stripped to be put under the Souldiours feete, that they might stand more steedily whiles they were whipping him. In semblable pride and violence hee handled other States and degrees of Citizens. Beeing disquieted with the stirre and noise that they kept, who by midnight tooke up their standings in the Cirque[3], which cost them nothing, hee drave them all away with cudgels: in which tumult and hurliburly, there were twenty Knights of Rome and above, crowded and crushed to death, as many matrones and wives also, besides an infinite number of the common multitude.

[1] Removed.   [2] *Essedum*, or *earroch*.   [3] Or shew-place.

23

THE HISTORIE OF

At the Stage Plaies, being minded to sow discord, and minister occasion of quarrell betweene the Commons and Gentlemen of Rome: he gave his Tallies[1] forth sooner than ordinarie[c]: to the end that the *Equestria*[2] might be possessed afore-hand even by the basest Commoners that came. At the sword-fight, he other whiles commaunded the Curtaines to be' folded up and drawne together, during the' most parching heate of the sunne: and forbad that any person should be let forth[3]: and then, removing and sending quite away the ordinarie furniture of shewes provided to make pastime, he put forth unto the people for to behold, poore wild-beasts and carian-leane, to bee baited: the basest sword-fencers also and worne with age, to combat: yea, and appointed housholders[4] such as were of quality and well knowne, but yet noted for some speciall feeblenesse and imperfection of body to goe under the *Pegmes*[5][d] and carie them. And divers times hee brought[6] a dearth and famine among the people, by shutting up the garners and Storehouses from them.

27

The crueltie of his nature he shewed by these examples most of all. When Cattell which were to feede wilde beasts prepared for baiting, grew to be sold very deere, he appointed malefactours found guilty to be slaughtered for that purpose. And in taking the review of Gaoles and prisoners therein, as they were sorted according to their offences: he, without once looking upon the title and cause of their imprisonment, standing only within a gallerie, commaunded al in the mids, *a calvo ad calvum*[7][a], *i.* from one bald-pate to another, to be led forth to execution. He exacted of him the performance of a vow, who had promised to doe his devoir in publick sword-fight for the recoverie of his health: and him he beheld fighting at sharpe: neither dismissed he

---

[1] Or Tickets. [2] Roomes and seates in the Theater appointed for the Gentlemen. [3] *Emitti*, some read *amiciri*, *i.* to be covered with Hat, veile, bonet of Bongrace against the sunne. [4] *i.* Citizens. [5] *Pegmatis*, in the dative case, or frames for Pageants. [6] *Induxit.* [7] *Medios*, a *calvo ad calvum.*

24

TWELVE CÆSARS

him before he was victour, and after many prayers. Another there was, who for the same cause had vowed to die. This man being not very forward to pay his vow, hee caused to be dight with sacred hearbs, and adorned with Infules [1], like a sacrifice; and so delivered him into the hands of boyes: who calling hard upon him for the discharge of his vow, should course and drive him through the streets of the City, untill he were throwne headlong downe the steepe Rampier [2]. Many honest Citizens of good calling and estate, after he had first disfigured with markes of branding yrons, he condemned to dig in mines, and to make high-waies, or to encounter with beasts; or kept them creeping with all foure like brute beasts within a cage for the nonce: or else slit them through the mids with a sawe. And those whom hee thus served, were not all of them guilty of any grievous offences: but sufficient it was, if they had a base conceite and spake but meanly of some shew that he exhibited: or because they had never sworne stoutly by his *Genius* [3 b]. Parents he forced to be present at the execution of their owne children. And when one Father excused himselfe by reason of sicknesse, hee sent a Licter for him: another of them immediatly after the heavie spectacle of his sonne put to death, he invited to his own bourd [c]; made him great cheere, and by all manner of courtesie provoked him to jocondnesse and mirth. The Maister of his sword-fights and beast baitings, he caused for certaine daies together to be beaten with chaines [d] in his owne sight: but killed him not quite, before himselfe could no longer abide the stench of his braine by this time putrified. A Poet, the Author of *Atellane Enterludes*, for a verse that he made implying a jest, which might be doubly taken, he burnt at a stake in the very middle shew-place of the Amphitheatre. A Gentleman of Rome, whom he had cast before wild beasts, when he cried out, that he was innocent, he commaunded

---

[1] Ribbands.   [2] Of Tarquinius, as some thinke.   [3] These *Genii* are of a middle essence, betweene men and Gods, called therefore, *Medioxumi*. It signifieth here, the Dæmon, Tutelar angel or spirit of the Prince. For the maner of the Romaines was in flattering wise, thus to sweare, as also by the helth, the life, the honour of their Emperours.

2 : D

to be brought back : and after hee had cut out his tongue, sent him among them againe, (to fight for his life or to be devoured).

28

Having recalled one from exile which had been long banished, he demaunded of him, what he was wont to do there, who made answere thus by way of flatterie, 'I praied,' quoth he, 'to the Gods alwaies that Tiberius[1] (as now it is come to passe) might perish, and you become Emperour.' Hereupon Caligula weening that those whom he had banished praied likewise for his death, sent about into the Ilands[2], to kill them every one. Being desirous to have a Senatour torne and mangled peecemeale, he suborned certaine of purpose, who all on a suddaine as he entred into the *Curia*, should call him enemie to the State, and so lay violent hands upon him : and when they had with their writing yrons[a] all to pricked and stabbed him, deliver him over to the rest, for to be dismembred and cut in peeces accordingly. Neither was hee satisfied, untill he saw the mans limmes, joints and inwards drawne along the streetes, and piled all on an heape together before him.

29

His deeds most horrible as they were, hee augmented with as cruell words. His saying was, That he commended and approved in his owne nature nothing more, than (to use his own terme) *adiatrepsian, i.* unmoveable rigour. When his Grandmother Antonia seemed to give him some admonition, he (as though it were not enough to disobey her), 'Go to dame,' quoth he, 'remember I may do what I wil against all persons whomsoever.' Being minded to kill his owne brother, whom for feare of poison he imagined to be fortified afore-hand with Preservatives[3]; 'What,' quoth he, 'is there any Antidote against Cæsar?' When he had banished his sisters, he threatned them in these termes, saying, That hee had not Ilands[a] onely at commaund but swords also.

[1] Who had banished him.   [2] Where they were wont to live banished.
[3] Or counter-poisons.

TWELVE CÆSARS

A certaine Citizen of Pretour's degree, desired oftentimes from the retiring place where he was at Anticyra [1][b], (into which Isle he went for his health sake) to have his licence continued [2]. But hee gave order he should be killed outright: adding these words therewith, that Bloud-letting was necessary for him, who in so long time had found no good by Hellebor [3]. Once every ten daies, his manner was to subscribe and write downe a certaine number out of the Gaole to be executed, and said withall, That hee cast up his reckonings, and cleared the booke of accompts. When hee had at one time condemned a sort of French-men and Greekes together, hee.made his boast that he had subdued Gallogræcia [4].

CAIUS
CÆSAR
CALIGULA

30

He would not lightly permit any to suffer death, but after many strokes given and those very softly, with this rule and precept evermore, which now became rife and well knowne, 'Strike so [5], as they may feele that they are dying.' Hee executed on a time one whom he had not appointed to die, by error onely and mistaking his name: 'But it makes no matter,' quoth he, 'for even he also hath deserved death.' This speech of the Tyrant [6] out of a Tragædie, hee often repeated, *Oderint dum metuant, i.·* ' Let them hate me so they feare me.' Many a time hee inveighed bitterly against all the Senatours at once, as the Dependants and adhærents of Sejanus, or the Informers against his mother and brethren; bringing forth those evidences which hee had made semblance before were burnt: and therewith excused and justified the cruelty of Tiberius as necessary: seeing he could not otherwise chuse but beleeve so many that made presentments unto him. The degree of Gentlemen he railed at continually, as devoted wholly to the Stage and shew-place. Being highly dis leased upon a time with the multitude favouring as they didp the contrary faction [7] to his [8], 'Would God,' quoth he, 'that the people of Rome had but one neck.' And when

---

[1] By letters or friends that he made.   [2] Renewed.   [3] *i.* By purging.
[4] A Nation mixt of French and Greekes.   [5] *Ita feri*, etc.   [6] Atreus.
[7] Of Chariotiers.   [8] For he favoured the greene Liverie.

THE HISTORIE OF

Tetrinius Latro[a] was by them called for to fight at sharpe
he said, That they also who called for him were *Tetrinii*[1]
every one. It fortuned that five of these *Retiarii*[2], fighting
in their single coates, and together by companies[3], had
without any combat yeelded themselves as overcome to as
many other Champions or Fencers called *Secutores*[4]. Now
when commaundement was given (by the people) that
they should be killed, one takes me up his Trout-speare
againe into his hand and slew all the other five who were
thought the Conquerours. This slaughter he both bewailed
in an Edict as most cruell, and also cursed them that endured
to see the sight.

31

Hee was wont moreover to complaine openly of the condition of his time wherein he lived, as not renowmed by any
publick calamities: whereas the raigne of Augustus was
memorable for the overthrow of Varus: that of Tiberius
ennobled by the fall of scaffolds in the Theater at Fidenæ.
As for himselfe, like hee was to be forgotten, (such was the
prosperity in his daies). And evermore he wished the
carnage and execution of his armies: Famine, Pestilence,
and Skarfires, or some opening chinks of the ground.

32

Even whiles he was at his recreations and disports, whiles
he set his mind upon gaming and feasting, the same cruelty
practised he both in word and deed. Oftentimes as hee sate
at dinner or banquetted, were serious matters examined in
his very sight by way of torture: and the Souldiour that had
the skill and dexterity to behead folke, then and there used

---

[1] Worthy and meet to be put to sword-fight.   [2] So named of a net
that they used in fight to catch their adversarie with: they handled also
a weapon with three tines or pikes like a Trout-speare. They were
called *Threcos*.   [3] *Grogatim dimicantes:* for distinction of those that
were called *Monomachi*, and imploied in single fight.   [4] Otherwise, *Mirmillones*. These were armed, whereas the *Retiarii* were lightly appointed,
and *Tunicati*, traversing their ground nimbly, and seeming otherwhiles
to flie: whereupon the others took their name, *Secutores*, as following
them.

TWELVE CÆSARS

to cut off the heads of any prisoners indifferently without respect. At Puteoli, when he dedicated the bridge, which as we noted before, was his owne invention: after hee had invited many unto him from the shore and strond, suddainly hee turned them all headlong over the bridge into the water. And seeing some of them taking hold of the helmes [1] for to save themselves, he shooved and thrust them off, with poles and oares into the sea. At a public feast [2] in Rome, there chaunced a servant [3] to pluck-off a thin plate [4] of silver from the table [5]: and for this, immediatly hee delivered him to the hang-man for to be executed; namely to have his hands cut off, and hung about his neck just before his brest with a written Title caried before him declaring the cause of this his punishment; and so to be led round about all the companies as they sat at meate. One of these Fencers called *Mirmillones* [6], comming out of the Fence-schoole plaied at wooden wasters with him, and there tooke a fall for the nonce, and lay along at his feete: him he stabbed for his labour, with a short yron skeine that hee had: and withall, after the solemne manner of Victors, ranne up and downe with his garland of Date tree branches. There was a beast brought to the Altar ready to be killed for Sacrifice: he comes girt in habite of these Beast-slayers [7], and with the axe head that he lifted up on high, knocked downe the Minister himselfe, who was addressed to cut the said beasts throat, and so dashed his braines out. At a plenteous feast where there was great cheere, he set up all at once an unmeasurable laughter: and when the Consuls who sate just by him asked gently and with faire language, Whereat he laughed so? 'At what else,' quoth hee, 'but this, That with one nod of my head, I can have both your throats cut immediatly.'

33

Among divers and sundry jests and merie conceites of his, as he stoode once hard by the image of Jupiter, he

---

[1] For this bridge was made of barks.   [2] A great dinner.   [3] Waiting at the bord.   [4] Or leafe.   [5] For tables in those dayes were laid and covered over with silver plates. Plin. lib. 33.   [6] Or *Secutores*, aforesaid.   [7] At sacrifice.

demaunded of Apelles an actour of Tragædies, whether of the twaine he thought to be the greater and more stately, Jupiter or himselfe. And whiles he made some stay ere he answered, he all to tare and mangled him with whipping cheere, praising ever and anone his voice crying unto him for mercy, as passing sweet and pleasant, even when he groned also under his lashes. So often as he kissed the neck of wife or concubine[1], he would say withall, 'As faire and lovely a neck as this is, off it shall goe if I doe but speake the word.' Moreover, he gave it forth many a time, That he would himselfe fetch out of his wife Cæsonia, though it were with Lute-strings[2], what was the reason that he loved her so entirely[a].

34

Neither raged he with lesse envie and spitefull malice, than pride and cruelty, against persons, in manner, of all times and ages. The Statues of brave and worthy men brought by Augustus out of the Capitoll Courtyard for the straightnesse of the place, into Mars-field, he overthrew and cast here and there in such sort, as they could not be set up againe with the Titles and Inscriptions whole: forbidding that ever after there should be any where Statue or Image erected unto any person living, without his advice asked and graunt passed. He was of minde also to abolish Homers verses: 'For why may not I,' quoth he, 'doe that which Plato lawfully did, who banished him[3] out of the Cittie that he framed and ordeined?' The writings likewise and images of Virgil and T. Livius, he went within a little of remooving out of all libraries. The one[4] of these he carped, as a man of no witte and verie meane learning: the other[5], for his verbositie and negligence in penning his Historie. Moreover, as touching Lawiers, (as if he meant to take away all use of their skill and knowledge) he cast out these words many times, That he would surely bring it to passe, they should be able to give none other answere nor councell than according to reason and æquitie[a].

---

[1] Or Paramour.   [2] By cramping and torturing her therewith.   [3] Being a Poet.   [4] Virgill.   [5] Livie.

TWELVE CÆSARS

35

He took from the noblest personages that were, the olde armes and badges[1] of their houses: from Torquatus the collar[2]: from Cincinnatus the curled lock of haire: and from Cn. Pompeius[3], of an ancient stocke descended, the surname of Magnus belonging to that linage. As for King Ptolemeus, (of whom I made report before) when he had both sent for him out of his realme and also honorably intertained him he slewe all of a sodaine, for no other cause in the World but for that as he entred into the Theatre to see the shewes and games there exhibited, hee perceived him to have turned the eyes of all the people upon him, with the resplendent brightnesse of his purple cassocke. All such as were faire, and caried a thick bush of haire growne long, so often as they came in his way, he disfigured by shaving their heads all behind. There was one Esius Proculus (whose father had beene a principall captaine of the formost cohort) for his exceeding tall personage and lovely favour withall named Colosseros[a]. Him hee caused sodainly to be pulled downe from the scaffold where he sat, and to be brought into the plaine within the lists: where he matched him in fight with a sword-fenser of that sort which be called *Threces*[b], and afterwards with another, all armed[4]. Now when he had given the foile twice[5], and gotten the upper hand, he commanded him forthwith to be pinniond and bound fast, and being put into foule and overworne clothes to be led round about the streets to be shewed unto women, and so to have his throat cut in the end. To conclude there was none of so base and abject condition, nor of so meane estate, whose commodities and good parts he depraved not. Against the great Prelat stiled by the name K. Nemorensis[c], because he had many yeares already enjoyed his sacerdotall dignitie he suborned under hand a comcurrent and adversarie mightier than himselfe. When as upon a certaine day of publike games[6], there was greater applause and more clapping

[1] Or Ensignes. [2] Or Cheine. [3] Who afterwards married the daughter of Claudius the Emperour. [4] *Hoplomacho*, with shield and helmet. [5] To the *Threx* and *Hoplomachus*. [6] To wit, sword fight.

THE HISTORIE OF

of hands than ordinarie at Popius the fenser[1], manumising his slave for joy of the fortunate combate which hee had made, he flung out of the Theatre in such hast, that treading upon his own gown skirt he came tumbling down the staires with his head forward: chafing and fuming, yea and crying out that the people of Rome, Lords of all nations, yeelded more honour, and that out of a most vaine and frivolous occasion unto a sword-fenser, than to consecrated Princes, or to himselfe there in personall presence.

36

No regard had he of chastitie and cleannesse, eyther in himselfe or in others. M. Lepidus Mnester the Pantomime[2], yea and certain hostages he kept and loved as the speech went, by way of reciprocall commerce in mutuall impurity, doing and suffering against kind. Valerius Catullus, a yong gentleman descended from a familie of Consuls degree, complained and openly cried out, that hee was unnaturally by him abused, and that his verie sides were weried, and tyred out with his filthie companie. Over and above the incests commited with his owne sisters, and his love so notorious of Pirallis that common and prostitute strumpet, there was not lightly a dame or wife of anie worship and reputation that hee forbare. And those for the most part would he invite together with their husbands to supper: and as they passed by at his feete, peruse and consider curiously; taking leasure thereto after the maner of those that cheapen and buy wares in ouvert market: yea and with his hand chocke them under the chin and make them to looke up, if happily any of them in modesty and for bashfulnesse held downe their faces. And then so often as he listed, out he goes from the refection roome, and when he had called her unto him apart that liked him best, hee would within a little after (even whiles the tokens were yet fresh testifying their wanton worke) returne: and openly before all the companie, eyther praise or dispraise her: reckoning up everie good or bad

[1] *Essedario*, or Champion that use to fight and play his prises out of a British or French Chariot called *Essedum*. [2] A player counterfeiting all partes, and kindes of gesture.

TWELVE CÆSARS

part of bodie and action in that brutish businesse. To some of them, himselfe sent bils of divorsement in the name of their husbands absent, and commanded the same to be set upon the file and stand in publike record.

37

In riotous and wastfull expense [a], he outwent the wits and inventions of all the prodigal spendthrifts that ever were; as having devised a new found manner and use of baines, together with most strange and monstrous kinds of meats and meales: namely, to bath with hote and cold ointments [1]: to drinke off and quaffe most pretious and costly pearles dissolved in vinegar: to set upon the bourd at feastes loaves of bread and other viands to them before his guests, all of golde, saying commonly withall, That a man must either be frugall or els Cæsar. Moreover for certaine dayes together, he flung and scattered among the common people from the Louver of the stately Hall Julia, mony in peeces of no meane valew. He built moreover tall galliasses of ceder timber [b], with poupes and sternes beset with precious stones, carying sailes of sundrie colours, conteining in them baines, large galleries, walking places, and dining chambers of great receit: with vines also and trees bearing apples and other fruit in as much varietie: wherein he would sit feasting in the very day time among quires of musicians and melodious singers, and so saile along the costs of Campania. In building of stately Pallaces and mannor houses in the countrey he cast aside all rules and orders as one desirous to do nothing so much as that which was thought unpossible to be done. And therfore he laid foundations of piles where the sea was most raging and deep withall, and hewed rocks of most hard flint and rag: plains also he raised even with mountaines and by digging down hill tops levelled them equall with the plaines: all with incredible celeritie: as punishing those who wrought but slowly even with death. In summ, (and not to reckon up everie thing in particular) that infinite wealth and masse of Treasure which Tiberius

[1] Or Oiles.

THE HISTORIE OF

CAIUS
CÆSAR
CALIGULA Cæsar left behind him valued at 2700 millians[1] of Sesterces, hee consumed to nothing, before one whole yeare was gone about.

38

Being exhaust therefore and growen exceeding bare, he turned his mind to rapine and polling by sundrie and most nice points; of forged calumniation, of sales, of imposts and taxes. He affirmed plainely, that those held not by lawe and rightfully the freedome of Rome Cittie, whose Auncestours had obtained the grant thereof in these tearmes, to them and their posteritie: unlesse they were sonnes: for, by *Posteri, i.* Posterity, quoth he, ought to be understood none beyond this degree of descent. And when the Letters-pattents and graunts of Julius and Augustus, (late Emperours of sacred memorie) were brought forth as evidences, he bewailed[2] the same as olde, past date and of no validitie. Hee charged those also with false valuation and wrong certificate of their estates[3], unto whom there had accrued afterward (upon what cause soever) any encrease of substance. The last willes and testamentes of such as had beene principall Centurions of the formost Cohorts, as many I say, as from the beginning of Tiberius Empire, had left neither the sayd Tiberius, nor himselfe Heire, he canciled for their unthankfulnesse: of all the rest likewise, he held the wils as voide, and of none effect: in case any person would come forth and say, that they purposed and intended, at their death to make Cæsar their Heire. Upon which feare that hee put men in, beeing now both by unknowen persons unto him, nominated Heire among their familiar friends, and also by pa   among their children, he tearmed them all mockerenated cousiners, for that after such nuncupative wils they continued stil alive: and to manie of them he sent certaine dainties[4] empoisoned. Now such causes as these above-saide he heard judicially debated: having before hand set downe a certaine rate and summe of money, for the raising whereof he sat judicially in Court: and when that

---

[1] *Vicies ac septies millies.* [2] *Deflebat,* or *deflabat, i.* he rejected and despised.
[3] *Perperam editi Census.* [4] *Macteas* or *Mattyas,* such as Marchpanes.

34

TWELVE CÆSARS

summe was fully made up, then and not before hee would
arise.   And (as he was one who in no wise could abide any
little delay) he condemned upon a time by vertue of one definitive sentence above fortie persons, liable to judgement for
divers and sundry crimes: making his boast withall unto his
wife Cæsonia newly wakened out of her sleepe, What a deale
he had done, while she tooke her noones repose.   Having
published an open port-sale of the residue remaining of
furniture provided to set out all shews and games, he caused
the said parcels to be brought forth and sold: setting the
prices thereof himselfe and enhaunsing the same to such a
prick, that some men enforced to buye certaine things at an
extreame and exceeding rate (whereby they were empoverished
and stript of all their goods) cut their owne veines and so
bled to death.   Well knowen it is that whiles Aponius
Saturninus tooke a nap and slept among the seats and stauls
where these sales were held, Caius put the Bedell[1] in mind
not to let slip and overpasse such an honorable person of
Pretours degree as he was: considering, quoth he, that
with his head he had so often nodded and made signes unto
him[2], and thus taking that occasion, he never rested raising
the price whiles he sat and nodded stil, untill there were
fastened upon the man, (ignorant God wote, altogether of
any such matter) thirteene sword-fensers, at nine millians
of Sesterces.

39

In Gaule likewise, when he had sould the jewels, ornaments, and houshold-stuffe of his sisters[3] by him condemned ;
their servants also and verie children at excessive high
prices: finding sweetnesse in the gaine growing thereupon
and thereby drawen on to proceede in that course, looke
what furniture belonged to the old imperiall Court, hee sent
for it all from the Cittie of Rome: for the cariage whereof,
hee tooke up even the passengers wagons that usually were
hired, yea the very jades which served mils and backe-
houses[4]: in so much, as manie times there wanted bread in

---

[1] Or Crier.   [2] As it were, to buy this and that.   [3] Livilla and
Agrippina.   [4] In grinding Corne, and carrying bread.

35

THE HISTORIE OF

Rome: and a number of Termers, such as had matters
depending in lawe, for that they could not make their
appearance in Court at their dayes appointed, by absence
lost their suits. For the selling of which furniture, there
was no fraude, no guile, no deceitful allurement to be devised
that he used not: one while checking each one for their
avarice, and rating them because they were not ashamed to
be richer than he: otherwhiles making semblance of repentance, in that he permitted persons to have the buying
of such things as belongd to the Empire: intelligence was
given unto him, that a certaine wealthy and substantiall
man in that province, had paide 200000 sesterces unto his
officers (who had the bidding of guests unto his owne table)
that by some suttle shift, himselfe might be foisted in among
other guests: neither was he discontented that the honor
of supping with him was prized so high. The morrow after
therfore, as this provinciall man was sitting at a publike
portsale, hee sent one of purpose to tender and deliver unto
him some frivolous trifle (I wot not what) at the price of
200000 sesterces: and withall to say unto him, That take
a supper he should with Cæsar, as a guest invited by his
owne selfe.

40

He levied and gathered new tributes and imposts, such
as never were heard of before: at the first by the hands
of Publicanes; and afterward (by reason of the excessive
gaines that came in) by the Centurions and Tribunes of the
Pretorian cohorts. For he omitted no kind of thing, no
manner of person, but he imposed some tribute upon them.
For all cates that were to be solde throughout the Citie,
there was exacted a certaine taxation and set paiment. For
actions, for suits, for judgements whersoever commensed or
drawn in writing, the fortieth part of the whole summe in
suite went to his share in the name of a tribute: not without a penaltie, in case anie one were convinced, to have
eyther growen to composition or given the thing in question. The eighth part of the poore porters and Cariers
daies-wages: out of the gets also and takings of common

TWELVE CÆSARS

strumpets, as much as they earned by once lying with a man, was payed *nomine tributi*. Moreover to the chapter of the law, this branch was annexed, that there should bee liable to this tribute, not onely the parties themselves that by trade of harlotry gat their living, but even they likewise who kept houses of bawderie: as also that wedded persons should paye for their use of mariage [1].

41

After these and such like taxes were denounced by proclamation, but not yet published abroad in writing, when as through ignorance of the written lawe many trespasses and transgressions were committed [a]: at length, upon instant demaund of the people, he proposed indeede the act, but written in very small letter and within as narrow a place, so that no man might exemplifie the same or copie it out. And to the end that there might bee no kinde of spoile and pillage which he attempted not, he set up a stewes and brothelhouse in the verie Palace, with many roomes and chambers therein distinguished asunder, and furnished according to the dignity and worth of that place. In it there stood to prostitute themselves, maried wives, youths and springals free borne. Then sent he all about to the frequented places as well markets as Halles of resort, certaine *Nomenclatours*, to invite and call thither by name, young men and olde, for to fulfill and satisfie their lust. All comers at their entrance payde money (as it were) for usurie and interest. Certaine persons also were appointed to take note in open sight, of their names, as of such as were good friends increasing the revenewes of Cæsar. And not disdeining so much as the lucre and vantage arising out of hazard and dice-play, hee gained the more by cogging, lying, yea and forswearing (of gamesters). And upon a time, having put over to his next fellow gamester his owne course, to cast the dice for him in his turne: out he goes into the court-yeard and foregate of the house: where, having espied two wealthy gentlemen of Rome passing by,

[1] *Nec non et matrimonia obnoxia essent.* Some interpret this of wedded folke playing false and committing adulterie.

he commanded them to be apprehended incontinently, and condemned in the confiscation of their goods: which done he returnd in againe, leaping for joy and making his vaunt, That he never had a luckier hand at dice.

42

But when he had once a daughter borne, complaining then of his povertie and the heavie charges that lay upon him not onely as Emperour, but also as a father, he gently tooke the voluntarie contributions and benevolence of men toward the finding of the girle her food, as also for her Dowry another day. He declared also by an edict, that he would receive newyeares gifts: and so he stood the first day of Januarie[1], in the porch or entrie of his house Palatine, readie to take what peeces soever of money came, which the multitude of all sorts and degrees, with full hands and bosomes[2] poured out before him. Finally, so farre was he incensed with the desire of handling money, that oftentimes he would both walke bare-footed up and down, yea and wallow also a good while with his whole body upon huge heapes of coyned gold peeces, spred here and there in a most large and open place.

43

In militarie matters and warlike affaires he never dealt but once: and that was not upon any intended purpose: but what time as he had made a progresse to Mevanta, for to see the sacred grove and river of Clitumnus; being put in mind to supply and make up the number of the Batavians whom he had about him for his guard, it tooke him in the head to make an expedition into Germanie. Neither deferred he this disignement, but having levied from al parts a power consisting of legions and auxiliarie forces; and taken musters most rigorously in every quarter, as also raised and gathered together victuals and provision of al sorts in that quantity, as never any other before him the like, he put himselfe on his journey. Wherein he marched, one while in such hurrie and haste, as that the Pretorian cohorts were

[1] Or *a Kalendis, i.* the first day, etc.   [2] Or laps of their clothes.

38

TWELVE CÆSARS

forced (against the manner and custome) to bestowe their
ensignes upon the sumpter beasts backs and so to follow
after: otherwhiles, after such a slow and delicate manner,
as that he would be carried in a litter upon eight mens
shoulders, and exact of the common people inhabiting the
neighbour cities adjoyning, that the high waies might be
swept and watered for the dust, against his comming.

44

After that he was arrived once at the campe, to the end
that he might shew himselfe a sharpe and severe Captaine:
those Lieutenants who had brought aid with the latest,
out of divers and dissituate parts, he discharged with ignominie and shame. But in the review of his armie the most
part of the Centurions who had alreadie served out their
complete time, yea and some whose terme within very few
dayes would have beene fully expired, he deprived of their
places: to wit, the leading of the formost bands, finding
fault forsooth with the olde age and feeblenesse of every one.
As for the rest, after hee had given them a rebuke for their
avarice, he abridged the fees and availes due for their service performed; and brought that same downe to the valew
of 6000 sesterces. And having atchieved no greater exploit,
than taken to his mercie, Adminius the sonne of Cinobel-
linus King of the Britains [1], who being by his father banished,
was fled over sea with a small power and traine about him,
he sent magnificent and glorious letters to Rome, as if the
whole Isle had beene yeelded into his hands: warning and
willing the carriers ever and anon, to ride forward in their
wagon directly into the market place and the *Curia*, and in
no wise to deliver the sayd messives but in the Temple of
Mars unto the Consuls, and that in a frequent assembly of
the Senate.

45

Soone after, when there failed matter of warre, he commanded a few Germanes of the Corps de guard [2], to be

[1] *Batavorum, i.* the Batavorians.   [2] *De Custodia*, or that were prisoners
and in ward.

THE HISTORIE OF

CAIUS
CÆSAR
CALIGULA

transported and hidden on the other side of Rhene, and that news should be reported unto him after dinner in most tumultuous manner, That the enemy was come: which done, he made what haste hee could, and together with some of his friends and part of the Pretorian horsemen he entred the next wood: where after he had cut off the heads of trees and adorned their bodies in manner of *Tropæes*, hee returned into the Campe by torch-light. As for those verily who followed him not in this service, he reproved and checked them for their timorousnesse and cowardise: but his companions and partners in this douty victorie, he rewarded with a new kind and as strange a name of Coronets: which being garnished and set out with the expresse forme of Sunne, Moone, and Stars he called *Exploratorias* ᵃ. Againe, when as certaine hostages were had away[1] perforce out of the Grammer schoole, and privily sent before, he suddenly left his supper, and with his men of armes pursued them as runawaies, and beeing overtaken and caught againe he brought them backe as prisoners bound in chaines, shewing himselfe even in this enterlude also, beyond all measure insolent and intemperate. Now after he was come backe to supper, those who brought him word that the battailes were rallied and come forward in safetie, hee exhorted to sit downe to meate armed as they were in their Corselets: yea and advertised them out of that most vulgar Verse of Virgil: *Durarent, Secundisque rebus se servarent, i.*

Still to endure in all assayes
And keepe themselves for better dayes.

Moreover, amid these affaires, he rebuked most sharply in a proclamation, the Senate and people both, in their absence: for that whiles Cæsar fought battailes and was exposed to so many perils, they could so unseasonably celebrate feastes, haunt also the Cirque, the Theatres, and their retyring places of solace and pleasure.

46

Last of all, as if he meant now to make a finall dispatch for ever of the warr, having embattailed his armie upon the

[1] By his means.

40

TWELVE CÆSARS

Ocean shore, planted his balists and other engins of Artillerie in their severall places, (and no man wist the while or could imagine what he went about) all at once he commanded them to gather fish-shels, and therewith to fill their headpeeces and laps, tearming them the spoiles of the Ocean, due to the Capitol and the Palatium. In token also and memoriall of this brave victorie, he raised an exceeding high turret, out of which as from a watch-towre, there might shine all night long lights and fires for the better direction of ships at sea in their course. And after hee had pronounced publikely a donative to his Souldiours, even an hundred good Deniers a peece; as if thereby hee had surmounted all former precedents of liberality, 'Now goe your waies,' quoth hee, ' with joy. Goe your wayes I say, enriched and wealthy[1].'

47

Turning his minde after this to the care of his Triumph, hee selected and set apart for the pompe (over and above the Captives and runnagate Barbarians) the tallest men of Stature also that were to be found in Gaule : and everie one that (as hee saide himselfe) was *axiothriambeutos*, that is, worthy to be seene in a Triumph, yea and some of the Nobles and principall persons of that Nation : whom hee compelled not onely to colour the haire of their heads yellow like burnished gold, and to weare the same long : but also to learne the Germaines language, and to beare barbarous names. He gave commaundement also, that the Gallies with three rankes of Oares, wherein hee had embarqued and entred the Ocean, should bee convaied to Rome, a great part of the way by land. Hee wrote likewise unto his procuratours and Officers, To provide the furniture of his triumph, with as little cost as might be: but yet the same in as ample manner as never before was the like, seeing they had both might and right to seize all mens goods into their hands.

48

Before his departure out of that Province, hee intended

---

[1] As if with 3l. 2s. 6 pence, they had beene made for ever.

2 : F   41

THE HISTORIE OF

the execution of an horrible and abhominable designement;
even to put to sword those Legions, which long a-goe upon
the decease of Augustus, had made a commotion: because,
forsooth, they had beset both his father Germanicus their
Captaine, and himselfe also, then an Infant. And being
hardly and with much a-doe reclaimed from such a rash and
inconsiderate project, yet could hee by no meanes be stayed:
but stifly persisted in a full minde and will to tith them [1].
When hee had summoned them therefore to a publique
assembly, unarmed, and without their swords which they had
put off and bestowed heere and there, he environed them
with his Cavallerie all armed. But seeing once, that many
of them suspecting where-about he went, slipped away in
sundry places for to resume their weapons if any violence
were offred, himselfe abandoned the assembly and fled,
taking his direct way immediatly to the Citie of Rome,
diverting all his bitternesse and crueltie upon the Senate:
whom, (to avert from himselfe the odious rumours of so great
and shamefull villanies) hee openly threatned; complaining
among other matters that he was by them defrauded and
put by his just and due triumph: whereas, himselfe but a
little before, had intimated and denounced upon paine of
death, that they should not make nor meddle in any matter
about his honours.

49

Being encountred therefore and met upon the way by
Embassadours from that most honourable Order [2], entreating
him to make speed: with a most loud voice, 'Come I will,'
quoth he, 'I will come, I say and this with me heere,' beating
oft upon the swords hilt [3], which he ware by his side. He
made it knowne also by an Edict, That he returned in deede,
but it was to them alone who wished it, namely, the degree
of Gentlemen and the common people. For himselfe would
be no longer a Citizen or Prince to the Senate. He commaunded moreover, That not one of the Senatours should
meete him. And thus, either omitting quite or putting of
his triumph, hee entred the Citie riding ovant, upon his

[1] *i.* To kill every tenth man of them.   [2] Of Senators.   [3] Or haft.

TWELVE CÆSARS

very birth-day: and within foure moneths after came to his end, having attempted and done notable outrages and very great villanies, but plotting still and practising much greater. For hee had purposed to remove his imperiall Court to Antium, and afterwards to Alexandria [1]: but having massacred first the most choise and chiefe persons of both degrees [2]. And that no man may seeme to doubt heereof, there were in his secret Cabinet found two bookes bearing divers titles. The one had for the Inscription *Gladius*, i. the sword: the other, *Pugio*, that is to say, the dagger. They contained both of them the markes and names of such as were appointed to death. There was found besides, a bigge chest full of divers and sundry poisons, which soone after being by Claudius drowned in the Seas, infected and poisoned the same, not without the deadly bane of fishes killed therewith, which the tide cast up to the next shores.

50

Of Stature hee was very tall, pale and wan-coloured: of body grosse and without all good making: his neck and shanks exceeding slender: his eyes sunke in his head, and his temples hollow, his forehead broad, and the same furrowed and frowning: the haire of his head growing thinne, and none at all about his crowne: in all parts else hairie he was and shagged. It was therefore taken for an hainous and capitall offence, either to looke upon him as he passed by from an higher place, or once but to name a Goate upon any occasion whatsoever. His face and visage being naturally sterne and grim, hee made of purpose more crabbed and hideous: composing and dressing it at a look-ing-glasse, all manner of waies to seeme more terrible and to strike greater feare. He was neither healthfull in body nor stoode sound in minde; being a child, much troubled with the falling sicknesse. In his youth, patient of labour and travaile: yet so, as that ever and anone upon a suddaine fainting that came uppon him, he was scarce able to goe, to

---

[1] Or Alexandrea is Antiochea in old Manuscripts. [2] Senatours and gentleman.

43

THE HISTORIE OF

stand, to arise, to recover himselfe and to beare up his head. The infirmitie of his minde, both himselfe perceived, and oftentimes also was minded to goe aside (unto Anticyra[1]), there to purge his braine throughly. It is for certaine thought, that poysoned he was with a Potion given unto him by his wife Cæsonia: which in deede was a love medicine[2], but such an one, as crackt his wits and enraged him. He was troubled most of all with want of sleepe[3]; for, he slept not above three honres in a night: and in those verily hee tooke no quiet repose, but fearefull; and skared with strange illusions and fantasticall imaginations: as who among the rest, dreamed upon a time that hee saw the very forme and resemblance of the sea talking with him. And heereupon for a great part of the night, what with tedious wakefulnesse and wearinesse of lying, one while sitting up in his bed, another while roaming and wandering too and fro in his Galleries (which were of an exceeding length) hee was wont to call upon and looke still for the day-light.

51

I should not doe amisse, if unto this mindes sicknesse of his I attributed the vices which in one and the same subject[4] were of a most different nature: to wit, excessive confidence, and contrariwise, overmuch fearefulnesse. For, hee that set so light by the Gods and despised them as hee did, yet at the least thunder and lightning, used to winke close with both eyes, to enwrap also and cover his whole head: but if the same were greater and somewhat extraordinarie, to start out of his bed, to creepe and hide himselfe under the bed-steede[a]. During his peregrination verily and travaile through Sicilie, after hee had made but a scorne and mockerie at the miracles and strange sights in manie parts there, he fled suddainly by night from Messana, as affrighted with the smoake and rumbling noise of the top of Ætna. And hee that against the Barbarians was so full of threats and menaces, when as beyond the river Rhene he rode in a

[1] An Isle, where grew the best Ellebor, a purgative meete for lunaticke and distracted persons. [2] Or drinke. [3] *Insomnia.* [4] Or person.

TWELVE CÆSARS

Germaines Chariot betweene the Streights, and the Armie marched in thicke squadrons together : by occasion onely that one saide, There would be no small trouble and hurliburly, in case the enemie from any place appeared in sight : forthwith hee mounted on horsebacke and turned hastily to the bridges : but finding them full of Camp-slaves and cariages wherewith they were choaked [1], as one impatient of any delay, he was from hand to hand and over mens heads conveied to the other side of the water. Soone after likewise, hearing of the revolt and rebellion of Germanie, hee provided to flie; and for the better meanes of flight, prepared and rigged shippes: resting and staying himselfe upon this onely comfort : That hee should yet have Provinces beyond sea remaining for him, in case the Conquerours following the traine of their victorie, either seized the Hill tops of the Alpes (as sometimes the Cimbrians), or possessed themselves of the very Citie of Rome, as the Senones in times past did. Heereupon I verily beleeve that the murderers of him afterwards devised this shift, namely to hold up his Souldiours with a loude lie when they were in an uprore, and to beare them in hand that hee laide violent hands on himselfe, affrighted at the fearefull newes of the field lost.

52

As for his apparrell, his shooes and other habite, hee wore them neither after his owne Country-guise, nor in a civile fashion, no nor so much as in manlike manner, nor yet alwaies, I may tell you, sorting with the state and condition of a mortall wight. Beeing clad oftentimes in cloakes of needleworke and embroidred with divers colours, and the same set out with pretious stones: in a coate also with long sleeves: and wearing bracelets withall, hee would come abroade into the Citie. Sometime you should see him in his silkes, and veiled all over in a loose mantle of fine Sendall [2] with a traine : one while going in Greekish slippers [3], or else in buskins: otherwhiles in a simple paire of broges or high shooes, such as common Souldiours emploied in espiall used.

[1] Or guarded. [2] Lawne or Tiffanie. [3] Or Pantofles.

THE HISTORIE OF

CAIUS
CÆSAR
CALIGULA
Now and then also was he seene shod with womens pumps[1]. But for the most part he shewed himselfe abroade with a golden beard[a] carying in his hand either a thunderbolt or a three-tined mace[4b], or else a warder or rod called Caduceus[c] (the ensignes all and ornaments of the Gods) yea and in the attire and array of Venus. Now, for his triumphall robes and ensignes hee used verily to weare and beare them continually, even before any warlike expedition: and sometime the cuirace withall of K. Alexander the great, fetcht out of his Sepulcher and monument.

53

Of all the liberall Sciences, hee gave his minde least to deepe literature and sound learning: but most, to eloquence: albeit he was (by nature) faire spoken and of a ready tongue[3]. Certes if it had beene to pleade and declame against one, were he angred once, he had both words and sentences at will. His action, gesture and voice also served him well: in so much as for very heate and earnestnesse of speech, uneth was he able to stand his ground and keepe still in one place, yet might hee bee heard nothlesse of them that stoode a farre off. When he was about to make an Oration, his manner was to threaten in these termes, namely, That he would draw forth and let drive at his adversarie the keene weapon and dart of his night-studie by candle light; contemning the milder and more piked kinde of writing so farre forth, as that hee said of Seneca, a writer in those daies most accepted, That his compositions which he made were plaine exercises to bee shewed onely: and was no better himselfe, than sand without lime. His wont was also, to answere by writing the Orations of those Oratours who had pleaded well and with applause: to meditate and devise as well accusations and defences of great persons and waighty matters in the Senate; and according as his stile framed, either to over-charge and depresse, or to ease and relieve every man with his sentence: having called thither

[1] Or pinsons.   [2] With three graines like an ele speare.   [3] *Quantumvis facundus:* or, beeing very faire spoken, etc.

46

TWELVE CÆSARS

by vertue of his Edicts, the degree also of Gentlemen to heare him speake.

54

The Arts moreover and maisteries of other kinds hee practised right studiously, even those of most different nature. A professed Sword-fencer [1] he was and a good Chariotier: a singer withall and a dauncer. Fight hee would even in earnest with weapons at sharpe: and runne a race with chariots in the open Cirque, which he built in many places. As for chaunting and dauncing, he was so hotly set thereupon, that hee could not forbeare so much as in the publick Theaters and Shew-places, but that hee would both fall a singing with [2] the Tragædian as he pronounced, and also counterfaite and openly imitate the gesture of the player [3], as it were by way of praise or correction. And verily, for no other cause proclaimed hee (as it is thought) a wake or Vigile all night long; that very day on which hee was murdred, but that by taking the opportunity of the nights licentiousnesse, he might therewith begin to enter upon the Stage. And divers times daunced he by night: but once above the rest, having raised out of their beds three honourable persons that had beene Consuls, and sent for them at the reliefe of the second watch into the Palace; whiles they were much afraid and doubted some extremity he caused them to be placed aloft upon a scaffold, and then suddainly with a great noise of hautbois and sound of shawlmes or Cimbals, out commeth he leaping forth with a palle and cassocke reaching downe to his ankles; and after hee had daunced out the measures to a song, vanished and went his way againe. Now, this man so apt a schollar as hee was to learne all other feates, had no skill at all in swimming [4].

55

Looke, whom he tooke a love and liking unto, he favoured them all exceedingly and beyond all reason. Mnester the

---

[1] *Thrax.*   [2] Or, to.   [3] Or Actour.   [4] A laudable exercise in Rome, as may appeare before in Augustus.

47

THE HISTORIE OF

famous Pantomime [1] he affected so much, as that he bashed
not to kisse him even in the open Theater; and if any
whiles he [2] was dauncing or acting a part, made never so
little noise and interrupted him, hee commaunded the party
to be pulled out of his place, and with his owne hand
scourged him. A Gentleman of Rome chaunced to keepe
some sturre whiles the said Mnester was upon the Stage:
unto him hee sent word peremptorily by a Centurion to
depart without delay, and goe downe to Ostia (there to take
Sea) and so to carie unto King Ptolomæus as farre as into
Mauritania his letters in writing tables, the tenour whereof
was this, 'To this bearer, whom I have sent hither to you,
see you doe neither good nor harme.' Certaine Fencers
called *Thraces* [3] hee made Capitaines over those Germaines
that were of his Guard and Squires to his body. As for
the *Mirmillones* [4], hee deprived them of their armour. One
of them named Columbus, fortuned to foile his concurrent,
howbeit hee had gotten before some small hurt: he made
no more adoe but put poison into the wound, which thereupon he called Columbinum. So much addicted and devoted was he, to the greene faction [5] of Chariotiers, that day
by day hee would take his suppers and make his abode in
their hostelrie [6]. Upon Eutychus a Chariot-driver [7], he bestowed in hospitall gifts at a certaine banquet, two millions of
sesterces. To one of their Chariot-steedes named Incitatus [8],
for whose sake (because he should not be disquieted), he was
wont the day before the games *Circenses*, by his Souldiours
to commaund the neighbours there adjoyning to keepe
silence, besides a Stable all built of marble stone for him,
and a manger made of Ivorie: over and above his caparison

---

[1] A Gesturer or dauncer that counterfaited all parts.   [2] The said Mnester.
[3] Or *Retiarii*, as some think. Others take it to be a generall name of all
Sword-Fencers.   [4] A faction or crew of fencers opposite to the *Thraces*
or *Retiarii*, whom in respect of the *Thraces*, he favoured not.   [5] *Prasina
factioni*.   [6] Or lodging.   [7] Of that green livery.   [8] *Incitato, equo, cuius
causa*, some interpret it otherwise thus: To Incitatus, for whose horse sake ::
taking Incitatus to be the name of the Maister, and not of the horse, because
in the Poet Martiall, there is mention made of Incitatus a famous Chariot
rider and a mulitier. Yet L. Verus Antoninus erected an Image of gold for
on horse that he had named Volucer whiles he lived: and a sepulcher when he
was dead. And why might not this braine-sicke Prince be as absurd?

48

TWELVE CÆSARS

also and harnois of purple, together with a brooch or pen-
dant Jewell of pretious stones at his poictrell: he allowed
an house and familie of servants, yea and houshold-stuffe
to furnish the same: all to this end, that guests invited in
his name might be more finely and gaily intertained. It
is reported moreover that he meant to preferre him unto
a Consulship.

56

As he rioted thus and fared outragiously, many there
were who wanted no hart and good will to assault his
person. But after one or two conspiracies detected, when
others for default of opportunitie held-of and made stay,
two at length complotted and imparted one unto the other
their designment, yea and performed it; not without the
privitie of the mightiest freed-men about him, and the
Capitaines of his Guard. The reason was, for that they
also, beeing nominated (although untruly) as accessarie to
a certaine conspiracie, perceived themselves suspected and
odious unto him therefore. For, even immediatly, by
sequestring them a part into a secret place he brought
upon them great hatred, protesting with his sword drawne,
That die he would upon his owne hand, if they also thought
him worthy of death. Neither ceased hee from that time
forward to accuse one unto the other, and to set them
all together by the eares. Now when these Conspiratours
were resolved and agreed to assaile him during the Palatine
games [a], as he departed thence out of the Theater at noone-
tide, Cassius Cherea Tribune of the Pretorian Cohort tooke
upon him to play the first part in this Action: even hee,
whom being now farre stept in yeeres Caius [1] was wont to
frump and flout in most opprobrious termes as a wanton and
effeminate person: and one while, when he came unto him
for a watch-word, to give him Priapus or Venus: another
while, if upon any occasion he rendred thanks, to reach out
unto him his hand, not onely fashioned but wagging also
after an obscœne and filthy manner.

[1] Caligula.

2 : G   49

THE HISTORIE OF

Many prodigious signes were seene, presaging his future death and murder. The image of Jupiter at Olympia, which his pleasure was to bee disjointed and translated to Rome, did set up all on a suddaine such a mighty laughter that the workmen about it, let their Engines and Vices slip and so ranne all away. And straight-waies came there one in place whose name also was Cassius, that avouched, he had warning and commaundement in a dreame to sacrifice a Bull unto Jupiter. The Capitol ᵃ in Capua upon the Ides of March was smitten with lightning. Likewise at Rome the Porters lodge belonging to the Princes Palace. And there wanted not some who gave their conjecture, that by the one Prodigie was portended danger to the Master of the house from his Guard and the Squires of his person: by the other some notable murder againe, such as in times past had beene committed upon the same day ᵇ. Also, Sulla the Astrologer, when Caius asked his counsell and opinion, as touching the Horoscope of his Nativitie, told him plaine, That most certaine and inevitable death approached neere at hand. Semblably the Oracle at Antium, gave him a caveat, to beware of Cassius. For which very cause, hee had taken order and given expresse commaundement, that Cassius Longinus Proconsull then in Asia, should bee killed: not remembring that the fore-saide Chærea had to name Cassius. The day before he lost his life, he dreamt that he stoode in heaven close unto the throne of Jupiter: and that Jupiter spurned him with the great toe of his right foote, and therewith threw him downe headlong to the earth. There went also for currant prodigies and fore-tokens of his fall, even those occurrents that hapned unto him that very day, a little before he was murdred. As himselfe sacrificed, bespreinct he was with the bloud of the foule Phænicopterus. And Mnester the skilfull Actour above named, represented that very Tragædie¹ which whilome Neptolemus the Tragædian acted at the solemnitie of those games, wherein Philip King of the Macedonians² was killed. And when

¹ *Cinyra.*   ² The sonne of Amyntas.

50

TWELVE CÆSARS

as in the shew or Enterlude entitled *Laureolus*ᶜ, wherein
the chiefe plaier making hast to get away out of the ruine[1],
vomited bloud, many more of the Actours in a second
degree strived a vie to give some triall and experiment
of the like cunning; the whole stage by that meanes flowed
with bloud. Prepared there was likewise against night
another shew, wherein the darke fables reported of Hell
and the Infernall Spirits there, were to be exhibited and
unfolded by Ægyptians and Æthiopians[2].

58

Upon the ninth day before the Kalends of Februarie[3],
about one of the clocke after noone: doubting with himselfe, whether he should rise to dinner or no (for that his
stomacke was yet rawe and weake upon a surfait of meate
taken the day before), at last by the perswasion of his
friends hee went forth. Now, when as in the very cloisture[4]
through which hee was to passe certaine boyes of noble
birth sent for out of Asia (to sing Himnes, and to skirmish
martially upon the Stage) were preparing themselves, he
stood still and staied there to view and encourage them.
And but that the leader and chiefetaine of that crew, said,
He was very cold, hee would have returned and presently
exhibited that shew. But what befell after this, is reported
two manner of waies. Some say, that as he spake unto the
said boies, Chærea came behind his back, and with a drawing blow grievously wounded his neck with the edge of his
sword, giving him these words before, *Hoc age, i.* Mind
this: wherupon, Cornelius Sabinus, another of the Conspiratours, encountred him a front, and ranne him through
in the brest. Others write, that Sabinus, after the multitude
about him was voided by the Centurions (who were privie
to the Conspiracie) called for a watch-word, as the maner
is of souldiers, and when Caius gave him the word, Jupiter,
Chærea cryed out alowde, *Accipe ratum, i.* Here take it sure:
and with that, as he looked behind him, with one slash cut
his chaw quite thorough: also as he lay on the ground and

[1] Of some house represented upon the Stage.   [2] Fit Actours and exposi-
tours of such an argument.   [3] 24 of Januarie.   [4] Or Vault.

51

THE HISTORIE OF

drawing up his limmes together cryed still, That he was
yet alive, the rest of their complices with thirtie wounds
dispatched and made an end of him. For, this mot, *Repete*,
i. Strike againe, was the signal of them all. Some of them
also thrust their swords through his privie members. At the
very first noise and outcrie, his licter-bearers came running
to helpe, with their litter-staves: soone after, the Germans
that were the squires of his bodie came in: and as they
slew some of the murderers, so they killed certaine Senatours
also that were meere innocent.

59

He lived 29 yeares, and ruled the Empire three yeares
10 moneths and 8 dayes. His dead corps was conveyed
secretly into the Lamian hortyards, where being scorched
onely, or halfe burnt in a tumultuary and hasty funerall
fire, covered it was with a few turfs of earth lightly cast
over it: but afterwards, by his sisters now returned out of
exile, taken up, burnt to ashes and enterred. It is for
certain knowen and reputed, that before this Complement
was performed, the keepers of those hortyards were troubled
with the walking of spirits and ghosts: and in that very
house[1] wherin he was murdred there passed not a night
without some terror or fearefull object, until the very house
it selfe was consumed with fire. There dyed together with
him, both his Wife Cæsonia, stabbed with a sword by a
Centurion, and also a daughter of his, whose braines were
dashed out against a wall.

60

What the condition and state was of those dayes, any man
may gather, even by these particulars. For neither, when
this massacre was divulged and made knowen abroad, men
gave credite by and by thereto; but there went a suspicion,
that Caius himselfe had feigned and given out a rumour
of this murder, by that meanes to sound mens minds, and
find, how they stood affected unto him: nor yet had those
conspiratours destined the Empire to anie one. And the

[1] Which hee called a vaut or cloyster, before.

52

TWELVE CÆSARS

Senators in recovering their antient freedome againe accorded so, as that the consuls assembled them not at the first into the *Curia*[1], because it bare the name Julia[2], but into the Capitol: yea and some of them, when their turnes came to speake, opined, That the memorie of the Cæsars should be utterly abolished and razed out, giving advise to pull downe their temples. Moreover, this hath beene observed and noted especially, That the Cæsars, who had to their forename Caius[3], beginning at him first who was slaine in the troublesome dayes of Cinna, dyed all of them a violent death.

CAIUS CÆSAR CALIGULA

[1] A new Senate house in liew of *Curia Hostilia*.   [2] For now the name of the Cæsars and their race became odious, as oppressers of the common weale.
[3] And yet wee reade not so much of Caius one of Augustus sonne, brother of Lucius.

THE HISTORIE OF

THE HISTORIE OF
TIBERIUS CLAUDIUS DRUSUS
CÆSAR

1

A.U.C. 714. S touching Drusus father to this Claudius Cæsar, which Drusus was in times past forenamed Decimus and afterwards Nero; dame Livia wedded unto Augustus even when she was great with child, brought him into the world within three moneths after the said mariage, and folke suspected that begotten he was in adulterie by his (supposed) father in law himself[1]. Certes presently after his birth, this verse went rife in every mans mouth, τοῖς εὐτυχοῦσι καὶ τρίμηνα παιδία,

> On persons great this fortune doth attend,
> That children they may have at three moneths end.

This Drusus in the honorable place of questure and pretureship, being L. Generall of the Rhætian, and so foorth of the Germane warre, was the first Romane Captaine that sayled in the North Ocean: and on the farther side of Rhene caste those trenches of a straung and infinite worke which yet at this day be called Drusinæ[2]. Many a time he put the enemy to sword, and when he had driven him as farre as to the inmost deserts, gave not over chasing and pursuing,

---

[1] Augustus: and not by Tiberius Nero, his mothers husband.　　[2] Or Drusianæ, Tacit.

TWELVE CÆSARS

untill there appeared unto him the likenesse of a Barbarian woman [1], more portly than a mortall wight, which in the Latine tongue forbad him to follow the traine of victorie anie farther. For which acts atchieved, he enjoyed the honour of a pety Triumph [2], and had the Triumphall ornaments graunted unto him. After his pretureship, he entred immediatly upon the Consulate: and having enterprised a second expedition thither, fell sicke and dyed in his summer campe, which therupon tooke the name of *Castra Scelerata* [3a]. His corps by the principall Citizens and Burgesses of the free-burrowes and colonies, by the decuries also and orders of the Scribes [4] (who met them in the way and received it at their hands) was conveied to Rome and buried in Marsfielde. Howbeit the armie reared in honour of him an honorarie tombe [5] (or stately herse) about the which every yeare afterwards upon a certain set day, the souldiers should runne at tilt, keepe jousting and turnament: the Citties likewise and States of Gaule, sacrifice and make publike supplications to the gods. Moreover the Senate among many other honors, decreed for him a Triumphant arch of marble, with Tropees thereto in the street [6] Appia: as also the surname of Germanicus to him and his posterity for ever. Furthermore he is thought to have caried a mind no lesse glorious than civil and popular. For over and above the conquests gained of his enemies, he wan also from them Royall spoyles [7]: and oftentimes to the uttermost hazard of his life coursed and chaced the General of the Germans all over the field: neither dissembled he, but gave it out, that one day he would restore unto the Commonwealth their ancient state and libertie againe. Whereupon, I suppose, some presume to write, that Augustus had him in jelousie and suspicion: called him home out of his Province: and because he lingred and delayed his returne, made him away by poyson. Which verily put downe I have, because I would not seeme to pretermit such a matter, rather,

TIBERIUS
CLAUDIUS
DRUSUS
CÆSAR

[1] Representing Germanie.   [2] Called Ovation.   [3] The wicked and mischievous camp.   [4] Or Chancelors.   [5] Which the Greeks call *Cenotaphium*, i. an empty tomb.   [6] Or port-way.   [7] Which he tooke from their cheife generals.

55

THE HISTORIE OF

than for that I thinke it either true or probable: considering that Augustus both loved him whiles hee was alive so
entirely, as that he alwayes ordained him fellow-heire with
his sonnes, (like as he openly professed upon a time in the
Senate house) and also commended him after his death so
highly, that in a solemne oration before the bodie of the
people he prayed unto the Gods, To vouchsafe his owne
Cæsars to be like unto him: and to grant himselfe one day
such an end as they had given him. And not contented
with this that he had engraven upon his tombe an Epitaph
in verse which he himselfe composed, he wrot also the historie of his life in prose. By Antonia the yonger, he
became father verily of many children, but three onely
hee left behind him at his death, namely, Germanicus,
Livilla, and Claudius.

2

This Claudius was borne at Lyons, in the yeare when
Julius Antonius and Fabius Africanus were Consuls, upon
the Calends of August, that very day on which the altar
was first dedicated there unto Augustus: and named he was
Tiberius Claudius Drusus: and a while after, when his elder
brother was adopted into the family Julia, hee assumed into
his stile the surname of Germanicus. Being left an infant
by his father, all the time in manner of his child-hood and
youth[1], piteously handled he was with sundrie diseases, and
those tough and such as stucke long by him: in so much
as being dulled and enfeebled thereby both in mind and
bodie, he was not thought in the very progresse of riper
age, sufficient and capable of any publike office or private
charge: yea and many a day after that hee came to full
yeares and had sued out his liverie, hee was at the dispose
of another, even under a pedagogue and governour; whom
in a certaine booke himself complaineth of, terming him a
barbarous fellow, and no better sometime than a mulitier[2],
set over him of purpose to chastice and punish him most
cruelly for everie light cause and occasion whatsoever. By

[1] Or growing age.   [2] *Olim superiumentarium*, rather a maister of
mulitiers.

TWELVE CÆSARS

reason of this his sicknesse, both at the sword-play which he and his brother joyntly exhibited in memoriall of their Father, he sat as president (not after the accustomed manner) lapt in a cloake; and also upon his commensement day, when he was to put on his virile gowne, about midnight without anie honorable attendance and solemne traine, brought he was in a licter into the Capitoll[a].

3

Howbeit, from his very child-hood, he employed no meane studie in the liberall sciences. And oftentimes gave good proofe even in publike place of his proceedings in them all: yet could he never for all that reach to any degree of dignity, or yeeld better hope of himselfe for the time to come. His mother Antonia, was wont to call him *Portentum hominis*, *i.* The Monster and fantasticall shewe of a man, as if hee had not beene finished but onely begunne by nature: and if shee reprooved anie one for his foolishnesse she would saie, Hee was more sottish then her Sonne Claudius. His Grandmother Augusta[1] thought alwaies most basely of him, as who used neither to speake unto him but very seldome, nor to admonish him, unlesse it were in some sharpe and short writing, or els by messengers going between. His sister Livilla, when she heard that he should be one day Emperour, openly and with a lowd voice detested and wished farre from the people of Rome so hard and miserable a fortune.

4

And no mervaile: for to the end that it might be more certainly knowen what opinion his great Uncle Augustus[2] had of him both wayes[3], I have set downe certaine Articles and principall pointes gathered out of his owne Epistles. 'I have,' quoth he, 'my good Livia talked and conferred with Tiberius as you charged me, about this, namely, What is to be done to your Nephew Tiberius, at the solemnity of the Martiall Game[4]. Now, wee are both agreed that it

---

[1] Otherwise called Livia and Julia the mother of Drusus.   [2] His Grandmothers brother by the mothers side.   [3] As well good as bad.   [4] In honour of Mars Revenger.

THE HISTORIE OF

must be determined and set down once for all what course
we should take and follow with him: for, if he be ἄρτιος[1],
and as I may so say ὁλόκληρος[2], what doubt need wee to
make, but that he is to bee trained and brought by the
same oportunities of time and degrees[3] by which his brother
was. But if we perceive him ἠλαττῶσθαι καὶ βεβλάφθαι
καὶ εἰς τὴν τοῦ σώματος καὶ εἰς τὴν τῆς ψυχῆς ἀρτιότητα[4] ::
we must not minister matter to men, τὰ τοιαῦτα σκώπτειν
καὶ μυκτηρίζειν εἰωθόσι[5], for to deride both him and us.
For we shall ever find trouble and vexation inough, in case
of every occasion of time presented unto us, we should deliberate, μὴ προϋποκείμενου ἡμῖν[6], whether wee thinke him
able to menage honorable Offices in the State or no. Howbeit for the present (concerning such things whereof youle
aske mine advise) I mislike it not, that he have the
charge of the Priests dyning chamber, during these Martiall
solemnities aforesayd, so that he wil suffer himselfe to be
admonished and schooled by Silanus sonne, a man allyed
unto him, that he do nothing, which may be noted[7], or
derided. That he should behold the games *Circenses* from
out of the Pulvinar[8], in no wise can I allow. For being exposed so, to the sight of men in the very forefront of the
Theatre, he wil be eyed and observed: neither like we in
any hand, that he should goe up the Albane mount, or
abide at Rome during the Latine Holy-dayes[9]. For if he be
able to accompany and follow his brother to that mountaine,
why is he not as wel made Provost of the Cittie the while?
Thus, my Livia, you have our opinions delivered, as who
are fully resolved, that once for al somewhat must be put
downe as touching the whole matter, least we be evermore
wavering between hope and feare. You may also if it
please you impart unto our (niece) Antonia thus much of
this our letter.' Againe, in another Epistle: 'As for young

[1] Sufficient. [2] Sound throughout and perfect. [3] Or steps. [4] To
be impaired or disabled and maimed, as wel for the sufficiencie of body as integrity of mind. [5] Who are wont to make good game and scoffe at such
things. [6] If it be not resolved upon and set downe aforehand by us.
[7] *Conspici* or *despui, i.* spit at. [8] A Bedloft at the Games *Circenses*,
whereon the images of the gods are layed. [9] In the absence of the Consuls
attending the sacrifice upon the Albane Hill.

58

TWELVE CÆSARS

Tiberius [1], I for my part whiles you are absent, wil dayly invite him to supper, that he may not suppe alone with his Sulpitius and Athenoderus. And I could wish with al my hart that he would more soundly and lesse μετεώρως [2] make choice of some special one, whose gesture habite and gang, hee might, silly soule as he is, imitate.

'Ατυχεῖ λίαν ἐν τοῖσι σπουδαίοις πάνυ.
He comes farre short (when he is matched) with men of deepe understanding.

But looke, when his mind is not wandering out of the way, the generosity of his heart appeareth sufficiently.' Likewise in a third letter: ' Your nephew Tiberius my sweet Livia, if I doe not wonder, that when he declamed that he could please and content me, I pray God I be dead. For how he that in his dayly talke speaketh so ἀσαφῶς [3] should be able when he declameth, to deliver his mind and what he hath to say σαφῶς [4] I cannot see.' Neither is there anie doubt to be made, but that after all this, Augustus ordained and left him indued with no honorable office, save only the Sacerdotall dignitie of Augurs: nay he nominated him not so much as his Heire, but in a third degree and descent, even among those that were well neere Strangers: and that in a sixth part onely of his substance: and by way of legacie bequeathed unto him not above 800000 sesterces.

5

Tiberius his unkle conferred upon him when he sued for honorable dignities the Ornaments of Consuls. But when he instantly demaunded still, not imaginary but true magistracies indeede, he wrote backe unto him in his writing tables thus much onely, That he had sent unto him fortie peeces of golde [5] to spend at the feast *Saturnalia*, and to bestow in puppets and trifling gaudes, at the same time. Then, and not before, casting aside all hope of preferment and reall dignities, hee betooke himselfe to rest and quietnesse of life, lying close, one while within hortyardes of pleasure and

---

[1] Claudius. [2] Superficially. [3] Darkly and confusedly. [4] Cleerely and plainely to bee understood. [5] Every one worth 15s. 7d. *ob*, or one hundred sesterces.

THE HISTORIE OF

in a manner house without the Cittie: and lurking other whiles in a withdrawing place out of the way in Campania. And by his daily acquaintance and companie keeping with most base and abject persons besides the olde infamous note of sluggardie and foolishnesse hee incurred an ill name for drunkennesse and Dice-play: notwithstanding, that all the while he thus led his life, he never wanted the publike attendance and reverent regard of men seeking unto him.

6

The order of Gentlemen elected him twice for their patrone, in an embassage that was to be sent and delivered in their owne behalfe: once when the Consuls required to have the cariage of Augustus his corps upon their own shoulders to Rome: a 2 time when they were to congratulate with the same Consuls for the suppressing of Sejanus. Moreover, they were wont in shewes, and in the Theatre, when he came in place, to arise up and lay off their mantels[1] in respective honour of him. The Senate also ordained, that to the ordinarie number of the Priests or Guild-brethren called *Augustales*, who were by lot chosen, he should be admitted extraordinarily: and soone after, that his house, which by misfortune of a skare-fire he had lost, should at the Cities charges be reedified; as also the priviledge to deliver his minde and opinion in the Senate, among those who had beene Consuls; which decree of theirs was reversed and annulled: whiles Tiberius[2] alleadged by way of excuse his imbecillity, and promised to repaire the foresaid losse out of his owne private purse and liberality. Yet when hee laye upon his death-bed, he both named him among his heires in a third raunge, and in a third part of his estate, and also bequeathed him a legacie of two millions of Sesterces: yea recommended him besides by name unto the armies, to the Senate likewise and people of Rome in the ranke of other his especiall friends and kinsfolke.

7

At length under Caius[3] his brothers sonne, who at his

[1] As wee use to veile bonet or do of our hats.   [2] The Emperour.   [3] Caligula.

TWELVE CÆSARS

first comming to the Empire sought by all manner of enticing allurements, to gaine the good opinion of a bountifull and gracious prince, he began first to beare office of state, and continued Consul together with him for the space of two moneths: and it fortuned at his first entrance into the Forum with his knitches of rods, that an Eagle soaring thereby, setled upon his right shoulder. He was pricked also and allotted unto a second Consulship, against the 4th yeare following. Divers times he sat as president of the solemne shewes in Caius his turne: what time the people cryed *Feliciter* [1], partly to the Emperours [2] Uncle, and in part to Germanicus his brother.

8

Yet lived hee neverthelesse subject to the contumelious reproches of the World: for if at anie time, hee came somewhat with the latest and after the houre appointed to a supper, hardly and with much adoe, was there any roome made for to receive him, and not before hee had gone round about the tables where guests were set, for to finde a place: likewise, whensoever he took a nap, and fel a sleepe after meate (which was an ordinarie thing with him) the buffons [3] and jesters about him, made good sport, pelling him with olive and date stones: other whiles also they would by way of merriment awaken him with the clappe of a ferula or lash of some whip. They were wont likewise to glove his hands (as he lay snorting a sleep) with his shoes [4], that as he suddenly awaked hee might rub his face and eyes therewith.

9

Neither verily could he avoide divers dangerous troubles: first in his very Consulship: for, beeing behind hand and over slacke in taking order with the workmen for the making and erecting of Nero and Drusus Statues, who were

---

[1] All haile or happinesse. [2] Caligula. [3] *A Copreis*: See Tiberius Nero Cæsar, cap. 61, *vel a Tropæis*, such as would play Bo-peepe and hide themselves when they had done some unhappinesse. [4] For whiles they sat or leaned upon pallets at their meat they put off their shoes.

THE HISTORIE OF

TIBERIUS
CLAUDIUS
DRUSUS
CÆSAR

Cæsars[1] brethren, hee had like to have beene remooved and put out of that honorable office: afterwards, as eyther anie stranger, or one of his own house informed ought against him, he was continually and sundry manner of waies molested. But when as the Conspiracie of Lepidus and Getulicus came to light, being sent among other Embassadours to congratulate Caius in the name of the City, hee was in jeopardy of his very life: whiles Caius chafed and fumed with great indignation, that his Unkle chiefly of all others was sent unto him, as it were to governe a child: in so much, as some have not stuck to report on writing, that hee was turned also headlong into the river in his cloathes and all as he came apparailed. From which time forward, never spake hee to any matter proposed in the Senate, but last of all those, that had beene Consuls, as being in reproachfull wise and to his disgrace asked his opinion after them all. There was received likewise against him the examination of a forged will, wherein himselfe also had beene a witnesse and put-to his seale. Last of all, hee was forced to disburse eight millions of Sesterces for a fine or Income at his entrance into a new Priesthood: by occasion whereof, his estate being so much decaied, driven he was to those streights, that for his disability to keepe credit and satisfie the debt due unto the Chamber of the City by an Edict of the Citie Treasurers[a] according to the law *Prædiatoria* hee hung up to be sold in *vacuum*[2].

10

Having passed the greatest part of his time in running thorough these and such like troubles, at length in the fiftieth yeere of age, hee attained to the Empire, and that by a strange and wonderfull hap. Being among others excluded by the Conspiratours that layed waite for Caius life, what time they voided all the Companie about his person, under a colour as if he desired to be a part himselfe alone in some by-place, this Claudius had stept aside and retired into a lodging or parlour called Hermeum: and not long after,

[1] Caius Caligula.   [2] His lands and goods were forfeited and so were published in table as voide and vacant.

62

TWELVE CÆSARS

being affrighted at the rumour of that murder, slily crept
forth and conveied himselfe up into a Solar[1] next adjoyning,
and there hid himselfe betweene the hangings that hung
before the dore. Whiles hee lurked close there, a common
Souldiour chauncing to runne too and fro that way, espied
his feete, and by earnest enquirie and asking who he was,
hapned to take knowledge of him : who having drawne him
forth of the place (when as for feare hee fell downe humbly
at his feete and tooke hold of his knees) saluted him by the
name of Emperour. From thence he brought him immediatly to his other fellow Souldiours, who as yet stoode
wavering and wist not what to doe but fare and fume. By
them was he bestowed in a Licter : and for that his owne
servants were fled scattering heere and there they also by
turnes one after another supported the said Licter upon
their shoulders : and so was he brought into the (Prætorian)
Camp, all sad and amazed for feare : pitied also by the
multitude that met him on the way, as if some innocent
had been haled to execution. Being received within the
trench and rampire, lodged he was alnight among the
souldiours-watch with lesse hope of his a good deale than
confidence. For the Consuls together with the Senate and
the cohorts of the citie-souldiers, seized the Forum and the
Capitol, with a purpose to claime and recover the common
libertie : and when himselfe was sent for, by a tribune of
the commons into the *Curia* to sit in consultation and give
his advise about those matters that were thought good to
be propounded, he made answere, That deteined he was
perforce and by constraint. But the next morrow, when as
the Senate grewe more colde and slacke in following and
executing their foresaid projects, (by reason of their tedious
trouble and discord who dissented in opinion) whiles the
multitude also standing round about, demaunded by this
time one Ruler and him[2] by name, he called the Souldiours
in armour[3] to an assembly, and suffred them to take their
oath of alleageance, and sweare to maintaine his imperiall
dignity : therewith promised unto them 1500 Sesterces[4] a

[1] A garret.   [2] Claudius.   [3] *Armatos*, or *armatus, i.* himselfe armed.
[4] *Quina dena Sestertia.* See Josephus.

63

THE HISTORIE OF

peece : the first of all the Cæsars that obliged unto him
the Souldiours fealty by a fee and reward.

11

Having once established his Empire, hee thought nothing
more deere and behovefull than to abolish the remembrance
of those two daies, wherein there was some doubtfull question
about the change and alteration of the State. Of all deedes
and words therefore, which had passed during that time he
made an Act there should be a generall pardon and perpetuall oblivion : which also hee made good and performed
accordingly. Onely, some few Colonels and Centurions, out
of that crew which conspired against Caius, he put to the
sword : as well for example sake, as for that he had certaine
intelligence, they required to have him also murdered.
Then presently turning and bending his minde to the duties
of pietie and kindnesse, hee tooke up no forme of oath,
either with more devout religion or oftener, than by the
name of Augustus. He gave order, that for his Grandmother Livia, there should be graunted Divine
honours ; as also in the stately pompe of the Cirque
Solemnities, a Chariot drawne with Elephants, like unto
that of Augustus : semblably, for the soules of his owne
parents departed, publick Dirges and Funerall feasts : and
more than so, particularly in the honour of his father Cirque-
Plaies and games every yeere upon his birth-day : and in
memoriall of his mother, a coach to be led and drawne along
through the Cirque : and the surname of Augusta, which
by his Grandmother was refused. In remembrance of his
brother[1] (to celebrate whose memoriall hee omitted no
occasion) hee exhibited a Greeke Comædie at the solemne
Games held in Naples : where, by sentence of the Umpiers
and Judges he received a coronet therefore. Hee suffered not
so much as M. Antonius to passe unhonoured, nor without
a thankfull mention and remembrance : protesting one time,
and that by an Edict, That so much the more earnest he
was, to have men celebrate the Birth day of his father
Drusus, because upon the same day, his Grandfather An-

[1] Germanicus.

TWELVE CÆSARS

tonius also was borne. The Marble Arch, decreed verily in times past by the Senate to be erected for Tiberius[1] neere unto the Theater of Pompeius, but for let, hee finished. And albeit hee abrogated and repealed all the Acts of Caius, yet the day of his death, although it were the beginning of his Empire, he forbad to be registred among feasts in the Kalendar.

12

But in honouring himselfe he was sparie, and caried a civile modestie. The fore-name of Emperour he forbare: excessive honours hee, refused: the Espousals[2] of his owne daughter, the birth-day also of his Nephew her sonne, he passed over in silence, onely celebrating it with some private ceremonie and religious complements within house. He restored no banished person, but by the authority and warrant of the Senate. That hee might bring with him into the *Curia*, the Capitaine of the Guard and Tribunes[3] of the Souldiours: Item, that those Actes might bee ratified and stand in force, which his Procuratours had set downe in judging of causes, hee obtained by intreatie. He made suite unto the Consuls for a licence, to hold Faires and Markets, for his owne private Manors and Lands. In Commissions and Examinations of causes held by the Magistrates, he would oftentimes be personally present and sit as one of the Commissioners. To the same Magistrates, when they exhibited any Plaies or Games, himselfe also with the rest of the multitude would arise up, and both with hand and voice[4] doe them honour. When the Tribunes of the Commons repaired unto him before the Front of his Tribunall, he excused himselfe unto them, for that by reason of straight roome hee could not give audience unto them otherwise than standing upon their feete. Therefore, within a small time hee purchased so much love and favour, as that when newes came (to Rome) that forlaied and slaine hee was in his journey to Ostia, the people in a great tumult and uprore, fell to banning and cursing both the Souldiours as Traitours,

---

[1] His Unkle.   [2] Or solemnity of nuptiall contract.   [3] Colonels.
[4] By applause and acclamation.

THE HISTORIE OF

and the Senate also as Paricides: neither ceased they thus
to force against them, untill first one messenger, and then
another, yea and soone after many more were produced by
the Magistrates to the publick Rostra, who assured them
that he was alive and approached homeward.

13

Yet continued hee not for all this secured every way from
the danger of secret practises and wait-laying : but assailed
hee was as well by private persons, as whole factions and conspiracies, yea and sore troubled in the end with civill warres.
For there was a man, one of the Commons, taken about
midnight neere unto his bed-chamber with a dagger. Found
there were likewise twaine of the Gentlemens degree, in the
open streete with a staffe having a blade in it [1], and a
Hunters wood-knife waiting for him : the one to assault his
person when he was gone forth of the Theater : the other
as hee sacrificed at the temple of Mars. Now there had
conspired to make an insurrection and to alter the State,
Gallus Asinius and Statilius Corvinus, the Nephewes of
Pollio and Messalla the Oratours, taking unto them for
their Complices many of his owne freed-men and servants.
As for civile warre, kindled it was and begun by Furius
Camillus Scribonianus, Lieutenant generall of Dalmatia :
but within five daies quenched cleane and suppressed; by
reason that the Legions, which had chaunged their oath of
alleageance, in remorce of conscience and touch of religion
repented, after that upon signification given of a journey
to their new Generall, neither the Ægles could bee dight
and trimmed, nor the militarie ensignes plucked up and
removed [2].

14

To his first Consulship he bare foure more : of which, the
two former jointlie and immediatly one after another: the
rest ensuing, with some time betweene, to wit, each one in
the fourth yeere : and as for the third, hee had no precedent
for it in any other Prince, as being substituted in the voide

---

[1] Some cal this a Jacobs staffe. [2] Ominous and unlucky signes.

66

TWELVE CÆSARS

place of a Consull deceased. A precise Justicer he was, ministring Justice, both when hee was Consull, and also being out of that Office, most painfully; even upon the solemne daies instituted for him and his: yea, and otherwhiles upon the auncient festivall daies and such as were religious. He followed not alwaies the prescript rule of lawes, moderating either the rigour or the lenity of penalties, by equity and reason, according as he stood affected to a cause: for, both unto those he restored their actions and gave leave to commense them a new, who in the Court before private Judges[1] had once lost their suites, by claiming more than was due: and also, such as were convict of some greater deceite and cousenage, he condemned to be cast unto wilde beasts: exceeding therein the ordinarie punishment by law appointed.

15

Moreover, in the examination, triall, and deciding of controversies, he was wonderous variable: one while circumspect, wary, and of great insight: otherwhiles as rash and inconsiderate: now and then also foolish, vaine, and like to one without all reason. When hee reviewed upon a time the Decuries of Judges, and put whom hee thought good from their Jurisdiction: one of them, who had answered to his name, and concealed the immunity and priviledge that he had by the benefit of children, he discharged quite, as a man desirous to be a Judge[2]. Another of them being molested and called into question by his adversaries before him, as touching a matter betweene him and them, and pleading withall for himselfe, That it was a case to be tried not extraordinarily (by Cæsar) but by the common course of Law, and in an ordinary Court of deputed Judges: he compelled immediatly to handle and decide his owne cause before him: as who in his proper businesse should give proofe how indifferent a Judge he would be heereafter in the matter of another. There was a woman that would not acknowledge her owne sonne. Now, when by evidences and arguments alleadged *pro et contra* on both sides, the

[1] Of private matters, as Prætours and Centumvirs.   [2] And therfore, ambitious.

67

THE HISTORIE OF

question rested in equall ballance doubtfull, he awarded, that she should be wedded to the young man[1]: and so forced her to confesse the truth and to take him for her child. Most ready he was to give judgement on their side, who made appearance in Court when their adversaries were absent: without any respect and consideration, whether a man slacked and staied by his owne default, or upon some necessitie. One cried out upon a forger of writings, and required, That both his hands might be cut off. Hee made no more a-doe, but forthwith called instantly, to have the hangman sent for, with his chopping knife and butchers block, to do the deed. There hapned one to be called judicially to the barre, For that being a forainer he bare himselfe as a Romaine Citizen: and when the advocates of both sides grew to some little variance about this circumstance, namely, Whether the party Defendant ought to make his answere and plead his owne cause in a gowne[2] or a cloake[3], he then, as if hee would make exceeding shew of pure and uncorrupt equitie, commaunded him to shift and change his habite often in the place, according as he was either accused or defended. Moreover, sitting in judgement to decide a certaine controversie, when he had heard what could be said, hee pronounced sentence out of a written table, as it is verily thought, to this effect, That hee judged on their side, who had alleadged the truth. For which prankes hee became base and contemptible, in so much as every where, and openly he was despised. One, to excuse a witnesse[4], whom Cæsar[5] had called for out of a Province, alleadged in his behalfe, and said, Hee could not possibly come in time and be present, dissimuling the cause thereof a great while: at length, after manie long demaunds, what the reason might be, 'Why,' quoth hee, 'the man is dead at Puteoli.' Another when hee gave him thankes, for suffering a person accused to have the benefite of a triall and to bee defended, added more-over these wordes, 'And yet this is an usuall and ordinarie thing.' Furthermore, I my selfe have heard olde folke say, that these Lawyers and Barristers were

---

[1] The plaintife himselfe. [2] As a Citizen of Rome. [3] As a forainer.
[4] Or deponent. [5] Claudius.

68

TWELVE CÆSARS

wont to abuse his patience so much, that as hee was going downe from the Tribunall[1], they would not onely call upon him to come backe againe, but also take hold of his gowne lappet and skirt, yea and otherwhile catch him fast by the foote, and so hold him still with them. And that no man need to mervaile heereat, there was one of these Greeke Lawyers, who pleading before him hapned in earnest altercation to let fall these words, Καὶ συ γέρων εἶ καὶ μωρός, i. Thou art both old, and a foole besides. And verily it is for certaine knowne, that a Gentleman of Rome, accused before him for his obscene filthinesse and unnaturall abuse of women, (although untruly) as having an enditement framed against him by his enemies that were mighty: when he saw common strumpets cited and their depositions heard against him, flung his writing steele and the bookes which he had in his hand, with great ubraiding of him also for his foolishnesse and cruelty, even at his very face, so as he rippled and hurt therewith his cheeke not a little.

16

He bare also the Censureship: an office that a long time had beene discontinued, after Paulus and Plancus the Censours: but even this very place he held with an uneven hand and as variable a minde, as the event and successe ensuing. In the review taken of Romaine Gentlemen, hee dismissed without shame and disgrace, a young man charged with many infamous villanies, howbeit one whom his owne father testified upon his knowledge and triall to bee right honest: saying withall, That he had a Censor of his owne. To another youth, who was in a very bad name for spoiling of maidens, and adulteries committed with wives, he did no more but give warning, either more sparily to spend him selfe in those young and tender yeeres of his, or else more warily at least-wise, to goe to worke: adding thus much beside, 'For why know I,' quoth hee, 'what wench thou keepest?' And when upon the intreaty of his familiar friends he had taken of the infamous note which was set upon the name of one, 'Well,' quoth he, 'let the blot yet

Marginal note: TIBERIUS CLAUDIUS DRUSUS CÆSAR

Marginal note: A.V.C. 800, 801.

[1] Or judgement seat.

THE HISTORIE OF

remaine still to be seene [1].' An honourable man and a principall personage of the Province Greece, howbeit ignorant
in the Latine tongue, he not onely rased out of the ranke
and roll of Judges, but also deprived of his freedom in
Rome, and made him a meere alien. Neither suffred he
any man to render an account of his life, otherwise than
with his owne mouth, as well as every one was able, and
without a patrone to speake for him. Hee noted many
with disgrace, and some of them without their knowledge,
as mistrusting no such thing: yea, and for a matter that
had no precedent, namely, because without his privity and a
pasport obtained they went forth of Italy: one also among
the rest, for that in the Province he accompanied a King in
his traine: alledging for example, that in his Auncestours
daies Rabirius Postumus for following of K. Ptolomæus into
Alexandria to save and recover the monie which he had lent
him, was accused before the Judges, of Treason to the State.
Having assaied to put many more to rebuke with great
imputation of the Inquisitours negligence, but with greater
shame of his owne: looke whomsoever he charged with
single life [2], with childlesse estate or poverty, those lightly
he found guiltlesse, as who were able to prove themselves
husbands, fathers, and wealthy. Certes, one there was, who
being accused to have laied violent hands upon himselfe,
and wounded his owne body with a sword, stript himselfe
naked, and shewed the same whole and sound, without any
harme in the world. Many other Acts he did of speciall
note whiles he was Censour as namely these: He commaunded a silver Chariot sumptuously wrought and set out
to sale in the streete Sigillaria, for to be bought and broken
all to peeces openly. Item, in one day he published 20
Edicts or Proclamations: and ij. among the rest: in the
one whereof hee gave the people warning, That when their
Vineyards bare Grapes plentifully, they should pitch [3] their
vessels very well within: in the other, he did them to
understand, That there was nothing so good against the
stinging of a Viper, as the juice of the Ughtree.

[1] *Litura tamen extet.* Some read *extat, i.* yet the blot remaineth: meaning the
filthines of the fact. [2] For these matters would beare action. [3] Or enhuile.

TWELVE CÆSARS

17

One expedition and no more hee undertooke, and that was
very small. When the Senate had by Decree allowed him
Triumphall ornaments, hee supposing that a bare title
of honour was inferiour to the majestie of a Prince and
Emperour, willing also to enterprise some exploit, whereby
he might win the due glorie of a complet triumph, made
choise before all other Provinces of Britaine; attempted by
none since Julius (Cæsar) of famous memorie, and at that
time in a tumultuous uprore, for that certaine revolts and
rebels fled from thence, were not rendred. As he sailed
from Ostia thitherward, twice had he like to have beene
cast away and drowned, by reason of the strong blustring
Southerne winde Circius, neere unto Ligaria, hard by the
Ilands Stoechades [a]. Having therefore travailed by land,
from Massiles as farre as to the Cape Gessoriacum [1], he
crossed the seas from thence into Britaine: and in very
few daies [2], without battaile or bloudshed, part of the Iland
yeelded to his devotion. So, in the sixth moneth after his
first setting forth hee returned to Rome, and triumphed
with most sumpteous pompe therefore prepared. To the
sight of which Solemnitie, hee suffred not onely the Presidents and Governours of Provinces to have recourse into the
Citie, but also certaine banished persons. And among the
enemies Spoiles, hee set up a navall Coronet, and fastened it
to the Finial of his house Palatine, hard by another civick
guirland, in token and memoriall of the Ocean by him sailed
over and subdued. After his triumphant Chariot rode
Messallina his wife in a Coach: then followed those gallants
also [3], who in the same warre had attained to triumphall
ornaments: the rest went on foote and in their rich robes
garded with purple: onely Crassus Frugi mounted upon a
brave Courser trimly trapped, and arraied himselfe in a
triumphant mantle of estate, for that now twice hee had
atchieved that honour.

---

[1] Where Calais standeth, or Bulloin, as som thinke.　[2] 16 according
to Dio.　[3] Mounted likewise.

THE HISTORIE OF

18

Hee was at all times most carefull and provident for the Citie¹, especially that the market might bee well served with victuals: what time, the Æmilian Ædifices (or Tenements) were on fire and continued still burning, hee remained two nights together in the place called Diribitorium: and when the multitude of Souldiours and household servants failed, hee called together by meanes of the Magistrates, the Commons of the Citie out of all the streetes and Parishes to come in and helpe, setting before him his chests full of money: exhorting them to doe their best for the quenching of the fire: and readie for to pay presently every one a good reward according to the paines hee tooke.   Now, when corne and victuals were growne very scarce, (such was the continuall unseasonable weather that brought barrainnesse)he was upon a time in the middes of the market place² deteined by the multitude and so assayled and pelled what with reviling taunts and what with peeces of broken bread, that hardly and with much adoe he was able to escape, and no otherwise than by a posterne gate, unto the Pallace.   Wherupon be devised all the means he possibly could to bring into the Citie provision of corne and victuals, even in the winter season.   For, he not onely proposed certaine set gaines to all cornemasters, that would venture for graine, undertaking himselfe to beare all the losse that should happen unto anie of them by tempest: but ordained also great fees and availes for those that would builde ships for such traffique and merchandise, according to the condition and quality of each one: Namely for everie Romane Citizen exemption from the lawe Papia Poppæa: for enfranchised Latines, the freedome of Romane Citizens: and for women, the priviledge and benefit of those that had 4 children, which constitutions stand in force and be observed at this day.

19

---

¹ When so ever you read in Suetonius (City) absolutely, understand therby Rome: *Kat' exocheen:* as one would say, The City of all Cities: an ordinarie phrase in other Romain writers: according as Virgil hath fitly expressed in this verse, *Eclog.* i.: *Urbem quam dicunt, Romam,* etc.
² Or Forum.

TWELVE CÆSARS

Many works he finished, and those rather for greatnesse, huge, then for use, needfull. But the chiefe and principall were these: The conduit of water begun by Caius. Item a scluse[1] to let out and draine the lake Fucinus; and the haven[2] at Ostia: although he knew well enough, that the one[3] (of the twaine) Augustus had denied unto the Marsians who continually entreated him about it: and the other[4] intended oftentimes in the designment of Julius Cæsar of sacred memorie, was for the difficultie thereof layde aside. The two colde and plenteous fountaines[5] of the water Claudia, of which the one beareth the name of Cæruleus, the other of Curtius or Albudinus, as also the new river of Anio[6] he conveied and brought to Rome all the way, within stone-work: and then derived and devided the same into many and those right beautifull pooles[7]. He went in hand with the mere Ficinus in hope of gaine as well as of glorie: when some there were, who would have bound themselves in covenant and promise, to draine the sayd marrish at their owne private charges, in case the grounds being once made drie might be graunted unto them in freehold. Now, for the length of three miles, partly by digging through the hill, and partly by hewing out the rocke before him, hee finished the channell at last with much adoe and after eleven yeares labour: albeit thirty thousand men were at worke continually about it and never rested between. The Pere at Ostia beforesayd he made, by drawing an arme of the sea about, on the left and right hand both: and with all, at the mouth and entrance thereof, where now the ground lay deepe, raising an huge dam or pile against it. For the surer foundation of which pile, he drowned before hand that ship, wherein the great Obelisk had beene trans-

---

[1] Or Gott.   [2] Or Pere.   [3] The drawing of the lake Ficinus.
[4] *Alterum, i.* the Pere at Ostia. But because there is no mention made in Julius Cæsars life of this Pere or haven, some read for *Alterum* in this place *Cæterum:* and then the word *Alterum* before, is meant of the second worke of these three, denied unto the Marsians, etc. *Cæterum, i.* but intended oftentimes in' the designement of Julius, etc.   [5] Or heads.   [6] *Novi Anionis:* some read *novi opere, i.* within new stonework.   [7] Or Cisternes.

THE HISTORIE OF

ported out of Ægypt: and when hee had supported it with buttresses of many stones, hee planted aloft upon the same an exceeding high watch-towre to the patterne of that Pharus at Alexandria, to the end that by the fires burning there, in the night season, vessels at sea might direct their course.

21

Hee dealt often among the people great doles and Congiaries. Many shewes and games likewise hee exhibited, and those magnificent: not such onely as were usuall and in accustomed places: but those that were both newly devised and also brought into use againe, whereas they had of auntient time beene discontinued: yea and where no man else before him had ever set forth anie. The games for the dedication of Pompeius Theatre, which being halfe burnt hee had reedified [1], he gave a signall to begin from out of his Tribunall [2] erected in the *Orchestra*: seeing that before time, when hee had sacrificed and done his devotions in the houses above and came downe from thence through the mids

of the Theatre and assembly, not one would once arise and give applause, but sat still and kept silence. He set out also the Secular games and playes [3], as if they had beene exhibited by Augustus over soone, and not reserved unto their full and due time: and yet himselfe in his owne histories writeth: That whereas the sayd solemnities had beene intermitted, Augustus long after by a most exact calculation of the yeeres reduced them into order againe. By occasion whereof, the voice of the cryer was then ridiculous and laughed at, when after the solemne manner he called the people, to behold those games and playes, which no man had once seene alreadie, or should ever see againe: whereas there survived yet many who had seene them before: yea and some of the actours, who in times past had beene produced, were then likewise brought forth upon the stage. Oftentimes also he represented the Circensian games

---

[1] For, the stage therof was consumed with fire.　　[2] Or seate of state.
[3] Which were solemnized once in the revolution of one hundred yeeres or one hundred and tenne as some write.

74

TWELVE CÆSARS

in the vaticane, and otherwhiles after every 5 courses[1] hee brought in the baiting of wild beastes. But in the greatest Cirque of all which was beautified with barr-gates of marble stone and goales all guilded (whereas before time they had beene made of soft sandstone and wood), hee appointed proper and peculiar places for the Senatours, who had wont before time to behold the same sports here and there. Beside the races for the prise of Chariots drawen with foure steeds: he represented also the warlike Troie pastime, and the baiting of Leopards: which the troup of the Pretorian horse-men slew, having for their leaders the Tribunes and the Captaine himselfe. Moreover, hee brought into the shewplace Thessalian men of armes, whose manner is to chase about the cirque wild buls, until they be tyred: then to mount them, and by the hornes to force them downe to the ground. As for shewes of sword-fensers, hee exhibited them in many places, and after divers and sundrie sorts. One, that was kept every yeare within the Prætorian camp, without any baiting and sumptuous provision of furniture. As for that, which was ordinarily set out and formally with baiting and other preparations in Mars field at the *Septa*: in the same place likewise, another extraordinary one and of short continuance, which he began to call *Sportula*, because he proclaimed at first when he exhibited it, That he invited the people thereto, as it were to a sodaine supper and short pittance, such as men use to bid themselves unto. And in no kind of sport or gaming represented unto them, was he more civile, familiar and better disposed to passe the time away: in so much as putting forth his left hand, he togither with the common sort, would both by word of mouth tell, and with his fingers also number the peeces of gold as he tendred them unto the winners; and many a time by way of exhortation and entreaty provoke the people to mirth; ever and anon calling them Sirs[2]: yea, and betweene whiles intermingling bald, and far fetcht jests. As for example, when the people called for one Palumbus[3 a] to play his prises, hee promised to let them have him, if he

---

[1] Of Chariot running. [2] Or, my maisters, *Dominos*. [3] The name of a fenser.

75

THE HISTORIE OF

were once caught. This also was but a simple plaine jest although to good purpose and in season delivered: when he had by a speciall indulgence, granted unto a Champion who fought out of a British chariot, (for whome his foure children made earnest suite and entreaty) that he should bee freed from that profession of sword-fight; and that with the great favour and liking of all men, he sent presently an admonition in writing: wherein he advertised the people, how much they should endeavour to get children, seeing, as they did, in what good steed they served, and how they procured grace even unto a sword-fenser. He represented also in Mars field a warlike shew of the winning and sacking of a towne: likewise the yeelding of the Princes of Britaine; where he sat himselfe as president in his rich Coat-armour. When he was about to let out the water of the mere[1] Ficinus, he exhibited in it a navall fight before: and as they who were to fight this battaile, cryed out unto him, '*Ave Imperator*, etc., *i*. All haile O Emperour; they salute thee and wish thy life who are ready to dye': and he againe made answere, '*Ávete*[2] *vos*.' After which word given, as if he had pardoned them this skirmish, there was not one of them would fight: he, sitting a good while in doubt and suspense with himselfe, whether he should destroy them al with fire and sword, at length leapt forth of his throne, and running to and fro about the circuit of the sayd lake (not without foule faltering of his legs under him) partly with threats, and in part by way of exhortation, constrained them to skirmish. At this brave shew, the Sicilian and Rhodian fleetes encountred: eyther of them consisting of twelve[3] gallies ruled with three rankes of oares a peece. To give the signall of battaile, there was a Triton of Sylver[4] arising out of the mids of the lake by a fabrieke artificially devised, to sound the trumpet and set them togither.

---

[1] Or Lake.   [2] This Verbe (*Avete*) signifieth here, farewell or adieu. But the Souldiours construed it in the better sense for theyr owne turns, (as they had used it before in saluting him) All haile ye also.   [3] *Duodenarum*. Some read *undevicenats, i.* 19, and out of Dio, *quinquagenarum, i.* 50.   [4] Resembling Neptunes Trumpetter.

TWELVE CÆSARS

22

Certaine pointes about religious ceremonies, touching the
state likewise of civill and militarie affaires, as also concerning all degrees of persons both at home and abroad, he
eyther reformed, or after long disuse forgotten, brought into
practise againe, or els instituted and ordained new. In the
election and admission of Priests throughout their severall
Colledges, hee nominated not one but he tooke his oath
first. He observed also precisely that so often as there was
an Earthquake in the Citie, the Pretour for the time beeing
should call a publike assembly of the people and proclaime
certaine holydaies: semblably, that upon the prodigious
sight of an unlucky foule[1] in the Capitol, there should be
held a solemne procession and supplication: wherein himselfe personally in the right of High priest, after warning
given unto the people from the *Rostra*, did read and pronounce a forme of prayers and they say after him. But
from this congregation hee sequestred and removed the
base multitude of mechanicall labourers and slaves.

23

The handling of causes and judiciall pleading in Courts,
devided before time into certaine moneths for winter and
summer, he conjoyned altogether. The jurisdiction as
touching feofments upon trust which was wont yeere by
yeere, and onely within the Citie to bee committed unto
the magistrates, hee ordained to hold by patent for ever:
and betooke the charge thereof unto the rulers and governours also of state in every province. That branch
annexed to the lawe Papia Poppæa[2 a], which emplyeth thus
much, That men threescore yeeres of age are disabled for
generation, he altered[3] by an edict[4]. He ordained that
unto Pupils[5], the Consuls should extraordinarily appoint

---

[1] Whether it were an Owle, or the birde named *Incendiaria*, see Plin.
lib. 10, cap. 13, and 12.   [2] That a Woman under 50 yeares of age, should
not bee wedded to a man that was threescore.   [3] *Edicto abrogavit*.
[4] Granting that men threescore yeeres olde might mary women under fiftie.
[5] Wards under age.

THE HISTORIE OF

Tutors and Guardians. That they also who by the head-
Magistrates were forbidden to make abode within any
provinces, should bee debarred likewise from the Citie of
Rome and Italie. Himselfe confined some after a strange
fashion and without any precedent, inhibiting them to
depart above three miles from the City. When he was to
treat of any great affaire in the *Curia*, his manner was to
sit in the Tribunes pue just in the midst betweene the
Consuls chaires. As for pasports[1] which the Consuls were
wont to be sued unto for, he would have the Citizens to bee
beholden unto himselfe onely therefore, and to crave the
same at his hands.

24

The badges and ornaments belonging unto the Consuls
he granted unto the Ducenarie Procuratours and Seneschals
of Provinces[2]. From as manie as refused the honorable
dignitie of Senatours, he tooke away also the worship of
the gentlemens degree. The right to weare the Laticlave[3],
(although hee promised at first not to chuse anie one
Senatour who could not reckon 4 lineall descents from a
citizen of Rome,) he allowed also to a libertines sonne: but
with this condition, if he were adopted before by a Gentleman of Rome. And fearing for all that, least he should be
blamed, he proved and shewed, that even Appius Cæcus the
cheife auncitour and Auctor of his owne race, being censor
elected and admitted into the Senate the sonnes of Libertines: ignorant as hee was, that in the dayes of the sayde
Appius, and in the times long after ensuing, those were
called Libertines, not onely who themselves were manumised
and enfranchised, but such also, as were free borne of their
progeny. The Colledge of Questours, insteede of paving the
streets and high-wayes he enjoyed to exhibite a game or
shew of sword-fensers: and in the lieu of the Provinces,
Ostia and Gaule[4] which he tooke from them hee restored

---

[1] Licences to be absent a time from Rome.   [2] Who received 200000
sesterces for salarie or might despend so much by the place.   [3] *i.* The
Senatours robe studded with purple.   [4] Cisalpina, which therupon was
called Provincia Quæstoria.

TWELVE CÆSARS

the charge of the publike Treasure in the temple of Saturne; which office in the meane space betweene[1], the Pretours for the time being, or those verely who had been Pretours before had borne. Unto Silanus espoused and betrothed unto his daughter, before he was undergrowen and 14 yeeres of age hee granted triumphall ornaments: but of elder persons to so many, as there is an Epistle extant written in the common name of the Legions wherein they make petition, That unto the Consuls Lieuetenants there might be granted together with the conduct of the armie, the sayde triumphall honours: to the end that they should not picke quarrels and seeke occasions of warre, they cared not how nor what way. Moreover to A. Plantius he gave by a decree the pety triumph *Ovatio*: and as he entred so into the Citie himselfe met him upon the waie: and both when he went into the Capitoll and returned also from thence againe, gave him the better hand[2]. Unto Gabinius Secundus, who had vanquished the Cauci a nation in Germanie, he permitted and gave leave to assume the surname Caucius in his style.

25

The horsemens service and their places he ordered so by degrees, as that after the charge of a cohort, he granted the leading of a wing: and after the commaund thereof, the Tribuneship or regiment of a Legion: he ordained their stipends also: and a kind of imaginary warrefare called *Supra-Numerum* (which they that were absent might execute) and in name or title onely. By vertue of a decree that assed even from the Nobles them selves, he prohibited all souldiours professed, to enter into any Senatours houses for to do their dutie and salute them. Those Libertines who bare them selves for Romane gentlemen he caused to forfeit their goods and bodies to the state. Such of them as were unthankful and of whom their patrons complained, he deprived of freedome and made them bound againe: yea and denied unto their

---

[1] From Augustus dayes.   [2] *Latus texit, i. lævus ei incedebat*, he gave him the right hand, and went on his left side.   *Vide* Eutropium.

THE HISTORIE OF

advocates, for to heare any plea and to sit in judgment
against their owne freed men. When some Masters there
were, that put forth their sick and diseased slaves into the
Isle of Æsculapius[1], for to avoid the tedious trouble of their
cures at home, he made an act and ordained, That all such
slaves should be free and not returne againe into the hands
of their Masters, in case they ever recovered: and if anie
Master chose to kill them outright, rather then thus to put
them forth, they should be guilty of murder. He gave warning by an edict, that no waifaring men should travaile
through anie towne in Italie, but either on foot or borne
in a chaire, or els carried in a licter[a]. In Puteoli and in Ostia
he placed severall cohorts, to put by all mischances of skarefires. He forbad all persons by condition aliens and forrainers,
to take upon them Romane names; those I meane onely that
distinguished houses and families. As manie of them as
usurped the freedome of Rome-Citie he beheaded in the
Esquiline fielde[2]. The two provinces Achaia and Mace-
donia, which Tiberius (the Emperour) had appropriated to
him selfe[3], hee yeelded up againe into the hands and dispose
of the Senate. The Lycians hee deprived of their freedome,
by occasion of the mortall discord and variance among them.
To the Rhodians, who repented for their olde trespasses hee
restored their libertie which they had lost. Hee forgave all
tributes to the Ilienses for ever, as to the first founders and
stocke-fathers of the Romane Nation: and to that purpose
hee red an olde letter in Greeke written unto K. Seleucus by
the Senate and people of Rome: wherein they promised to
entertaine amitie and league with him upon this condition,
that hee would graunt unto the Ilienses, their naturall kinsfolke, immunitie from all taxes and tributes. The Jewes[4][b]
who by the instigation of one Chrestus were evermore
tumultuous, he banished Rome. The Embassadours of the
Germanes hee permitted to sit in the *Orchestra*[c] (with the
Senatours) beeing mooved so to doe at their simplicitie and

---

[1] Otherwise called Tiberina.   [2] Without the gate Esquilina.   [3] And
his successours.   [4] This some thinke is to bee understood of Christians
whom we find in the Ecclesiasticall writers to bee misnamed by the Ethnicke
Infidels, *Chrestiani*, like as Christ himselfe *Chrestos*, in skorne.

confident boldenesse, for that beeing brought into the *Popu-* TIBERIUS
laria[d] and perceiving Parthians and Armenians sitting among CLAUDIUS
the Senatours, they of their owne accord had remooved and DRUSUS
passed to that quarter: giving out these words withall, that CÆSAR
their valour and condition of estate was nothing inferiour to
the others.   The religion of the Druidæ among the French-
men, practising horrible and detestable cruelty and which
under' Augustus, Romane Citizens onely were forbidden to
professe and use, he quite put downe and abolished.   Contrariwise, the sacred rites and holy Cæremonies (of Ceres)
called *Eleusinia*, hee attempted to transferre out of the
Territorie Attica to Rome.   The Temple likewise of Venus
Erycine[e] in Sicilie, which in continuance of time was decayed
and fallen downe, hee caused to bee repayred and built againe
at the common charges of the people of Rome: hee made
Covenants and league with forraine Kings, by the complements of killing a sowe[1] in the Forum, and using withall
the sentence or preface that the Heraulds[2] in old time
pronounced: but both these affaires and others besides, the
whole Empire also in a manner or a great part thereof he
managed not so much after his owne minde, as by the direction and wil of his Wives and freed-men: beeing verely affected
and framed for the most part so, as stood eyther with their
profit or good pleasure.

26

When he was a very youth, he had espoused two maidens,
namely Æmilia Lepida neice to Augustus once remooved,
likewise Livia Medullina, surnamed also Camilla, a Ladie
descended from the auntient house of Camillus the Dictatour.
The former of these twaine, because her parents had offended
Augustus he cast off remaining as yet a Virgin: the latter, hee
lost by occasion of sicknesse, upon that very day which was
appointed for the mariage.   After this, he wedded these
wives, to wit, Plautia Herculanilla[3], whose father had
triumphed; and not long after, Ælia Pætina, whose father
had beene Consul.   Both these he divorsed: Pætina upon
light offenses and small displeasures: mary, Herculanilla he

---

[1] *Porca.*   [2] Or Fecials. See Livie, lib. i.   [3] Or Urgulanilla.

THE HISTORIE OF

TIBERIUS
CLAUDIUS
DRUSUS
CÆSAR
A.U.C. 801.

put away for her filthy lust and whorish life; as also for suspicion of a murder. After these he tooke to wife Valeria Messallina, the daughter of Barbatus Messalla his cousin german: whom when hee found once, over and beside the rest of her abominable vices and dishonesties, to have been wedded to C. Silius[1], and that with a dourie assured unto her and signed among the Auspices[2], he put to death. And in a speech that he made openly before his Pretorian Souldiours, avowed that because his mariages proved so bad, he resolved to remaine unmarried and live a single life: and if he did not continue so for ever, hee would not refuse to be stabbed by their very hands. Neither could he endure, but forthwith treat upon conditions of mariage even with Pætina, whom long before hee had put away: yea and with Lollia Paulina wife some time to C. Cæsar. But through the entieing allurements of Agrippina[3], the daughter of Germanicus his owne brother, what by the meanes of kissing courtesies, what by the opportunities of other daliances, being drawen into love and fancie with her, at the next Session of Senate he subborned certaine of purpose to opine and give advice, to compell him for to make her his Wife, as being a matter of right great consequence, and which most of all concerned the State: that other men also might be dispensed with and licenced to contract the like mariages[4] which until that time were reputed incestuous. And so, himselfe staied hardly one day between, before hee dispatched the wedding: but none were found that followed the precedent, except one libertine and another who had been a principal Centurion in the formost Cohort, at whose mariage even himself in person together with Agrippina was present to do him credite and honor.

27

Children he begat of 3 wives. By Herculanilla he had Drusus and Claudia: by Pætina he was father of Antonia: and Messallina bare unto him Octavia and a son, whom first he named Germanicus and afterwards Britannicus. As for

---

[1] Whiles she was Empresse and wife to Claudius.   [2] The handfasters or makers of the mariage.   [3] His owne neipce.   [4] With their brothers or sisters daughters.

82

TWELVE CÆSARS

Drusus, he lost him at Pompeii¹ before he was 14 yeares of age by occasion that he was choaked with a peare which in play and pastime beeing tossed aloft into the aire, fell just into his mouth as he gaped wide for it : unto whom also but few daies before, hee had affianced in mariage the daughter of Sejanus: which maketh mee more to mervaile that some have written, hee was treacherously killed by Sejanus. His (supposed) daughter Claudia, who in deede was conceived by his freed man Boter, although shee was borne before the fifth moneth after the divorse, and began to be nourced and reared, yet hee commaunded to be laid at her mothers dore and starke naked to be càst forth. Antonia his daughter, he gave in mariage to Cn. Pompeius Magnus: afterwards to Faustus Sulla ij. right noble yong gentlemen : and Octavia he bestowed upon Nero² his wives sonne, notwithstanding she had been promised, and betrothed before unto Silanus. His sonne Britannicus, whom Messallina bare unto him the twentieth day after he came to the Empire and in his second Consulship, being yet a very babe he recommended continually both to the souldiours in open assembly, dandling him in his owne hands, and also to the common people at the solemnities of games and plaies, holding him either in his bosome or just before him, whiles the multitude with great acclamations, all good words and fortunate osses seconded him. Of his sonnes in Law who matched with his daughters, he adopted Nero: Pompeius and Silanus he not onely cast off and rejected but murdred also.

TIBERIUS
CLAUDIUS
DRUSUS
CÆSAR

A.U.C. 773.

A.U.C. 806.

A.U.C. 803.

28

Of all his freed men hee esteemed especially Posides the Eunuch³, unto whom also in his triumph over Britaine, among martiall men and valiant Souldiours, he gave a speare without an yron head⁴ : and no lesse account made he of Fælix⁵ : whom first he ordained Capitaine over the Cohorts and Cornets of Horsemen, yea and ruler of the Province Jurie ; the husband of three Queenesᵃ. As also of Harpocras,

¹ *Pompeiis impuberem amisit.*   ² Emperour after him.   ³ Or gelded man.   ⁴ *Hasta pura donavit:* for his great valour forsooth.   ⁵ Of this Fælix mention is made in the Acts of the Apostles.

83

THE HISTORIE OF

unto whom hee graunted a priviledge to be caried in a Litter
through the Citie of Rome, and to set out Games and Plaies
in publick[b] : and besides these, hee affected with much respect
Polybius, the guide and directour to him in his Studies, who
oftentimes would walke cheeke by jole betweene the two
Consuls. But above all these, he held in greatest esteeme
Narcissus his Secretarie or enditer of Epistles, and Pallas
the Keeper of his bookes of accounts: whom by vertue of a
Decree also which went from the Senate, he suffred willingly
to be not onely rewarded with rich Fees, but also to be
adorned with the Honours of Questure and Pretureship:
likewise to get, to pill and poll by hooke and crooke so
much, as that when himselfe complained upon a time how
little treasure hee had in his Coffers, one made answere unto
him not absurdly, That hee might have store enough and
plenty, in case his two freed men[1] would admit him to share
with them.

29

To these (freed men) and to his wives as I said before,
being wholly addicted and enthralled, hee bare himselfe not
as an absolute Prince, but as their Minister and Servitour[a].
According as it was behoovefull and commodious to any of
these, or stoode with their affection and pleasure, hee graunted
honourable dignities, conferred the conducts of Armies, and
awarded impunities and punishments: yea, and for the most
part, I assure you when himselfe was altogether ignorant
and wist not what hee did.   And not to reckon up particularly, every small thing, to wit, his liberalities and gifts
revoked, his judgements reversed, his Patents and Writings
concerning the graunts of Offices either foisted in or plainly
altered or chaunged by them: hee slew his brother Appius
Silanus[2]: the ij. Juliæ, the one daughter of Drusus[3], and
the other of Germanicus[4], upon bare imputation of a crime,
without any ground: not allowing them so much as lawfull
triall and libertie to plead in their owne defence: likewise

---

[1] Narcissus and Pallas.   [2] *Consocerum :* so called for that their children
maried together : and such with us, name one another brethren.   [3] The
sonne of Tiberius.   [4] Who is called also Livilla.

84

TWELVE CÆSARS

Cn. Pompeius, husband to his elder daughter, and Lucius
Silanus espoused to the other (and all through their sug-
gestions and informations). Of which, Pompeius was stabbed
even as he lay in bed with a beloved youth and Catamite of
his: Silanus was forced to resigne up his Pretureship foure
daies before the Kalends of Januarie, and to loose his life[1]
in the beginning of the yeere on the very wedding day of
Claudius and Agrippina. To the execution of 35 Senatours,
and above an hundred Romaine Gentlemen so easily was
hee induced, as that, when the Centurion brought word
backe, as touching the death of one who had beene Consull,
saying, That the deede was done which he had commaunded,
he flatly denied that he gave any such warrant. Neverthelesse the thing he allowed : whiles his freed men aforesaid standing by, avouched, That the Souldiours had done
their devoir, in that they ran willingly of their owne heads
to revenge their Emperour. For, it would be thought
incredible if I should relate, how even for the very mariage
of Messallina with the Adulterer Silius : his own self sealed
the Writings for assurance of the Dowrie, being perswaded
and brought thereunto, as though the said wedding was but
colourably, of purpose pretended to avert forsooth and
translate the danger, that by certaine prodigies were portended to hang over his owne head.

30

Right personable hee was, and caried a presence not
without authorite and majestic, whether he stoode or sate ;
but especially when he was laid and tooke his repose. For,
of stature hee was tall, and nathlesse his body not lanke and
slender. His countenance lively, his gray haires beautifull,
which became him well, with a good fat and round neck
under them. Howbeit, both as he went his hams being
feeble failed him: and also whiles he was doing ought, were
it remissely or in earnest, many thinges disgraced him : to
wit, undecent laughter and unseemely anger, by reason, that
hee would froth and slaver at the mouth, and had evermore his nose dropping : besides, his tongue stutted and

[1] Tacitus writeth, that hee killed himselfe upon that day.

THE HISTORIE OF

stammered: his head likewise at all times, but especially if he did any thing were it never so little used to shake and tremble very much.

31

Concerning his bodily health, as before time he used to be grievously sick, so being once Emperour exceeding healthfull he was and stoode cleere of all diseases save onely the paine of the stomacka, in a fit whereof hee saide, hee thought to have killed himselfe.

32

Hee made feasts, and those very great and ordinarily; yea, and in most open and large places, such as for the most part would receive sixe hundred guests at one sitting. Hee feasted also even upon the Sluce of the Lake Fucinus: what time hee had like to have beene drowned, when as the water let out with a forcible violence reflowed backe againe. At everie supper his manner was to have also his owne children, who together with other noble mens children as well boyes as girles, should after the olde manner sit and feede at the tables feete[1]. One of his guests, who was thought to have closelie stollen away a cup of gold the day before, he re-invited against the morrow: and then he set before him a stone pot[2] to drinke in. It is reported moreover, that he meant to set forth an Edict, wherein he would give folke leave to breake winde downward and let it goe even with a crack at the very bourda; having certaine intelligence, that there was one who for manners and modestie sake, by holding it in, endaungered his owne life.

33

For appetite to meate and drinke his stomacke served him passing well alwaies, and in every place. Sitting upon a time judicially in Augustus Hall of Justice, to heare and determine causes, and senting there the steime of a dinner, that was a dressing and serving up for the Priests Salii[a]

---

[1] Or at a Settle at the tables end.   [2] Or earthen pot.

TWELVE CÆSARS

in the temple of Mars[1] next adjoyning, he forsooke the Tribunall, went up to the said Priests, and there sate downe with them to meate. Lightly you should never have him goe out of any dining roome, but with his belly strutting out, well whitled also and drenched with wine: so, as straightwaies, whiles hee layd him downe along upon his backe and tooke a sleepe gaping, there was a feather put ordinarily into his mouth wide open for to discharge his stomack. Hee tooke very short sleepes: for commonly before midnight hee awaked: yet so, as otherwhiles he would catch a nap in the day time, as he sat to minister justice: and scarcely could bee awakened by the Advocates at the barre, who of purpose raised their voices and pleaded the lowder. Hee was excessively given to the wanton love of women. As for the preposterous abuse of malekind, he was altogether unacquainted therewith. Hee plaied at dice most earnestly (concerning the Art and skill whereof, he published also a little booke) being wont to plie that game even whiles hee was caried up and downe, having his Carroch and Dice-bourd so fitted, as there might be no confusion nor shuffling at all in play.

34

That cruell he was and given to bloudshed naturally, appeared in great and very small matters. As for tortures used in examinations, and the punishments that Paricides suffred.[a], hee exhibited and exacted the same to be done without delay, and openly in his owne presence. Being desirous upon a time to behold an execution performed after the auncient manner at Tibur, when as (the malefactours standing bound already to a stake), there wanted the butcherly executioner to doe the feat, he staied there still in the place, and waited untill evening, for one that was sent for out of Rome. At all Swordfights, whether they were set forth by himselfe, or by others, he commaunded as many of the Champions as chaunced onely but to stumble and fall therewith, to have their throats cut:

[1] Revenger, situate neere to the Hall: for distinction of another Temple bearing that name, in the Capitoll mount.

THE HISTORIE OF

especially the Fencers called *Retiarii*[1] : and why! because forsooth hee would see their faces as they lay gasping and yeelding up their breath. It fortuned, that a couple of these fighting at sharpe wounded and killed·one another : thereupon hee commaunded little knives to bee made of both their blades, for his owne proper use. Hee tooke such pleasure in those that fought with wild beasts[2 b], as also in the sword fights ordinarily about noone, that he would by breake of day go downe to the Theater for to behold the one : and at noone dismisse the people to their dinners, and sit it out himselfe to see the other : yea, and besides those that were appointed to such combats, upon any slight and suddaine occasion set some to fight for their lives, even out of the number of Carpentars, Servitours, and such like emploied about these games : if happily any of those artificiall motions[c] that goe by vices, or a pageant in frame[3], or some such fabrick proved not well. Hee fetcht in also one of his owne Nomenclatours[4] even in his gowne as he went to fight for his life[5].

35

But it passed, how timorous and diffident hee was. At his first comming to the Empire (how ever as we said before, he bragged and stoode upon his civill and familiar behaviour) he durst not for certaine daies goe to any feast, dinner or supper, without Pensionars standing about him with their speares and Javelins, and his Souldiours waiting at the table : neither visited hee any sicke person, unlesse the bed-chamber where the party lay, were first searched ; the beds, bolsters, pillowes, Coverlets and other cloathes were groped, felt, and throughly shaken before hand. All the time after, hee appointed evermore certaine searchers for them all, that came to salute him, sparing not one, and such searchers as were most cruell. For, long it was first, and that with much adoe, ere hee graunted that women, young boyes in their embroidred coates, and maidens,

---

[1] The adverse faction to the *Mirmillones* whom he favored.   [2] Which combats were usually in the morning.   [3] Or Pegme.   [4] Prompters of names.   [5] With wilde beasts or otherwise.

TWELVE CÆSARS

should not bee handled and felt in this manner: that any mans Attendants likewise or Clerks might not have their Pensheathes and Penknife-cases taken from them [a]. In a civile commotion, when Camillus, (making no doubt but that without any warre at all hee might be terrified) willed him in a contumelious, menacing, and malapert letter, to resigne up the Empire, and to leade a quiet life in private estate, hee called his Nobles and chiefe personages about him, to counsell, and put to question, whether it were best to hearken unto him or no.

36

At the headlesse report and flying newes of some treason that should bee practised against him, he was so affrighted, that hee went about to lay downe his Imperiall dignity. By occasion, that one (as I related before) was taken with a weapon upon him, about his person as hee sacrificed, in all hast he sent out the Bedels and called the Senate together: before whom, with teares and loude out-cries hee bewailed his owne piteous case, as who no where could make account of any safety: and thereupon for a long time forbare to come abroad. His affectionate love also to Messallina, most fervent though it were he renounced and cast cleane from her, not so much for any indignity of the dishonourable wrongs she offred unto him, as upon very feare of daunger, as fully perswaded that shee practised to bring the Empire into Silius the Adulterers hands. At which time in a great fright he fled in shamefull manner to the camp, asking and enquiring all the way nothing else, but whether the Empire remained still safe to his behoofe.

37

There arose no suspition, there came forth no Author so light and vaine, but gave him a bone to gnaw upon, and put no small toyes in his head: wherby he was forced to beware and seeke revenge. One of those, that had a matter depending in Court before him, taking him a side, when hee came by way of salutation to doe his duty, avowed unto

2 : M

THE HISTORIE OF

TIBERIUS
CLAUDIUS
DRUSUS
CÆSAR

him, that he dreamed, How hee was killed by one. Then within a while after, the same party, (as if he had now taken knowledge who that one was that should murder him) pointed unto his owne adversarie, even as hee tendered a supplication unto Claudius, and said, ' This is he.' Whereupon immediatly apprehended he was, and haled to execution. After the semblable manner by report, came Appius Silanus to his death. For, when Messallina and Narcissus had conspired to worke his overthrow and finall destruction, they complotted thus, that Narcissus betimes in a morning before day light rushed like a man amazed and astonied into the bedchamber of his Patrone (Claudius) relating unto him his dreame, namely that Appius had laid violent hands upon him: and Messallina for her part, composing and framing her selfe as if shee wondered greatly thereat, reported, How shee likewise had seene already the same vision for certaine nights together. And not long after this, word came, (as it was before agreed betweene them) that Appius was comming to rush in among them: who in deed had beene bidden the day before to be present at the same instant. Whereupon, as if the said dreame had now proved true and beene plainly represented in effect, order was given for Appius, to be endited, arraigned, and to suffer death. Neither doubted Claudius the morrow after to report the whole storie and the order thereof unto the Senate: and withall to give thanks unto his freedman [1], for being so vigilant and watchfull in his very sleepe for his sake.

38

Being privie to himselfe of passionate anger [2] [a] and bearing malice, he excused them both in an Edict, distinctly

---

[1] Narcissus.   [2] *Iræ atque Iracundiæ.* The manner is of this Author throughout his story to set those points downe first in a word, whereon he meaneth to stand, and then in order to particularize presently upon them. By which method of his, it appeareth in this place, that hee meaneth by *Ira*, the momentarie passion of anger, which we call heat and ·choler, soone up and as soone downe, quickly kindled and as quickly quencht : by *Iracundiæ*, the habite of inveterat wrath continuing still untill revenge be had : which we call malice and rancour. Howsoever our modern Lexicographers have in their Dictionaries put downe the contrary.

90

TWELVE CÆSARS

promising that the one of them verily should be but short and harmlesse, the other not unjust nor causelesse. Having sharply rebuked the men of Ostia, because they had not sent boats and barges to meet him as he came upon the river Tiberis: and that in such odious termes as these, That he was now become base and abject in their eies: all on a suddaine, he pardoned them upon the submission and readinesse to make satisfaction. Some there were, whom in the very open street he thrust from him with his own hand, comming unto him somewhat out of season. Semblably he confined and banished the Court a Scribe who had been Questour: a Senatour likewise that had born the Pretureship, both of them without their cause heard and altogether guiltlesse, for that the one [1] pleading in Court as an Advocate against him when he was a private person, had caried himselfe not so modestly as he should: and the Senatour in his Ædileship had amerced and fined certaine tenants of his dwelling upon his lands, for selling boiled meats contrary to the law expresly forbidding so to do: and withall whipped his Bailife comming betweene [2] (to intercede for them). For which cause also, he tooke from the Ædiles their authority to punish the disorder of those that kept Tavernes and victualing houses. But as touching his owne foolishnes, he concealed it not, but gave it out and protested in certaine short orations, That he counterfaited himselfe a foole for the nonce during Caius daies; because otherwise he should not have escaped, nor attained to that (imperiall) place which hee aimed at and was now entred upon. Howbeit, he could not make the world beleeve so much, untill there was a book put forth within a short time after, entituled μωρῶν ἀνάστασις, i. The resurrection (or Exaltation) of fooles. The argument and matter whereof was, That no man faigneth folly [b].

TIBERIUS
CLAUDIUS
DRUSUS
CÆSAR

39

Among other thinges, men wondered at him for his oblivion and unadvisednesse, or (that I may expresse the same in Greeke) his μετεωρίαν καὶ ἀβλεψίαν, i. his grosse over-sight or forgetfulnes, and inconsiderate blindnes. When

[1] The Scribe.   [2] To intercede for them.

91

THE HISTORIE OF

Messallina was (by his owne commaundement) killed, within a while, after he was set in his dining parlour hee asked
why his Lady[1] came not.   Many of those whom he had
condemned to death, the very morrow immediatly after, he
commaunded to have warning both to sit in counsell with
him, and also to beare him company at Dice-play: yea, and
by a messenger chid and checked them as drowsie and sloth-
full for staying so long and making no better hast.   Being
minded to take Agrippina to wife against all law of God
and man, he ceased not in all his speech to call her, his
daughter[2] and nourceling: to give out also, That she was
borne and brought up in his bosome.   Having a purpose to
admit Nero into the very name of his owne house and family,
as if he had not incurred blame enough already for adopting
(him) his wives son, having a naturall sonne[3] of his owne who
was now of ripe yeeres, he eft-soones divulged, That never
any one had beene by adoption inserted or incorporate into
the family of the Claudii.

40

He shewed oftentimes so great negligence and carelesnes
what he said or did, that he was thought not to know nor
consider, either who made any speech, or among whom, or
at what time, and in what place?   When there was some
question and debate about Butchers and Vintnars, he cried
out in the Senate house, 'I beseech you[4], my Maisters, who
is able to live without a little piece or morsell of flesh?' and
withall described the abundance[5] of the olde Tavernes[a],
from whence himselfe also in times past was wont to bee
served with wine.   As touching a certaine Questour, who was
a Candidate of his and by him recommended: among other
reasons why he favoured him, he alleadged this, Because
his Father had quickly and in due time given him
lying sick, cold water to drinke.   Having in the Senate
brought in a woman to depose, 'This,' quoth he, 'was my
mothers freed woman, and she that kept her ornaments, and

---

[1] Or Mistres of the house, *Domina Græce*, δέσποινα.   [2] And in deede
he was her Unkle.   [3] Britannicus.   [4] *Rogo vos*, or I demaund of you.
[5] Or excessive number.

92

TWELVE CÆSARS

used to deck and dresse her: but she alwaies tooke me for her Patrone. This have I,' quoth he, 'delivered of purpose because there be some yet in mine house, who think me not to be her Patron.' Moreover, sitting upon the Tribunall, when he was in a great chafe, and the men of Ostia requested at his hands (I wot not what) in the name of their towne, he cried out aloud, That he knew nothing wherefore he should oblige them unto him: 'And if any man else,' quoth he, 'I also am free and at mine owne liberty.' As for these words of his which now I will relate, they were rife in his mouth daily, yea every houre and minute therof: 'What doest thou take me for Theogonius and λογιώτατος[b]?' beside many such foolish termes, not beseeming private persons, much lesse a Prince, otherwise not uneloquent nor unlearned: nay, rather one eagerly given to his booke, and a great Student in the liberall Sciences.

41

In his youth, he attempted to write an Historie, exhorted thereto by Titus Livius; and having the help besides of Sulpitius Flavus. And when he put the same first to the triall and judgement of men in a frequent auditorie, hardlie and with much a-do he read it through, being often in the while coldly heard, by an occasion that himselfe gave. For, when, (as hee began his reading) there was set up a laughter, by reason that many of the seates brake with the weight of a certeine corpulent and fat swad, he was not able to hold, no not after the tumult appeased, but eftsoones ever and anon call to minde that accident and fall afresh to unmeasurable laughing. During his Empire likewise, hee both wrote much and also rehearsed the same continually by his reader. The beginning of his foresayd historie he tooke from the time presently ensuing the murder of Cæsar Dictator: but hee passed over to the latter dayes: and began againe at the civill pacification: perceiving that it was not left in his power and libertie to write of the occurrents in those former times, as who was often checked both by his mother[1] and

---

[1] Antonia the Triumvirs daughter.

THE HISTORIE OF

also by his grandame[1]. Of the former argument he left
behinde him two volumes, of the later, fortie-one. Hee compiled of his owne life eight bookes: a report not so wisely
and discreetly put downe, as otherwise elegantly penned:
Item, an Apologie or defense of Cicero against the bookes of
Asinius Gallus: a peece of worke full enough of learning.
He devised moreover three new characters or letters in the
(Latine) Alphabet[a], and put them to the number of the olde
as most necessarie. And having published whiles he was
yet a private person, concerning the reason of those letters,
one booke: soone after beeing Emperor he easily effected
that they should be brought into use also indifferently with
the rest. And verely such manner of writing with those
characters is now extant to be seene in many bookes of
records in Journels, and titles or inscriptions of works.

42

With no lesse diligence studied hee the Greeke disciplines,
professing as any occasion was offered, his affectionate love
to that tongue, and the excellency thereof. When a certaine Barbarian discoursed in Greeke and Latine, 'See you be
skilfull,' quoth he, 'in both our languages'; and in recommending Achaia unto the LL. of the Senate, he sayde it was a province that he affected well and delighted in, for the commerce
and society of studies common to him and them: and many
a time he answered their embassadors in the Senate, with
a long and continued oration (in Greeke). But upon the
Tribunall he used very much verses also out of Homer.
Certes whensoever he had taken revenge of enemie or traytor,
he lightly gave unto the Tribune over the Sentinels and
guard of his person, calling unto him after the usual manner
for a watchword, none other but this:

"Ἄνδρ' ἐπαμίνασθε ὅτε τις πρότερος χαλεπήνῃ.
Resist, revenge with maine and might,
When one provokes thee first to fight.

To conclude, in the end he wrote Greeke histories also, to
wit twentie books entituled *Tyrrhenicoon*[2], and 8 entituled

[1] Octavia the wife of Antonie or Livia Augusta her selfe.   [2] Of Tuskane
affaires.

94

Carchedoniacoon[1]. In regard of which histories, unto the auntient schoole at Alexandria he adjoyned another bearing his owne name[2]: and ordained it was, that every yeare in the on of them his books *Tyrrhenicoon*; and in the other his *Carchedoniacoon* upon certaine daies appointed therefore should (as it were in a frequent Auditorie) be read whole through by severall single readers in their turnes.

43

Toward the end of his life, hee shewed certaine signes and those evident enough, that he repented both his mariage with Agrippina, and the adoption also of Nero. For by occasion that his freed-men made mention and gave their commendation of a judiciall proceeding of his, wherein he had condemned the day before, a Woman in the case of adulterie, hee avouched that the destinies likewise had so or-dained, that all his mariages[3] should bee unchaste howbeit not unpunished: and soone after, meeting his sonne Britannicus and embracing him harder and more closely than his manner was, 'Growe apace,' quoth hee, 'and take account of me for all that I have done.' Using withall these Greeke words, ὁ ἔρως δ' ἐπείγεται, *i.* love enforced me[4]. And when he had fully purposed to give him being as then very young and of tender yeeres his Virile Robe, seeing that his stature and growth would beare and permit it ᵃ, he uttered these words moreover, 'To the end that the people of Rome may·yet at last have a true and naturall Cæsar.'

44

And not long after this he wrote his wil and signed it with the seales of al the head-magistrates: whereupon before that he could proceed anie further, prevented hee was and cut short by Agrippina. Whom they also who were privie to her and of her councell[5], yet neverthelesse enformers,

---

[1] Of Carthaginian matters. [2] Called Claudium. [3] *Matrimonia,* or Wives like as *Coniugia proconiugibus.* [4] Or rather, ὁ τρώσας καὶ ἰάσεται, *i.* He that wounded will also heale. I that have done thee wrong wil make amends. [5] *Conscii :* some read *Conscientia quoque,* even his owne conscience.

TIBERIUS
CLAUDIUS
DRUSUS
CÆSAR

accused besides all this of many crimes. And verely it is agreed upon generally by all, that killed he was by poyson: but where it should be, and who gave it, there is some difference [a]. Some write, that as he sat at a feast in the (Capitoll) Castle with the priests, it was presented unto him by Halotus the Eunuch his taster: others report that it was at a meale in his owne house by Agrippina herselfe, who had offered unto him a mushrome empoisoned; knowing that he was most greedy of such meats. Of those accidents also which ensued hereupon, the report is variable. Some say, that streight upon the receipt of the poyson he became speechlesse, and continuing all night in dolorous torments, dyed a little before day. Others affirme, that at first he fell a sleepe: and afterwards, as the meate flowed and floted aloft vomited all up, and so was followed againe with a ranke poyson [1]. But whether the same were put into a messe of thicke gruell, (considering hee was of necessitie to be refreshed with food beeing emptied in his stomacke) or conveied up by a clister, as if being overcharged with fulnesse and surfeit, he might be eased also by this kind of egestion and purgation, it is uncertaine.

45

His death was kept secret until all things were set in order about his successour. And therefore, both vowes were made for him as if hee had lyen sicke stil, and also comicall Actours were brought in place colourably to solace and delight him, as having a longing desire after such sports. He deceased

A.U.C. 807.

three dayes before the Ides of October, when Asinius Marcellus and Acilius Aviola were Consuls: in the 64th yeere of his age, and 14th of his Empire. His funerals were performed with a solemne pompe and procession of the Magistrates: and canonized he was a Saint in heaven: which honor forlet and abolished by Nero hee recovered afterwards by the meanes of Vespasian.

46

Especial tokens there were presaging and prognosticating

---

[1] *Toxico.*   [2] The 13th of October.

TWELVE CÆSARS

his death: to wit the rising of an hairy[1] starre which they call a Comet: also the monument[2] of his father Drusus was blasted with lightning: and for that in the same yeere most of the Magistrates of all sorts were dead[a]. But himselfe seemeth not either to have beene ignorant that his end drew neere, or to have dissimuled so much: which may bee gathered by some good arguments and demonstrations. For both in the ordination of Consuls hee appointed none of them to continue longer then the moneth wherein he dyed: and also in the Senate, the very last time that ever he sat there, after a long and earnest exhortation of his children to concord, he humbly recommended the age of them both to the LL. of that honourable house: and in his last Judiciall Session upon the Tribunal once or twice he pronounced openly, That come he was now to the end of his mortalitie: notwithstanding they that heard him, greived to heare such an Osse, and praied the gods to avert the same.

[1] Or blazing.　　　[2]. Or tombe.

THE HISTORIE OF

THE HISTORIE OF
NERO CLAUDIUS CÆSAR

1

A.U.C. 586.

UT of the Domitian stocke and name, there sprung two famous families, to wit, the Calumi and the Ænobarbi. These Ænobarbi have for the first Author of their originall, and surname likewise, L. Domitius: whome, as he returned in times past homeward out of the countrey, two yong men twinnes[1], carying with them a venerable presence and countenance more then ordinary, encountred, by report, and commanded to relate unto the Senate and People of Rome, newes, of that victorie ·whereof as yet they stood in doubt: and for the better assurance of their divine majestie stroke his cheekes so, as that therewith they made the hayre[2] of blacke, redd[3], and like in colour to brasse[4]. Which marke and badges con- tinued also in his posterity; and most of them have such red[5] beardes. Moreover, having borne seven Consulships, triumphed likewise and beene Censors twice, and therwith bin chosen into the ranke of the *Patritii*, they remained al in the same surname. Neither were they known by any other forenames than Cneus and Lucius: and the same in variety worth the noting and observation: one while con- tinuing either of the sayd names in three persons together: otherwhiles changing alternatively one after another in every descent. For, we have heard say, that the first, second and

A.U.C. 593, 632, 658, 660, 700, 722, 785, 632, 639, 663.

---

[1] Castor and Pollux resembling two yong men. [2] *Capillum, i. Pilum.* Gellius. [3] Or ruddy. [4] Or Copper. [5] Or ruddy.

98

third of these Ænobarbi were forenamed Lucii: and againe, the three next following them in order were Cnei. All the rest no otherwise then by turnes one after another had their forenames, first Lucii and then Cnei. That many persons of this house descended should be knowen, I suppose it very pertinent and materiall: whereby it may the better appeare, that Nero degenerated from the Vertues of his Auncestors so, as yet he caried away and resembled the vices of them all, as infused into him and inbred by nature.

2

To fetch the beginning therefore of this our discourse somewhat farther of, his great Grandfathers Grandfather [1] Cn. Domitius, beeing in his Tribunate much offended at the Pontifies [2], for electing any other but himselfe into his fathers place, transferred the right and power of subrogating priests in the roome of those that were deceassed, from their Colledges to the bodie of the people. But in his Consulship having vanquished the Allobroges and the Arverni, he rode through his province [3] mounted upon an Elephant, whiles the whole multitude of his souldiours attended upon him in a traine after the manner of a solemne triumph. This Domitius it was, whom Licinius Crassus the oratour in a certaine declamation sayd, It was no mervaile he had a brasen beard whose face was made of Iron, and heart of lead. His sonne being Pretour was the man, who as Cæsar [4] went out of his Consulship (which he was thought to have borne against the *Auspicia* [5] and the lawes) convented him before the Senate to be by them examined, tried and censured. Afterwards when he was Consull he attempted to fetch him backe, Lord Generall as he was of an armie, from his forces in Gaule: and being by the adverse faction [6] nominated his successour in that province, was in the beginning of the civil warre taken prisoner before Corfininum: from whence being dismissed and set at libertie, after he had by his comming to the Massilians streightly

A.U.C. 632.

A.U.C. 696.

A.U.C. 700.

---

[1] *Atavus eius*, his Grandfather 4 degrees of.   [2] High Priests.   [3] Gallia Narbonensis.   [4] Jul. Cæsar Dictator.   [5] Approbation of the gods.
[6] The Pompeians.

THE HISTORIE OF

beleagured, much strengthened them, sodainely he forsooke them: and in the end, at the battaile of Pharsalia lost his life : a man not very constant and resolute, but with all of a fell and savage nature. Being driven to utter despaire, he was so much afraid of death, which for feare he had desired, that after a drawght of poyson hee repented the taking thereof and cast it up againe ; yea and enfranchised his Phisitian, who wittingly and of purpose had so tempered it that it might do him no great harme. And what time as Cn. Pompeius put to question what should be done to those Neuters that stood indifferent and sticked to no part: he alone opined, That they were to be reckoned enemies and proceeded against accordingly.

3

Hee left behind him a sonne, worthy without question, to be preferred before all others of his name and linage. This man being among those that were privie to Cæsars death, and of that conspiracy, standing condemned (though A.U.C. 720. guiltlesse) by the law Pædia[1], when he had betaken himselfe to Cassius and Brutus his neere kinsfolke, after the end of them both, held stil in his hand the fleet committed before time to his charge, yea and augmented the same : neither yeelded he it up to M. Antonius before his owne side was every where quite overthrowen: which he then did of his owne accord ; and so, as that Antonius took himselfe highly beholden unto him therfore. He only also of all those who by vertue of the like law stood condemned, being restored into his native countrey, went through the most honorable offices of state: soone after likewise, when civil dissension was kindled againe and renewed, being in quality of Lieu-tenant to the said Antonie, what time the soveraigne Empire was offered unto him by those who were ashamed of Cleopatra[2], not daring to accept thereof nor yet to refuse it resolutely, by occasion of sodaine sicknesse wherewith he was surprised, went and sided with Augustus, and within few dayes after departed this life : being himselfe also noted

[1] Which Q. Pædius made against the murderers of Cæsar.   [2] The present state governed according to his wil and pleasure.

100

TWELVE CÆSARS

with some infamie: for, Antonie gave it commonly forth, NERO
That for the love of one Servilia Nais whom he kept, he fled CLAUDIUS
to Augustus side.
CÆSAR

4

From him came that Domitius, who soone after had the
name abroade to have beene the chapman of Augustus
goods and substance left by his wil and testament [1]: a man
no lesse renowmed in his youth for good skill in ruling of
Chariots and running with them a race, as afterwards for
the triumphant ornaments achieved by the Germaine warre;
but arrogant of spirit, wastefull in expence, and therewith
cruel. When he was Ædile he forced L. Plancus that had
beene Censor [2], to give him the way. Bearing the honorable
offices of Preture and Consulate, hee produced upon the
stage to acte a Comicall and wanton Enterlude, the gentlemen and dames of Rome. He exhibited baiting of wilde
heastes both in the cirque and also in every quarter of the
City, yea and a shew of sword-fight: but with so great
cruelty, that Augustus was compelled of necessitie to
restraine him by an edict, since that no secret warning nor
admonition at his hands would prevaile.

5

Of Antonia the elder, hee begat the father of Nero: an
impe in all the parts of his life ungracious and detestable.
For accompanying Caius Cæsar [3] in his youth into the East-
parts, where he killed a freed-man of his owne, because he
refused to quaffe as much as he was commanded, being discharged therfore out of the cohort of his friends, he led his
life never a whit more modestly: but both within a village
standing upon the street Appia, sodainely put his horses to
gallop, and not unwittingly rode over a little child and
trode him to death: and also at Rome in the midst of the
Forum plucked a Romane gentlemans eye out of his head,
for chiding him somewhat over boldly. So false and per-

---

[1] *Dicis causa, i.* by an imaginarie bargaine of sale to have bought them to
the behoofe and use of the heyre.   [2] *Censorium*, not *Censorem*.   [3] Sonne
of M. Agrippa and Julia, adopted by Augustus.

101

THE HISTORIE OF

fidious beside, that he defrauded not onely the bankers and money changers of the   of such commodities as they had bought up, but also when he was Pretour put the runners with Chariots besides the prises of their victories. For which prankes, reproved he was merily even by his owne sister (Lepida) and upon complaint made by the Masters of the foure factions[a] hee enacted, That from thence-forth ever after, the said prises should be presently payed. Being accused likewise for treason to the State and many adulteries, as also for incest committed with his sister Lepida a little before the decease of Tiberius, yet escaped he the danger of Law by the alteration of the times, and died at Pyrgæ of the Dropsie [1][b], when Agrippina daughter to Germanicus had brought him a sonne named Nero.

6

This Nero was borne at Antium, nine moneths after that Tiberius departed this world, eighteene daies before the Kalends of Januarie, just as the Sunne was newly risen, so as his beames light [2] well neere upon him before they could touch the earth [3]. As touching his Horoscope [4], many men straightwaies gave many guesses and conjectures of fearefull events. And even a very word that his father Domitius spake, was taken to be a presaging osse. For when his friends by way of gratulation wished him joy of his sonne new born, he said, That of himselfe and Agrippina there could nothing come into the world but accursed, detestable and to the hurt of the weale publick. Of the same future infortunity there appeared an evident signe upon his naming day[a]: for Caius Cæsar (Caligula) when his sister (Agrippina) requested him to give the Infant what name [5] he would, looking wistly on Claudius his Unkle, (by whom afterwards being Emperour (the child) was adopted), said he gave him his name. Neither spake hee this in earnest, but merily in boord: and Agrippina scorned and rejected it, for that as

---

[1] *Morbo aquæ intercutis:* that kind of dropsy wherein water runneth between the fell and the flesh all the bodie over, *Leucophlegmatias* in Greeke.
[2] Or shone.   [3] Dio sayth, hee was compassed with the sunne beames: and yet no sunne appeared above the Horizon.   [4] Or Nativitie.   [5] Forename.

TWELVE CÆSARS

then, Claudius went for a foole, and one of the laughing
stocks of the Court. At three yeeres of age he became
fatherlesse: and being his fathers heire but of one third
part, yet could not he touch so much as that, full and
whole, by reason of Caius his coheire, who had seized upon
and caught up before-hand all the goods: and for that his
mother also was soone after confined and packt away, he
being in manner destitute of all helpe and very needy, was
fostered in his Aunt Lepidæs house under two Pædagogues,
a dauncer and a Barber. But when Claudius was come once
to the Empire, hee not onely recovered his patrimonie[1], but
also was enriched by the inheritance of Crispus Passienus
his mothers husband, that fell unto him. And verily through
the grace and power of his mother now called home againe
and restored to her estate, hee flourished and grew so great,
that commonly it was bruted abroad, That Messallina the
wife of Claudius sent some of purpose to take the opportunity of his noones sleep, and so to smuddre and strangle
him, as the onely Concurrent of Britannicus[2], and one that
eclipsed the light of his glorie. Now in the tale it went,
besides: that the said parties tooke a fright at a Dragon
issuing out of his pillow, whereupon they fled backe and
forsooke the enterprise. Which fable arose upon this, that
there was in deede found the slough[3] of a serpent in his bed
about the bolsters. And yet, this slough he enclosed within
a bracelet of gold (as his mother willed him) and wore it
a good while after, upon his right arme: and at length,
wearie of any memoriall and monument of his mothers flung
it away: but in his extreamity and despaire of his estate
sought for the same againe in vaine.

7

In his tender yeeres, and whiles hee was yet a boy of no
full growth, hee acted at the Circeian Games the warlike
Troy fight most resolutely, with great favour and applause
of the people. In the eleventh[4] yeere of his age adopted
he was by Claudius and put to schoole unto Annæus Seneca,

---

[1] Fathers goods.   [2] Her Sonne.   [3] Or skinne.   [4] *Undecimo:* some
reade rather *tertio et decimo, i.* the thirteenth.

THE HISTORIE OF

even then a Senatour, for to be trained up in good literature. The report goes, that Seneca, the next night following, dreamed as hee lay in bed, that hee was teaching C.[1]
Cæsar: and shortly after Nero proved his dreame true, bewraying the fell stomacke and shrewd nature of the said
Prince, by the first experiments that he could give thereof.
For when his brother Britannicus saluted him after he was
once adopted, (as his wonted manner was before) by the
name of Ænobarbus, hee went about to lay this imputation
upon him before his Father, that he was some Changeling
and no sonne of his as he was reputed. His Aunt Lepida likewise being in trouble, hee deposed against, in the open face
of the Court, thereby to gratifie his mother her heavie friend,
and who followed the suite hotly against her. Being honour-
ably brought into the Forum[2], the day of his first plea and
Commencement, hee promised publiquely for the people a
Congiarie, and Donative for the Souldiours. Having proclaimed also a solemne Justing[3], himselfe rode before the
Pretorian Souldiours bearing a shield in his owne hand.
After this, hee solemnly gave thanks to his Father in the
Senate. Before whom being then Consull, hee made a Latine
Oration in the behalfe of the Bononians, and for the Rhodians and Inhabitants of Ilium, another in Greeke. His
first Jurisdiction hee began as Provost of the Citie[a],
during the celebration of the Latine holidaies: what time
the most famous Advocates and Patrones in those daies strove
a vie, who could bring before him most accusations[4] and
longest[5]; not (as the manner was) such as were ordinarie
and briefe: the expresse commaundement of Claudius forbidding the same, notwithstanding. Not long after, hee
tooke to wife Octavia: and for the good health of Claudius,
exhibited the Cirque Games and baiting of wild beasts.

8

Being seventeene yeeres olde, so soone as it was knowne
abroad that Claudius was dead, hee came forth to those (of
the Pretorian Cohort) that kept watch and ward, betweene

---

[1] Caligula. [2] Or Hall of Justice. [3] Or running at tilt. [4] Or
declarations. [5] Drawne in large bookes.

TWELVE CÆSARS

the sixth and the seventh houre of the day[1]: for by reason
that the whole day beside was ominous and dismall, there
was no time thereof thought more auspicate and convenient
than it, to enter upon the Empire : and so before the Pallace
staires being proclaimed and saluted Emperour, he was in a
Licter brought to the Camp[2]: and hastily from thence,
after a short speech made unto the Souldiours, conveied
into the *Curia*. From whence he departed home in the
evening : and of those exceeding and infinite honours which
were heaped upon him, hee refused onely the Title in his
stile of *Pater Patriæ*[3], in regard of his young yeeres.

9

Beginning then with a glorious shew of Piety and Kindnes,
at the Funerals of Claudius[4], which were most sumptuously
performed, he praised him in an Oration and consecrated
him a God. In the memoriall of his owne Father Domitius,
he did him right great honour. His mother he permitted
to have the whole regiment of all matters as well publick
as private. The very first day also of his Empire, when the
Tribune of the Sentinels[5], asked of him a watchword, he
gave unto him this Mot, *Optima mater* (my best mother),
and afterwards many a time she accompanied him through
the Streetes, in his owne Licter. He planted a Colonie
at Antium, enrolling therein the old Souldiours out of the
Prætorian cohort, and joyning with them (by translating
their habitations) the richest Centurions who had beene
Leaders of the formost bands : where also hee made a Pere[6],
a most sumptuous peece of worke.

10

And to shew a surer proofe still of his towardnesse, after
profession made to governe the Empire according to the
prescript rule of Augustus, he omitted no occasion to shew
either bountifulnesse or clemencie, no nor so much as to
testifie his gentlenesse and courtesie. Those tributes and
taxes which were any thing heavie he either abolished quite

---

[1] Betweene noone and one of the clock. [2] Pretorian. [3] Father of
his Countrey. [4] The Emperour. [5] Or *corps de guard*. [6] Or haven.

THE HISTORIE OF

or abated. The rewards due unto Informers as touching the Law Papia[1], hee reduced to the fourth part onely of the penalty. Having dealt among the people 400 Sesterces[2] for every poll: to as many Senatours as were most nobly descended (howbeit decaied and weakned in their estates) he allowed yeerely Salaries, and to some of them 500000 Sesterces[4]. Likewise for the Pretorian Cohorts hee ordained an allowance of Corne monthely gratis[5]. And whensoever he was put in minde to subscribe and set his hand to a warrant (as the maner is) for the execution of any person condemned to die, hee would say, 'Oh, that I knew not one letter of the booke.' Manie times he saluted all the Degrees of the Citie one after another, by rote and without booke. When the Senate upon a time gave him thanks, hee aunswered '(Doe so) when I shall deserve.' To his exercises in Mars field he admitted the Commons also, yea and declaimed often publiquely before them. He rehearsed his owne verses likewise, not onely within house at home, but also in the Theater: and that with so general a joy of as many as heard him, that for the said rehearsall, there was a solemne procession decreed: and some of his said verses written in golden letters were dedicated to Jupiter Capitolinus.

11

Many and sundry kindes of shewes he set forth: to wit, the Juvenall sports[a], the Circeian Games, and the Stage-playes: also a Sword fight. In the Juvenall pastimes, he admitted old men even those of Consuls degree: aged women also and matrones to disport themselves. At the *Circenses*, he appointed places for the Gentlemen of Rome a part by themselves: where hee put also to runne a race for the prise chariots drawne with foure Camels. In the Stage plaies, (which beeing instituted for the eternizing and perpetuitie of his Empire hee would have to be called *Maximi*), very many of both degrees[6] and sexes plaied their parts upon the Stage. A Romaine Gentleman of very

---

[1] Poppæa.   [2] 3l. 2s. 6d. starling, a Romaine pound.   [3] Annuities.
[4] More by a fourth part, than the State or worth of a Gentleman of Rome.
[5] Without paying mony.   [6] Gentlemen and Senatours.
106

TWELVE CÆSARS

good note and especiall marke, mounted upon an Elephant ranne downe a rope [1]. There was brought upon the Stage to be acted the Romaine [2] Comædie of Afranius entituled *Incendium*: and graunted it was unto the Actours therein to rifle all the goods and implements of the house as it burned, and to take the same as their owne. Scattered also abroad there were for the people Missils [3], during the whole time of those Plaies : to wit, a thousand birds every day of all kindes : Cates and viands manifold : Ticquets and Tallies for corne, apparell, gold, silver, pretious stones, pearles, pictures upon tables : slaves, labouring garrons and beasts also tamed : last of all, ships, isles, lands and possessions, according to their Tallies.

12

These Games hee beheld from the top of the *Proscenium* [4]. At the Swordfight which hee exhibited in the Amphitheatre built of Timber in one yeeres space within the ward of Mars field hee suffred not one man to be killed, no not so much as a guilty malefactour. Moreover, hee brought into the Lists for to fight at sharpe even 400 [5] Senatours and 600 [6] Gentlemen of Rome. Some of good wealth and reputation, out of the same degrees, he caused to come forth into the Shew-place, for to kill wild beasts, and performe sundry services therto belonging. He represented also a Naval fight upon salt water from the Sea, with a devise to have sea beasts [7] swimming therein. Semblably, certaine Pyrrhick [8] daunces in armour, sorted out of the number of young Springals : and after their devoir done, he gave freely unto every one of them patents and graunts to be enfranchized Citizens of Rome. Betweene [9] the arguments of these Pyrrhick daunces, devised it was, that a Bull should leape Pasiphæ [a] hidden within a frame of wood resembling an Heiffer [10], which was acted so lively, that many of the

---

[1] *Per Catadromum*, for there were *Elephanti Funambuli, vide* Galb. cap. 6, *et* Xiphilinum.   [2] Or Latine.   [3] Or gifts.   [4] The fore-stage.   [5] *Quadringenos*, rather *quadragenos, i.* 40.   [6] *Sexacentosque*, rather *Sexagenos, i.* 60, according to Justus Lipsius.   [7] Or great fishes.   [8] Warlike.   [9] Or, among.   [10] To the likenesse of that which was devised by Dædalus.

107

THE HISTORIE OF

beholders beleeved verily it was so in deede. As for Icarus, at the first attempt to flie, hee fell presently downe hard by his owne[1] Bed-chamber[2][b] so that he bespreint him with blond. For very seldome had he used to sit as President at these Games: but his manner was, to behold them as he lay upon his bed[3]. First through little loope holes: but afterwards setting the whole gallerie open from whence he looked. Hee was the first moreover that instituted at

Rome, according to the Greeke fashion, Quinquennal games of three kinds, to wit, of Musick and Poetrie, of Gymnick maisteries and of Horsemanship[4]: which Games he called Neronia. After he had dedicated the Baines, and a place therein for Gymnick exercises[c], he allowed the oyle that went thereto both for the Senate and also for the Gentlemen. He ordained Maisters and Wardens of all this Solemnity, especiall persons of Consular degree, chosen by lot to sit as over-seers in the place of Pretours[5], and then came downe himselfe into the *Orchestra*[6] and the Senatours quarter. And verily the victorious coronet for the Latine tongue, both in prose and verse, about which the best and most worshipfull persons had contended, when it was graunted unto him with their owne consents he received: and the harp presented unto him by the Judges he adored, and commaunded that it should bee caried to the Statue of Augustus. At the Gymnick Games which he exhibited in the *Septa*, during the solemne preparation of the great Sacrifice Buthysia, hee cut off the first beard that he had, which he bestowed within a golden box, adorned it with most pretious pearles and then consecrated it in the Capitol[7]. To the shew of wrestlers and other Champions he called also the vestall virgins, because at Olympia the priestesses like-wise of Ceres, are allowed to see the Games there.

13

I may by good reason, among other Shewes by him ex-

---

[1] Of Nero.   [2] Or pavilion.   [3] Or a pallet.   [4] Or Horse running.
[5] Where they were wont to sit as Presidents at other games and playes.
[6] *In Orchestram, Senatumque aliter, per Orchestram in scenam*, by the *Orchestra* to the very stage.   [7] To Jupiter Capitolinus.

TWELVE CÆSARS

hibited, reckon also the entrance into Rome City, of Tiri- dates: whom being King of Armenia hee had sollicited by large promises. Now, when hee meant to shew him unto the people upon a set day appointed by an Edict, and was driven to put it off, (the weather was so cloudy) he brought him forth before them to be seene upon the best and most opportune day that hee could finde; having bestowed about the temples situate in the Forum[1], cohorts of Souldiours armed, and sitting himselfe upon his yvorie curule chaire of Estate before the *Rostra* in triumphall habite, among the militarie Ensignes, banners, guidons and streamers. And as the King came up towards him by the ascent of the steepe pulpit, he admitted him first to his knees; and then raising up with his right hand kissed him: afterwards as he was making his praier unto him, having taken off his Tiara[2], he did the diademe on[3]. Whiles one who had been Pretour, pronounced unto the multitude the Suppliants words, as they were by an Interpretour delivered unto him. Being brought after this into the Theater and making supplication againe, he placed him on his right side next to himselfe. For which he was with one accord saluted Emperour: and so bringing with him the Lawrell branch into the Capitoll, he shut both dores of double faced Janus temple, as if no reliques of warre remained behind[4].

14

Foure Consulships he bare: the first for two moneths: the second and last for three: the third for foure. The middle twaine he continued without any intermission: the rest he varied with a yeeres space betweene.

A.U.C. 808, 810, 811, 813.

15

In his ordinarie Jurisdiction, he lightly gave no answer to the Proctours before the day following, and that was by writing. In extraordinary Commissions and trials this

---

[1] Or Market place. [2] Resembling a cap of maintenance, or as some thinke, a Turkish tuffe or Turbant. [3] Which he had laid off again as it shold seeme, like as when he was vanquished by Corbito, he laid downe before the Image of Nero. [4] *Tanquam nullo residuo bello.*

THE HISTORIE OF

course he held, namely to decide every cause by it selfe one after another upon certaine daies of the Session; and to surcease quite the hudling up and debatements of matters one in the neck of another: so often as he went aside to consult, he did deliberate and aske advise of nothing either in common or openly: but reading secretly to himselfe the opinions written by every counsellour, what liked his owne selfe, that pronounced hee, as if many more thought well of the same. For a long time hee admitted not the sonnes of Libertines into the *Curia*: and to those that were admitted by the Emperours his predecessours hee denied all honorable Offices. If there sued for Magistracies more then could speed, or were places void; to comfort their harts againe for delaying and making them to stay longer, he gave unto them the conduct of Legions. He graunted for the most part all Consulships for six moneths terme. And if one of the two Consuls hapned to die about the Kalends of Januarie[1], hee substituted none in his steede: as misliking altogether the old precedent of Cannius Rebilus, who was Consul but one day[2]. Triumphall ornaments he gave even unto those that had borne Questours dignity only: yea and to some of the Gentlemens degree, and verily not alwaies for any militarie service[3]. His Orations[4] sent into the Senate concerning certaine matters, hee caused for the most part to be read and rehearsed by the Consuls, passing by the Questours Office[5].

16

He devised a new forme of the City buildings: and namely, that before the Ædifices standing by themselves[6], and other houses, likewise there should be Porches[7]. From the Solars whereof, all Skarefires might be put by and repelled[8]; and those he built[9] at his owne charges. Hee had an intention once to set out and enlarge the walls of

---

[1] Somewhat before.   [2] Or rather, one peece of a day: See Julius Cæsar cap. 76.   [3] Or upon occasion of war.   [4] Which else where be called Epistles.   [5] Unto whom properly it appertained.   [6] *Ante Insulas.*
[7] Foregates, or Gatehouses.   [8] From the front of such Ædifices.   [9] Or promised rather to build.

TWELVE CÆSARS

Rome, even as farre as to Ostia; and from thence by a Fosse to let the Sea into old Rome [1]. Many matters under him were both severely punished and also restrained, yea and likewise newly ordained. Expences in his daies had a gage and stint set upon them [2]. The publick suppers[a] were brought downe to small Collations. Forbidden it was that any thing sodden [3], but only pulse, and worts [4] should be sold in Taverns and Cookes houses; where as before time, there was no maner of viands but it was set out to sale. The Christians, a kinde of men given to a new, wicked and mischievous Superstition, were put to death with grievous torments. The sports of Chariotiers, wherein by an old and licentious custome they had been allowed to range up and downe, to beguile folke, to pilfer and steale in merriment, were prohibited. The factions[b] of the Pantomimi [5] together with the Actours themselves were banished and sent away.

17

Against forgers of writings, then first came up this invention that no books or instruments should be signed unlesse they were hoared and had a thred three times drawne through the holes. Provided it was, That in Wills the two first [6] parts [7] thereof should be shewed as blanks, unto those that came to seale the same: having the Testatours name onely written therein. Item, that no Clerk or Notarie, who was to draw and write another mans will, should put downe any Legacie for himselfe. Item, that they who had sutes depending in Court, should pay the certaine due fee set downe by Law, for pleading of their causes: but for the Benches [8][a] nothing, considering the Chamber of the Citie allowed the same gratis and to be free. Item, that in the pleading and deciding of controversies all causes debated afore time before the Maisters of the Exchequer or Citie Chamber should bee removed unto the Common Hall [9], to

---

[1] To bring an arme of it thither.   [2] In costly and excessive fare at the table.   [3] *Ne quid cocti*.   [4] As Potherbs.   [5] Cunning Actours, playing all parts, and resembling all gestures.   [6] Or uppermost.   [7] Or cered tables.   [8] Pues or seats, some expound this of the Judges Bench, as if their sentences should not be bought and sold.   [9] Or Pleas.

111

THE HISTORIE OF

be tried before the Commissioners and Delegates called
Recuperatores. Finally, that all appeales from the Judges
should be made unto the Senate.

18

Having no will, no motion, nor hope at any time, to pro-
pagate and enlarge the Empire, he thought once to have
withdrawne the forces even out of Britaine: neither gave he
over that intent of his, but onely for very shame; least
he might be thought to deprave the glory of his Father
(Claudius). Onely the realme of Pontus with the leave of
Polemon ᵃ, as also the Kingdome of the Alpes, by the death
of King Cottius hee reduced into the forme of a Province.

19

Two voyages and no more he undertooke, the one to
Alexandria, the other into Achaia. But his journey to
Alexandria hee gave over the very day of his setting forth:
by occasion that he was disquieted at once, both with a
religious scruple and also with some perill. For when hee
had gone in procession about all the temples, and sitten
downe within the Chappel of Vesta, as he was rising up,
first the hem[1] or edge of his Gowne stucke to the seate, and
after this, arose so darke a mist before his eyes, that uneth
he could see and looke about him. In Achaia hee attempted
to digge through Isthmus ᵃ, and in a frequent assembly
made a speech unto the Pretorian Souldiours, exhorting
them to begin the worke: and having given the signall by
sound of trumpet, himselfe first brake up the ground with a
little spade[2]; and when hee had cast up the earth, caried
it forth upon his owne shoulders in a scuttle. He prepared
also an expedition to the Caspian gates: for which hee
enrolled a newe Legion of Italian young Souldiours six
foote high[3]: this Legion hee called the Phalanx or
Squadron of Alexander the Great. These particulars pre-

[1] Jag, welt or fringes.   [2] *Rastello, i. ligone*, the same that *Dikella* in
Greeke with a cloven bit.   This by some Writers, was of gold.
[3] *Senum pedum*, some read *senum millium peditum*: *i.* of 6 thousand
footmen.

112

TWELVE CÆSARS

mised, partly deserving no blame, and in part worthy even of no meane praise, have I collected together, that I might sever and distinguish them from his villanies and wicked acts, whereof from henceforward I wil make report.

20

Among other arts and sciences, beeing in his childhood trained up in the skill also of musick: no sooner attained he to the Empire, but he sent for Terpnus the harper, renowmed in those dayes for his cunning above all other. Sitting by him as he played and sung, day by day after supper until it was far in the night, himselfe likewise by little and little began to practise and exercise the same: yea and not to let passe anie meanes that expert professours in that kind were wont to do, eyther for preserving or the bettering and fortifying of their voices: even to weare before him upon his brest a thin plate or sheet of lead: to purge by clystre or vomit: to absteine from apples and fruite, with all such meates as were hurtfull to the voice: so long, untill his proceedings stil drawing him on, (a smal and rusty [1] voice though he had) he desired to come forth and shew himselfe upon the open stage, having among his familiar companions this Greeke proverbe evermore in his mouth, That hidden musicke was nought worth [a]. The first time that he mounted the stage was at Naples, where he gave not over singing, (albeit the Theatre was shaken and ready to fall by a suddaine earthquake) before he had finished the song begun. In the same place he chaunted often and many dayes together. Moreover, after some short time betweene taken to repaire his voice (as one impatient of keeping within house) from the baines there he passed directly to the Theatre [2]: and having in the midst of the *Orchestra* before a frequent multitude of people feasted and banquetted, made promise in the Greeke tongue, that if he had sippled a little and wet his whistle, he would ring out some note more fully and with a stronger brest. Now, beeing much delighted with the Alexandrines [3] praises in

[1] Or hoarse.   [2] At Naples.   [3] *i.* Ditties.

2 : P   113

THE HISTORIE OF

prict song[1], who newly in a second voiage had with their fleet conflowed to Naples[b], he sent for more of them out of Alexandria. And never the later he chose from all parts youths of Gentlemens degree, and not so few as 5000 of the lustiest and strongest young men out of the commons, who beeing sorted into factions[2] should learne certaine kinde of shouts and applauses, which they tearmed *Bombos*[c], *Imbrices*[d] and *Testas*[e] : also that deft and trim boyes, such as had the thickest bush of haire upon their heads[3][f], and were set out in most excellent apparell, and not without a ring on their left hands[4], should give their attendance upon him as he sung. The cheiftaines and leaders of these had for their stipend 400000 sesterces[5].

21

Esteeming so highly as he did of singing, he solemnized at Rome also againe the foresaid games called *Neroneum* before the day and time by order appointed[6]. And when all the people called upon him for his celestial voice[a], he made answere: That he verily would do them that pleasure (being so willing and desirous as they were to heare him): but it should be in his Hortyards. Howbeit, when the corps de guarde of the (Pretorian) Souldiers which at that time kept watch and ward seconded the praiers of the common people, willingly he promised to fulfill their minds out of hand in the very place; and without any farther delay caused his owne name to be written in the roll of other professed minstrels and singers to the harpe. Thus having put his lot into the pitcher with the rest, hee entred the stage when his turne came : and withall the Capitaines of the Guard supporting his harpe : after them the tribunes militarie[7], and close unto them his most inwarde friendes and Minions. Now when hee had taken up his standing, and ended his Proœme, he gave publike notice and pronounced by

---

[1] Tuned and composed to the rules and measures of Musick, in the praise of him, by the merchants of Alexandria. See cap. 98, August.   [2] Or Crewes.   [3] *Pinguissima coma.*   [4] *Nec sine anulo lævis*, or, clean con-trarie, *ac sine anulo leves, i.* wearing no rings at all.   [5] A Knights living.   [6] Every fifth yeares.   [7] Or Colonels.

TWELVE CÆSARS

the voice of Cluvius Rufus, (no meaner man than of Consuls degree) that he would sing and act the storie of Niobe [1]: and so continued hee well neere unto the tenth houre of the day [2]: which done he differred the Musicke Coronet due for the present victorie, together with the residue of that gaming unto the next yeare following; and all because he might have occasion oftener to chaunt. But bethinking himselfe that the time was long, hee ceased not to come ever and anon abroade to shew his skill in open place. Hee stucke not also in private shewes and games [3] to doe his devoire, even among common Actors and Stage players: and namely, when one of the Pretours [4] made offer of a milian of Sesterces. Hee sung moreover, disguised, Tragæ-dies of the worthies and gods: of noble Ladies likewise in olde time and of goddesses, having their visards [5] framed and made to the likenesse of his own face and of some woman whom hee loved. Among the rest he chanted the tale of Canace travailing in child-birth [b]: of Orestes who killed his own Mother [c]: of Œdipus that plucked out his own eyes [d], and of Hercules enraged [e]. In the acting of which Tragædie, the report goes, that a novice [6] placed to keepe and guard the entrie of the stage, seeing him dressed and bound with chaines (as the argument of the sayd Tragædie required) ran in a good [haste] to helpe him.

22

Exceedingly given hee was of a boy to delight in horse-manship, and with the love of charioting mightily inflamed: and very much would he be talking (forbidden though he were) of the Circeian games. And one time as hee was making mone, and bewailing among his skoole-fellowes, the hard fortune of a chariot driver, one of the greene-coate

---

[1] Wife of Amphion King of Thebes, who priding herself in her faire issewe 6 sonnes and as manie daughters durst compare with Latona, the mother of Apollo and Diana, but she with her arrowes killed them al, and turned her into a stone. [2] Foure of the clocke after noone. [3] Of other magistrates, who in respect of the Prince are accounted private. [4] Larcius, Lydus, Xiphilin. [5] Or Masques. [6] Or young untrained souldiers.

115

THE HISTORIE OF

NERO
CLAUDIUS
CÆSAR

faction, drawen and dragged by his steedes[1], being chidden therefore by his schoole-master, he had a lye ready, and said that he spake of Hector[2]. But, as about his first entrance to the Empire, his custome was daily to play upon a chess-bourd with ivory horses[3] drawing in chariots, so he used to resort also from his retiring place of pleasure[4], to all the Circeian games, even the very least and meanest of them. First by stealth and privily: afterwards in open sight; so as no man made doubt, but at such a day he would be sure alwaies there to be. Neither dissimuled he that hee was willing to augment the number of the prises. And therefore the shew of Chariot running was drawen out in length and helde untill late in the evening, by occasion of manie more courses than ordinarie: so as now the Masters of every faction deigned not to bring forth their crues and companies[5] unlesse they might run the whole day through[6]. Soone after himselfe also would needs make one and be seene oftentimes to play the Chariotier. And when he had tryed what hee could doe, and performed, as it were, his first Actes in (private) hortyardes among verie slaves and the base commons, he proceeded to shew himselfe in the greatest Cirque in all mens eyes, appointing one of his freedmen to put out a (white) towell for a signall, from the place where Magistrates are wont to doe it. But not content with this, that he had given good proofe of his progresse in these feats at Rome, hee goes, as I sayde before, into Achaia, moved especially upon this occasion. Those Cities and states where solemne gamings of musicke are usually held, had brought up a custome to sende all the Coronets of harpe-players unto him. This he accepted so kindly, that he not onely admitted at the very first to his presence the Embassadors who brought the same, but also placed them among his familiar guestes at the table. And being requested by some of them to sing at supper time, and highly praised with

---

[1] Or sore wounded and bruised with the wheeles running over him. See Plin. *Nat. Hist.* lib. 28 cap. 17.   [2] Who was likewise, *Raptatus Bigis* as Virgil writeth.   [3] Or Chariots, to expresse those games *Circenses.*
[4] *Secessu*, or by way of retyring and recreation.   [5] *Greges*, either *agitatorum, i.* of chariot drivers: or *equorum quadrigariorum, i.* of steeds, both to one effecte.   [6] Which was their greater gaine.

116

TWELVE CÆSARS

excessive applause, he came out with this speech, That æcians were the onely skilfull Hearers, and the men alone worthie of his studies. Neither made he anie longer stay, but tooke his voyage: and no sooner was hee passed over the sea to Cassiope[1], but presently he began to sing at the altar there of Jupiter Casius.

CLAUDIUS
CÆSAR

23

After this, he went to all the games of prise, one after another: for even those that usually are celebrated at most remote and distant times he commanded to be reduced all into one yeare[2], and, some of them also to be iterated[3]. At Olympia likewise hee caused, (contrarie to the manner and custome of that place) a game of musick to be held. And least whiles he was busied about these matters, anie thing might either call him away or detaine him: when he was advertised by his freed-man Helius, that the Citie affaires required his presence, hee wrot backe unto him in these words: 'Albeit your councell to mee at this present and your willing desire is, that I should returne with all speede, yet ought you to advise me and wish rather, that I may returne worthy my selfe, that is to say Nero.' All the while hee was singing, lawefull it was not for anye person to depart out of the Theatre, were the cause never so necessarie. Whereupon reported it is, that some great bellied women falling into travaile were delivered upon the very skaffolds: yea and many men besides, wearie of tedious hearing and praysing him, when the towne gates were shut, eyther by stealth leapt downe from the walles, or counterfeiting themselves dead were caried forth as corses to bee buried. But how timorously, with what thought and anguish of minde, with what æmulation of his concurrents and feare of the Umpiers, hee strove for the Mastery, it is almost incredible. His manner was to deale with his adversaries, as if they had been but his æquals and of the same condition with him, in this sort: namely, to observe, watch and mark their behaviours; to ly in the wind for to catch advantage: to

[1] A towne in Corcyra.   [2] Wherein hee thither came.   [3] Solemnized twice in the same yeare.

117

defame them under hand, other whiles to raile at them and give them hard tearms as they came in his way : yea and to corrupt with bribes[1] and giftes such as excelled in skill and cunning. As for the Judges and Umpiers aforesaid, hee woulde speake unto them in all reverence before he begun to sing, using these tearmes : That hee had done whatsoever was to be done : howbeit, the issue and event was in the hand of Fortune : they therefore, as they were wise men and learned ought to except and barre all chaunces and mishaps. Now upon their exhortations unto him for to be bold and venturous, he would indeed goe awaye from them better appaied, but yet for all that, not without pensive care and trouble of minde : finding fault also with the silence and bashfull modestie of some, as if the same argued their discontented heavinesse and malitious repining, saying withall, That he had them in suspicion.

24

During the time that hee strove for to winne any prise, so strictely obeyed hee the lawes of the game, that hee never durst once spit and reach up fleame : and the very swet of his forehead hee wiped away with his arme onely[2]. Moreover in the acting[3] of a Tragædie, when he had quickly taken up his staffe againe[a], which he happened to let fall, being much dismaied and in great feare, least for that delinquencie hee should be put from the stage : by no meanes tooke he heart againe, until an under actor or prompter standing by sware an oth that it was not espied and marked for the shoutes and acclamations of the people beneath. Now, whensoever he wan the victorie, he used to pronounce himselfe victour. For which cause, he contended also in every place for the Criers coronet[4][b]. And to the end, there should remaine extant no memoriall or token of any other victours[c] in these sacred games beside himselfe, hee commanded all their statues and images to be overthrowen, drawen with a drag and so flung into sinkes and privies.

---

[1] Thereby to make them relent and not to do their best.   [2] Or sleeve and not with anie handkercheife.   [3] Chaunting.   [4] Due to him that had the lowdest voice.

TWELVE CÆSARS

Furthermore, he ran with chariots for the best game in many places, and at the Olympicke solemnities with one that had a teeme of tenne steedes, notwithstanding he reproved the very same in K. Mithridates as appeared by certaine verses of his owne making. But being once shaken and hoisted out of his Chariot and set therein againe, howbeit not able to hold out, he desisted and gave over, before he had runne the race through. Yet was he crowned neverthelesse. After this, at his departure from thence, he enfranchised the whole Province throughout: and withall, the judges of these Games he endowed with the freedome of Rome, and rewarded with great summes of money. Which benefits of his himselfe published with his owne voice from the middle of the race, upon a day of the Isthmian games.

25

Beeing returned out of Greece hee entred Naples, mounted upon a Chariot drawne with white horses: for that, in the said Citie he had made profession first of his skill, (in musicke) and a part of the wall was cast downe against his comming, (as the manner is of all victours in those sacred games). Semblably rode he into Antium, and from thence into Albanum and so forward into Rome. But he entred Rome in the very same Chariot, wherein sometime Augustus had rode in triumph, clad in a purple cloke [1], and the same garnished with starres embrodered in golde : wearing upon his head the Olympicke Coronet [2], and bearing in his right hand the Pythisk [3] : with a pompe and gallant shewe of the rest before him [4], together with their titles and inscriptions testifying, where, and whom, in what kinde of songe or fabulous argument, hee had wonne : not without a traine also of Applauders [a], following his Chariot, after the manner of those that ride ovant in petie Triumph setting up a note, and crying with a lowde voice, That they were Augustians, and the souldiers of his triumph. From thence he rode forward, and having throwen downe the Arch of the greatest Cirque, he passed on through the

[1] Or Mantell. [2] Made of the wilde Olive branches. [3] Of Lawrell.
[4] Isthmian, of Pine, and Nemean of smallach or persley.

119

THE HISTORIE OF

Velabrum and market place, up to the Palatium and so to the temple of Apollo. To do him honor all the way as he went, were beasts killed for sacrifice, and saffron eftsoones strewed along the streets. Birdes were let flie, ribbands also and labels yea and sweete banketting junkets cast among. As for the sacred Coronets and guirlands aforesayde, he bestowed them in his owne bed-chamber round about his beds : likewise his owne statues pourtraied in the habit of an harper [1], and with that marke stamped he his money. And after all this, (so farre was he from letting slacke and remitting one jote his ardent study of his musicke profession) that for the preservation of his voice he would never make speech unto his souldiours, but absent [2] : or having another to pronounce his words for him [3] ; nor yet do ought in earnest or mirth without his Phonascus [4] by, to put him in minde for to spare his pipes and hold his handkerchiefe to his mouth : and to many a man hee eyther offered friendship, or denounced enmitie, according as every one praised him more or lesse.

26

His unruly wildnesse, unbridled lust, wastfull riotousnesse, avarice and cruelty, he practised verely at first, by leasure closely, as the trickes of youthfull folly : yet so, as even then no man might doubt, that they were the inbred vices of nature, and not the errors of young age. No sooner was it twi-light and the evening shut in but p   n   he would catch up a cap [5 a] on his head, and so disguisedly goe into tavernes and victualling houses : walke the streetes playing and sporting all the way, but yet not without shrewd turnes and dooing mischiefe. For he used to fall upon those that came late from supper and knocke them soundly : yea and (if they strugled with him and made resistance,) to wound and drowne them in the sinkes and towne ditches : to breake into petie shops also, and rifle them : for he had set up in his house at home a faire [6 b], there to receive the price of the

---

[1] Or Minstrell.   [2] i. Per Nuntios by messengers sent betweene.
[3] When himself was present.   [4] A moderatour of his voice.   [5] Or hood.
[6] Or market.

120

bootie which hee had gotten, and was to bee solde to who would give most and bid best therefore.   But many a time at such brawles and skufflings aforesaied, he endangered his eyes, yea and his life too; being once beaten well neere to death by a certaine young gentleman of Senatours degree[c], whose wife he had misused with uncleane handling.   Where-upon, never after durst he goe abroad into the streets at that houre of the night, without his militarie Tribunes fol-lowing after him aloofe and secretly.   In the day time also, beeing caried close in a chaire[1] into the Theatre, hee would be present in person, and from the upper part[2] of the *Pro-scœnium*[3] both give a signall to the seditious factions of players (setting them together by the eares) and also behold them how they bickered.   Now when they were come once to plaine fight, skirmishing with stones and fragments of broken seates, skaffolds, himselfe stucke not to fling apace at[4] the people, in so much as once he brake the pretours head.

27

But as his vices grewe by little and little to get head, he laide aside these wilde trickes by way of sport and in secret: and without all care of concealing and dissimuling the matter, broke out openly to greater outrages.   His meales hee drewe out at length[a] : eating and drinking from noone to midnight, dowssed and fomented oftentimes in cesternes of hote waters, and in sommer season within bathes altered and made colde with snowe.   His suppers hee tooke divers times abroade also in publike place, to wit, in the Naumachia[5] shut up and enclosed; or in Mars fielde; or else in the greatest cirque: where hee was served and attended upon by all the common Queanes of the Citie, and stinking strumpets[b] of the stewes.   So often as hee went downe the River Tiberis to Ostia, or sayled along the Baian Creeke[6], there were pro-vided in divers places of the strond and bankes, boothes to baite in, conspicuous brothell houses and taverns; where stood maried dames after the manner of hostesses and

---

[1] Or Licter.   [2] Or loft.   [3] The forestage.   [4] Or among.   [5] A broad place, wherein a Naval fight had sometime been exhibited but then filled up, yet it caried the former name still.   [6] Or Bay.

THE HISTORIE OF

victualling wives[c] calling unto him ; some here, some there
on both sides of the bankes, intreating him to land and
turne in to them. His manner was also to give warning
unto his familiar friends, and bid him selfe to supper : and
one of them it cost in sweet meats 4 millians[1] of sesterces[d] :
and another a good deale more in rose water and odoriferous
oyles or perfumes of Roses from Syrtium[e].

28

Over and besides the unnaturall abusing of boyes free-
borne, and the keeping of mens wives as his concubines, he
forced also and defloured Rubria, a vestale Virgin. Acte
a freed woman he went very neere to have wedded as his
lawefull wife[2] : suborning certaine men who had beene Consuls, to avouch and forsweare, That she was of Roiall bloud
descended. A boy there was named Sporus[a], whose Genitories
he cut out, and assayed therby to transforme him into the
nature of a woman. Him he caused to be brought unto
him as a bride, with a dowry, in a fine (yellow) veile, after
the solemne maner of mariage : not without a frequent and
goodly traine attending upon him : whom he maintained as
his wife. Hereupon there goes abroad a pretie conceited
jest of a pleasant fellow, That it might have beene wel and
happie with the World, if his father Domitius had wedded
such a wife. This Sporus trimly set out with the jewels,
decked with the ornaments of the Empresses, and caried in
a licter, hee accompanied all about the shire-townes of great
resort and market burroughes of Greece : yea and afterwards
at Rome, up and downe the street Sigillaria, manie a time
sweetly kissing him by the way. For, that he had a lust to
ly with his owne mother, and was frighted from it by some
depraving backe-friendes of hers ; for feare, least the proude
and insolent dame might by this kind of favour grow too
mightie, no man ever made doubt : especially after that he
entertained among his Concubines an harlot, most like in all
points (by report) unto Agrippina. It is affirmed moreover,
that in times past, so often as hee rode in a licter together
with his mother, hee played the filthy wanton, and was

---

[1] *Quadragies* HS.   [2] Which had beene a great disparagement.

TWELVE CÆSARS

bewrayed by the markes and spottes appearing upon her vesture.

29

As for his owne body, certes, he forfeited the honour thereof, prostituting it to bee abused so farreforth, as having defiled in manner all the parts of it, at the last, he devised a kind (as it were) of sport and game : that being covered all over in a wilde beastes skin, hee should be let loose forth of a cage[1] and then give the assault upon the privities of men and women both as they stood tyed fast to a stake : and when he had shewed his rage to the full, be killed, forsooth by Doriphorus[a] his freed-man, unto whom him selfe also was wedded like as Sporus unto him : insomuch as hee counterfeited the noise and cries of maidens, when they bee forced and suffer devirgination[2]. I have heard of divers that he was fully perswaded, No man nor woman was honest, or in any part of their bodies pure and cleane, but most of them dissimuled their uncleannesse and craftily hid it. As many therefore as professed[3] unto him their obscœne filthinesse, he forgave all other faults and trespasses whatsoever.

30

The fruite of richesse and use of money, he tooke to be nothing else but lavish expense : thinking them to be very base niggards and mechanicall pinch-pennies, that kept any account or reckoning what they spent and layde out : but such only passing rich and right *Magnificoes*, who mispent and wasted all. He praised and admired his uncle Caius in no respect more, than for that hee had lashed out and consumed in a short space an huge masse of wealth, left unto him by Tiberius : hee kept therefore no meane, nor made anye end of prodigall giving and making away all. Hee allowed unto Tiridates[a] (a thing almost incredible) 800000 Sesterces, day by day, for his expenses, and at his departure bestowed upon him not so little as one hundred milians. Menecrates the harper, and Spicillus the sword-

---

[1] Or grate. [2] I wish that both Suetonius and Dio had in this place and such like been altogether silent. [3] Confessed of themselves and their owne accord.

fenser hee enfeoffed in the livings, patrimonies and houses of right noble personages, who had triumphed. Cerco-pithecus, whom hee had enriched with the lands and houses, (as well within the Citie as Countrey) of Panercos the Usurer, he honoured like a Prince at his funerals; and enterred with the charges well neere of a royall sepulture. No garments did hee on his backe twice: at hazard when he played, he ventured no lesse than 400000 sesterces at a cast, upon every point or pricke of the chaunce[1][b]. Hee fished with a golden net[2] (drawen and knit) with cords twisted of purple and crimsen silke in graine. He never by report when he made anie journey, had under a thousand carroches in his traine. His mules were shod with silver. His mulitiers arraied in fine (red) Canusme cloth: and attended he was with a multitude of Mazaces[3] and Curreurs gaily set out with their bracelets and riche Phalers[c].

31

In no one thing was hee more wastefull and prodigall then in building. Hee made an house, that reached from the *Palatium* to the *Esquiliæ*: which at first he called his Transitorie[4]: but when it had been consumed with fire and was reedefied hee named his golden ædifice. As touching the large compasse and receit, the rich furniture and setting out whereof, it may suffice to relate thus much. The porch[5] was of such an heigth as therein might stand upright the geant-like image representing his owne person, an hundred and twentie foote high. So large was this house, as that it con-teined three galleries of a mile a peece in length[6]. Item, a standing poole like unto a sea, and the same enclosed round

---

[1] *Quadringenis Sestertiis.* Take *Sestertium* here in the newter gender: otherwise, it were but a meane venture for such an one as Nero: as amounting not above 3l. 2s. 6d. Whereas now, it ariseth to 3125l.
[2] *Aurato rete.* Orosius saith more expresly, *retibus aureis.* [3] Horse men of Africke and Cappadocia. [4] As one would say, the passage from one hill to another. [5] Or fore-gate. [6] *Porticus triplices milliarias.* If a man expound it thus: Galleries with three rows of pillers, or as many yles, a thousand foote in length, it wold be more consonant to the truth I suppose. And yet the proportion that followeth is very strange and answerable to the vulgar and received exposition.

about with buildings in forme of Cities. It received more-over · graunges with cornefields, vineyards, pastures and woodes to them stored with a multitude of divers and sundry beasts both tame and wilde of all sorts. In all other parts thereof, all was laide over with golde, garnished with precious stones and shels of pearle[1]. As for the par-lours, framed they were with enbowed roufs, seeled with pannils of Ivorie, devised to turne round and remove so as flours might be skattered from thence: with a devise also of pipes and spouts to cast and sprinkle sweet oyles from aloft. But of al these parlours and banqueting roomes, the principall and fairest was made rounde, to turne about con-tinually both day and night, in manner of the World[2]. The banes within this house flowed with salte water de-rived from the sea, and with fresh from the rivers Albulæ. This ædifice finished after such a fashion as this, when he dedicated[3], thus farre forth onely he liked, as that hee sayd, He now at length began to dwell like a man. Furthermore, hee began a poole[4] reaching from Misenum to the Meere[5] Avernus, covered all above head, enclosed and environed with Cloistures[6]: into which all the hote waters that were in the Bathes of Baiæ might bee conveied. Likewise he cast a fosse[7] from the sayde Avernus, as farre as to Ostia, and the same navigable: that men forsooth might saile in ships, and yet not be upon the sea. This caried in length 160 miles, and bare that breadth, as gallies with 5 ranks of oares might passe to and fro thereupon. For the perform-ing of these workes, he had given commandement, that all prisoners wheresoever should be transported into Italie: and that no person attaint and convict of anie wicked act, should be condemned otherwise, but to worke thereat.

32

To these outragions expenses, beside the trust and con-fidence he had in the revenewes of the Empire, put forward hee was upon a certaine unexpected hope also that he

---

[1] Mother of pearle.   [2] Or heaven.   [3] Made his first entrie into it after a solemn and festivall manner.   [4] *Piscinam.*   [5] (Or lake.)   [6] Or Walk-ing places.   [7] Or ditch.

THE HISTORIE OF

conceived, of finding a world of wealth: and that through intelligence given unto him by a gentleman of Rome, who assured him upon his knowledge, that the rich treasure and old store of silver and gold both, which Queene Dido flying out of Tyros caried away with her, lay buried in Affricke within most huge and vaste caves under the ground, and might be gotten forth with some small labour of those that would goe about it. But when this hope failed him and came to nothing, being now altogether destitute, and so far exhaust and bare of money, that of necessity even souldiours pay, and the fees due unto olde servitours in the wars for their service must run on stil and be differred, he bent his mind to promoting of false imputations, to pilling also and polling. First and formost hee brought up this order, that out of the goods of freedmen deceased in steed of the one half, three 4th parts should be exacted and gathered for him, of as many, I say as without publike cause bare that name, which anie of those families did, whereunto himselfe was allied. Afterwards, that their wils should be forfaite and confiscate, who were unthankful to the Prince [1]. Item, that Lawiers should not escape free and go cleere awaie, who had drawen and written such wils: as also, that all deeds and words should bee brought within the compasse of treason: if there could be found but anie promoter to give information. He called moreover after a long time passed, for the rewards and Coronets due to victours, which ever at any times the Cities and States had presented or decreed unto him at the games of prise. And whereas hee had prohibited the use of the Amethist [2] and purple colours, he suborned one of purpose under hand to sell upon a market day [3] some few ounces therof, and thereupon made stay of all occupiers and chapmen [4] whatsoever, and laid them fast. Furthermore, having espied once (as he was singing) a dame of Rome from the skaffolds in the Theatre, arraied in purple forbidden by the law [5], himselfe pointed at her (as it is verily thought) and shewed her to his Procura-

---

[1] Remembred him not in their wils and made him not an heyre.　[2] Or violet in graine.　[3] Or faire.　[4] Who had bought the saide colours.　[5] Julia: which Cæsar Dictator made. See in Jul. Cæs. cap. 43.

tours[1]: and presently caused the woman to be haled from thence and turned out, not only of her garments but also of all the goods shee had. He assigned an office to no man, but he used these words withall, Thou knowest what I have neede of. Also, Let us looke to this, that no man may have[2] anie thing. To conclude, he robbed the Temples of many giftes and oblations: the Images likewise therein made of golde or silver he melted into a masse: and among the rest, even those of the Tutelar gods (of Rome)[3]: which soone after Galba restored and erected againe in their places.

33

As touching his Parricides and murders hee began them first with Claudius: of whose death although he were not principall author, yet he was privie and accessarie thereto. Neither dissimuled he so much, as who afterwards was wont by a Greek by-word[4], to praise mushromes, (in which kinde of meat Claudius had taken his bane), as the foode of the gods[5]. Certes, be abused him after hee was dead in most spitefull and contumelious manner, both in word and deede, every way: taunting and twitting him, one while with his folly, another while with his crueltie. For, in scoffing wise he would say of him that hee had left now *morari*[a] anie longer among mortall men, using the first sillable of the sayd word long. And many of his decrees and constitutions he annulled as the acts of a doltish and doting man. Finally, he neglected the place of his funerall fire[6b]: suffering it to be empaled[7], but with sleight stuffe and low railes of timber. As for Britannicus, not so much for envie that he had a sweeter and pleasanter voice than himselfe, as for feare least another day he should bee more gracious then he among men, in remembrance of his Father, he attempted to make him away by poison. This poison, Nero had received at the hands of one Locusta, a woman who appeached and

---

[1] Procters or Factours. [2] Or possesse. [3] Apollo, Neptune, Jupiter, Juno, Minerva. [4] Or Proverbe. [5] θεῶν βρῶμα, alluding to the deification after his death. [6] *Bustum.* [7] As the manner was for certaine daies before the ashes and reliques were gathered up.

brought to light divers confectioners of poysons: and seeing it wrought later than he looked it should doe, and prooved not to his mind, by reason that it mooved Britannicus to the stoole onely and caused a laske, he sent for the said woman, and beate her with his owne hands: laying hardly to her charge that in steede of a poyson she had given him a remedie and holsome medecine. Now when shee alleaged for her excuse that she gave him the lesse dose[1], thereby to colour and cloke the odious fact, which would have bred much anger and hatred: 'Why! then belike,' quoth he, 'I am affraide of the lawe Julia'[2]. And so hee forced her before his face in his owne bed-chamber to compound and seeth a poison that should be most quieke and of present operation. And then having made triall thereof in a kid, after he saw once that the beast continued five houres before it dyed, he caused the same to be boyled againe and manie times more, and so he set it before a pig. And when the pig dyed presently upon the taking thereof, hee commanded it should be brought into his refection chamber, and given unto Britannicus as he sat at supper with him. No sooner had he tasted it but hee fell downe dead. Nero readily made a lye and gave it out among the rest of his guests, that Britannicus was surprised by a fit of the falling sicknesse, as his manner was to be. But the next morrow, in all hast hee tooke order for his corps to bee caried forth to buriall, with no better funerals than ordinarie; and that, in an exceeding great storme of raine. Unto the sayd Locusta, for her service done, he granted impunitie[3]: he endued her also with faire lands: yea and allowed her to have schollers for to be trained up under her in that feat.

34

His owne mother, for looking narrowly into him, and examining his words and deedes somewhat streightly; for seeming also to correct and reforme the same, thus farre forth onely at the first he was grieved and offended with, as that eft-soones he made her odious to the world, pre-

---

[1] In quantitie. [2] *De Veneficiis.* [3] For her former practise of poisoning, by which she stoode condemned.

tending that he was about to resigne up the Empire and depart to Rhodes[1]. Soone after, he deprived her of all honour, dignity, and authority: and removing from about her the guard of Germaine Souldiours[2] that attended upon her person, hee banished her out of the same house with him, and so forth out of the precincts of the Palace: neither cared he what he did, so he might molest and trouble her: suborning some of purpose, both to disquiet her whiles shee abode in Rome with suites and actions; and also when shee was desirous of repose and ease in a retiring place out of the way, to course her with reproachfull taunts and flouting scoffes as they passed that way either by land or sea. But beeing terrified with her threats and violent shrewdnesse, hee determined to kill and dispatch her at once. Having attempted it with poison thrice, and perceiving that shee was defended with antidotes and preservatives, he provided a bed-chamber for her, with so ticklish an arched roufe over her head, as beeing easily unjoincted, the frame thereof might fall in peeces in the night, and light upon her as she lay a sleepe. When this dessigne could not be kept close, but was revealed by some of the complices privie thereto, hee devised a ship, so made, as that quickly it should cleave a sunder: that either by the wrack, or fall of the fore-deck aloft, she might come to a mischiefe and perish. And so, making a semblance of a Love-day and reconciliation, hee sent for her by most sweet and kinde Letters, training her unto Baiæ, there to celebrate with him the solemnity of the *Quinquatrian*[3]. And having given order before hand to certaine Maisters of Gallies for to split the Foist[4] wherein she was embarqued, as if by chaunce they were run full upon her, he made it late ere he went to the feast, and sat long at it. Now when she was to returne back againe unto Bauli, in lieu of that vessell thus shaken and crackt, he put unto her the other abovesaid made with joints and vices, easie to fall in pieces: and so, with a cheerefull countenance accompanied her (to the

---

[1] As if she were the cause therof.   [2] *Militum et Germanorum :* Hen dia duo.   [3] A feast in the honour of Minerva, beginning five daies before the Ides of March, *i.* the 11 of March.   [4] Or Pinnace.

2 : R

129

THE HISTORIE OF

water side[1]) and at the parting also kissed her paps. All
the time after, he lay awake in great trouble and feare,
waiting for the issue of these enterprises. But when he
understood that all went crosse, and that she was escaped
to land by swimming; being altogether to seeke what course
to take, as L. Agerinus, her freed-man brought word with
great joy, How she was escaped alive and safe, he conveied
privily a dagger close by him[2]; and as if he had been
suborned and hired secretly (by her) to kill him, caused the
said Agerinus to be apprehended and bound with chaines:
and withall, his mother aforesaid, to be murdred: pretending, as if by voluntary death she had avoided the odious
crime thus detected, and so made her selfe away. Worse
matter yet than all this and more horrible, is reported
beside, and that by Authors of good credit and who will
stand to it: namely, That he ran in all hast to view the
dead body of his mother when she was killed: that he
handled every part and member of it: found fault with
some, commended others: and being thirsty in the meane
time[3], tooke a draught of drink. Howbeit, notwithstanding hee was hartned by the joyous gratulation of Souldiours,
Senate, and People, yet could he not either for the present
or ever after, endure the worme and sting of conscience for
this foule fact, but confesse many a time, that haunted and
harried he was with the apparition of his mothers ghost:
tormented also with the scourges and burning torches of
the Furies. Moreover, with a sacrifice made by direction
of magicians, he assaied to raise up her soule and spirite,
and to intreate the same to forgive him. Verily as hee
travailed through Greece, at the sacred Eleusine ceremonies
(from the institution and professing wherein all impious,
godlesse, and wicked persons are by the voyce of a cryer
debarred[a]) he durst not be present. To this parricidy of
his mother, he adjoyned also the murder of his aunt[4]. For
when upon a time he visited her lying sicke of a costive
bellie[5], and she a woman now well stept in yeares, in handling

---

[1] Or to the staires.   [2] Betweene his feete. Tacit.   [3] About midnight
it was.   [4] Domitia by his fathers side.   [5] *Ex duritia alui, alias enim
cibum non transmittit*, as Plinie writeth, 26 lib.

130

TWELVE CÆSARS

the tender downe of his beard new budding forth, chanced, NERO CLAUDIUS CÆSAR
(as the manner is) by way of pleasing speech, to say, ' Might
I but live to take up this soft haire when it fals[1], I would
be willing to dye '; he turning to those that stood next
unto him, in derision and scoffing manner sayde, ' Mary and
even streight wayes I will cut it of (for her sake),' and so
made no more adoe but gave order[2] unto the Phisitian to
plye the sicke woman still with stronger purgatives[3]. For,
even before she was through dead, he laide sure hold of
her goods, and suppressed her last wil that nothing might
escape his clutches.

• 35

Besides Octavia[4], he maried afterwards two wives: to wit,
Poppæa[5] Sabina the daughter of one[6] who had beene Questor,
and the wedded wife before of a romane Knight[7]: then,
Statilia Messallina, neice[8] in the third degree removed of
Taurus[9], twice Consul, who had once triumphed. For to
have and enjoy her, he murdred her husband Atticus Vestinus A.U.C. 815.
then Consul, even during the time of that honorable Magistracie. Soone wearie he was of Octaviæ's companie and
forsooke her bed. And when some friends reproved him for
it he made answere, that the jewels and ornaments only of a
wife ought to content her. Soon after, when he had assayed
many times (but in vaine) to strangle her, he put her away,
pretending she was barraine. But when the people misliked
this divorse, and forbare not to raile upon him for it, he proceeded, even to confine and banish her quite. In the end he
murdred her, under a colourable imputation of divers adulteries, charged upon her so impudently and falsely, that when
al generally who were by torture examined upon the point,
stood stoutly to the very last in deniall, he suborned and
brought in Anicetus[10] his own Pædagogue against her, who

---

[1] As if she wold say, If I might see thee once a man growen, etc., for he
came to be Emperour before he was 18 yeere olde. [2] You must suppose,
he sent for the barber first, etc. [3] As purging was the cure, so it was the
colourable means wherby she was killed. [4] The daughter of Claudius.
[5] Or Pompeia as some read. [6] Titus Ossius. [7] Rufus Crispus. [8] In
the right line of descent. [9] Statilius who in Augustus time built the great
Amphitheatre in Rome, bearing his name. [10] Who had brought him up
in his childhood.

131

THE HISTORIE OF

should slander himselfe with her and confesse that by a wile he had abused her bodie. The twelfth day after the said divorcement of Octavia, he espoused and maried the afore-said dame Poppæa, whom he loved intirely; and yet even her also he killed with a kicke[1] of his heele, for that, being big with child and sickly withall, she had reviled him and given him shrewd words, for comming home so late one night, after his running with chariots. By her he had a daughter named Claudia Augusta, whom he buried when she was a very infant. There was no kinde of affinitie and consanguinity were it never so neere, but it felt the waight of his deadly hand. Antonia, the daughter of Claudius, refusing after the death of Poppæa to bee his wife, he slew, under a pretense as if she went about to conspire against him and to alter the state. Semblably, he killed all the rest, that were either allied unto him or of his kinred. Among whom, A. Plautius a young gentleman was one. Whose bodie, after he had by force filthily against kind abused before his death: 'Let my mother go now,' quoth he, 'and kisse my successors sweet lips': giving it out, that he was her welbeloved dearling, and by her set on to hope and gape after the Empire. His sonne in law Rufinus Crispinus, the son of Poppæa[2] being yet of tender yeeres and a youth under age, because the report went of him, that in game he would play for Dukedomes[3] and Empires, he gave order unto his owne servants for to drowne in the sea, whiles he was there fishing. Tuscus his nources sonne he confined and sent away, for that being his pro-curatour in Ægypt, he had bathed in those baines which were built against his comming. His Preceptor and Schoole-master Seneca he compelled to dye[4]: albeit he had sworne unto him very devoutely, (when he made suite many times for a licence to depart the Court, and yeelded up therewith all his goods into his hands) That he[5] had no cause to suspect him: for he would rather lose his owne life then doe him anie hurt. Unto Burrhus, Captaine (of the guarde)[6] he pro-

---

[1] Or spurne.   [2] His wife, by Rufius Crispus a former husband.
[3] *Ducatus* or Captainships.   [4] To cut the master veines of armes and legs and so to bleed to death.   [5] Seneca.   [6] *Eparchos Ton doruphoron.*

mised a medicine to heale his swollen throat[1], and sent him the rank poison Toxicum for it. His freedmen[2], that were rich and olde, whose favour, friendship and directions had stood him in good steede for procuring unto him in times past adoption, and afterwards the Imperial rule, he cut short every one by poyson, partly put into their meats and partly mingled with their drinks.

36

With no lesse cruelty raged hee abroad even against strangers and meere forainers. A blazing hairy starre, commonly thought to portend death and destruction to the highest poures, began to arise, and had appeared many nights together. Beeing troubled therewith, and enformed by Babilus the Astrologer, that Kings were wont to expiate such prodigious signes with some notable massacre, and so divert the same from themselves, and turne all upon the heads of their Peeres and Nobles, he thereupon projected the death of all the Noblest personages in the Citie. And verily, so much the rather, and, as it were, upon just cause, by reason of two conspiracies by him published and divulged abroad: of which, the former and the greater, bearing the name of Piso[3], was plotted and detected at Rome: the latter going under the name of Vinicius[4] at Beneventum. The conspiratours had their triall, and pleaded bound with three-fold chaines: and as some of them confessed the action of their owne accord, so others[5] said moreover, That he was beholden unto them for it, because they could not possibly doe a cure upon him by any other meanes, (disteined as he was and dishonored with all kinde of wicked actes) but onely by death. The children of the condemned were expelled the Citie, and then, dispatched with poison or hunger-starved. It is for certaine knowen, that some of them with their pædagogues and booke-keepers tooke their bane all at one dinner togither, others were restrained for seeking and earning their daily food.

---

[1] A squinancie.   [2] Namely, Doriphorus and Pallas: Tacit.   [3] And his friends, *Pisoniana*.   [4] And his adherents, *Viniciana*.   [5] And by name Sulpitius Asper.

133

THE HISTORIE OF

After this without all choise and respect, without all
measure in his hand, he spared none : he put to death whomsoever it pleased him, and for what cause it skilled not. But
not to make long relation of many, it was laid to Salvidienus
Orcitus charge, that he had set and let three shops out of
his house about the forum, unto the Cities and States abroad
for (their Embassadours) for to make their abode and converse in. To Cassius Longinus the lawier (a man bereft of
both his eyes) objected it was, that in the antient pedigree
of his own house and linage, he had set up againe the images
of C. Cassius, one of them that murdred Cæsar. To Pætas
Thraseas, for having a sterne and severe countenance like a
Pædagogue. When these with other were appointed once
to dy, he allowed them no more then one houres respite to
live after, and because no further delay might come between,
he put unto them Chyrurgians (in case they lingred and made
no hast) to cure them out of hand, (for that was the term
he used) meaning thereby, to cut their veines and let them
bleed to death. It is verily thought also, that to a certein
great eater [1] (an Ægyptian borne) that used to feed on raw
flesh and whatsoever was given him, he had a great desire to
cast men alive, for to be quartered cut in peeces and devoured
by him [a]. Being lifted and puffed up, with these as it were,
so great successes [2], he said that no prince ever knew [3] what
he might do : and oftentimes he cast out many words betokening very significantly, that he would not spare the
Senators remaining behind, but one day utterly rase that
order and degree out of the common-wealth, and permit the
gentlemen of Rome and his freed-men only to rule provinces
and have the conduct of armies. Certes, neither at his comming home nor going forth any whether, vouchsafed he to
kisse any one of them, no nor so much as once to resalute
them : and when with formall complements he entred upon
his worke of digging through Isthmus [4], he wished and praied
alowd before a frequent audience, That the enterprise might

---

[1] *Polyphago cuidam*, or glutton.   [2] Or prosperity.   [3] Or none of the
Emperors knew.   [4] In Achaia, nere Corinth.

TWELVE CÆSARS

speed well and turne to the weale of himselfe and the people of Rome, concealing and suppressing al mention of the Senate [1].

38

But yet for al that, he spared not the people nor forbare the very wals and buildings of his country the Citie. When one in common talke upon a time chaunced to say,

'Ἐμοῦ θανόντος γαῖα μιχθήτω πυρί [a],

When vitall breath is fled from me,
Let earth with fire imingled be:

'Nay rather,' quoth he, ''Ἐμοῦ ζῶντος,'

Whiles vital breath remains in me, etc.

And even so he did indeede: for being offended, as it were with the ylfavoured fashion of the olde houses, as also with the narrow, crooked and winding streets, he set the citie of Rome on fire so apparantly, that many Citizens of Consuls degree, taking his chamberlaines [2] in the maner with matches, touchwood and hurds in their messuages (within the Citie) would not once lay hand on them but let them alone: yea and certein garners and store houses about his golden Ædifice (for that the plot of ground on which they were situate, his mind stood most unto) were by war-engins forcibly shaken, throwen down and fired, by reason they were built with stone wals. For 6 days and 7 nights together raged he in this wise making havocke of all, and driving the common-people to take up their Innes [3] and shrowd themselves the while about the toumbs and moniments of the dead. During this time, oeside an infinit number of houses standing apart from others [b], the goodly ædifices and buildings of noble capitains in old time, adorned stil and beautified with the spoiles of enemies, the stately temples also of the gods, vowed and dedicated by the auntient kings first, and afterwards in the Punick and French wars [4]; burned all, on a light fire: and in one word, whatsoever remained from old time worth the

[1] Comprising therein the gentlemens degree: not *Senatui, populoque Rom.* as the manner had beene. [2] *Cubiculares, i.* the grooms of his chamber.
[3] Or lodgings. [4] With the Carthaginians.

135

THE HISTORIE OF

seeing and memorable was consumed. This fire, beheld he daily out of Mæcenas high toure [c]: and taking joye (as he sayd himselfe) at the beautiful flame that it made, chaunted the winning and destruction of Troie, in that Musitians habit wherein he was wont to sing upon the stage. And because he would not misse, but lay fast holde upon all the bootie and pillage which possibly hee could come by, even from thence also, having promised free leave to cast forth dead karkasses, and rid away the rammell of the ruines, looke what reliques remained of all their goods and substance unburnt, he permitted not one to goe unto it. Finally, not onely by receiving, but also by exacting Contributions from all parts, he beggered well neere the provinces and consumed the wealth of private persons.

39

To amend the matter well, unto these barmes and reprochefull dishonors (of the State) so great as they were arising from the Prince, there happened also some other calamities by chance and fortune: to wit, a pestilence continuing one autumne, whereby thirtie thousand burials were reckoned in the record[1] of Libitina[2a]; an unfortunate losse in Britaine, wherein two principall townes of great importance were sacked[3], with great slaughter besides of Romane Citizens and Allies: a shamefull disgrace received in the East by reason that the Romane Legions in Armenia were put under the yoke as Slaves, and Syria was hardly and with much adoe kept in tearmes of allegeance. But a wonder it was to see, and a thing especially to be noted, that amid all these infortunities hee tooke nothing lesse to the heart, than the shrewd checks and reviling taunts of Men: and was to none more milde, than to such as had provoked him, either with hard speeches, or opprobrious verses. Many infamous libels and defamatorie words, both in Greek and Latine, were publikely

---

[1] As we say in the Church booke.   [2] In whose temple were to be bought or hired, whatsoever pertained to funerals and burials: Varro.   Plutarch taketh her for Venus.   [3] *Camelodunum et Londinium coloniæ*, etc. Tacitus. *i.* Maldon and London ij. Colonies; and togither with them, Verulamium a Burrough free town, (in the ruines wherof S. Albanes now standeth) in which places 7000 (by report) were slain of Citizens and Alies.

TWELVE CÆSARS

written, or otherwise cast and spred abroad against him [b], as for example these :

Νέρων, Ὀρέστης, Ἀλχμαίων, μητροκτόνοι.
Νεόνυμφον, Νέρων ἰδίαν μητέρα ἀπέκτεινεν.

Nero, Orestes [c], Alcmæon [d], did shorten mothers life :
  Nero slew his [1], when newly her he wedded as his wife.

Quis neget Æneæ magna de stirpe Neronem ?
  Sustulit hic matrem, sustulit ille patrem.

Who can deny, of great Ænea our Nero sprung to be
  That rid his mother of her life, as Sire [2] from fire did hee [e] ?

Dum tendit citharam noster, dum Cornua Parthus,
  Noster erit Pæan, ille Hecatebeletes.

Whiles our Nero bendeth his harpe [3] while Parthian his bow ;
  Our prince shall be Pæan. Hee Hecatebeletes [f].

Roma Domus fiet : Veios migrate Quirites
  Sinon et Veios occupet ista domus.

Rome will become a dwelling house [g] : to Veii flit a pace.
  Quirites, least this house before ye come take up the place.

But no search made he after the authours hereof, and some of them being by the Appeacher convented before the Senate, he would not suffer to sustaine any grievous punishment. As he passed by in the open street, Isidorus the Cynick [4], had checked him alowd in these tearmes, That he used to chaunt the calamities [5] of Nauplius [h] very well, but disposed of his owne goods as badly. And Datus, a plaier of the Atellane Comædies [6] in a certein Sonet singing these words [i], *Hugiaine pater,* i. Farewel father, Ὑγιαῖνε μῆτερ, i. Farewel mother, had acted the same so significantly, as that he feigned the one drinking and the other swimming, to expresse thereby the end of C. Claudius [7] and Agrippina [8] : and in the last conclusion of all, with these wordes,

  Orcus vobis ducit pedes,
  Now Pluto leadeth forth your feet [k],

in plaine gesture noted the Senate. The Actor [9] and

---

[1] To wit Agrippina.   [2] Anchises.   [3] Hexametre and Pentametre.
[4] Philosopher.   [5] Or evils.   [6] Which were very lascivious and licentious.   [7] Whose son he was by adoption, for some report, he tooke his poison in a cup of drinke and not in a mushrom.   [8] Who was thought to have perished in the sea : and indeede she hardly escaped drowning by swimming.   [9] Datus.

THE HISTORIE OF

Philosopher[1] Nero did no more unto, but banish them Rome
and Italie: either for that he set light by all shame and
infamie; or els least in bewraying anie griefe, he might stir
up and provoke pregnant wits to worke upon him.

40

Well, the world having indured such an Emperour as
this, little lesse than 14 yeares, at length fell away and forsooke him cleane. And first the French began, following
as the ringleader of their insurrection Julius Vindex, who
that very time governed the Province[2], as Propretour. Foretold it had been long agoe unto Nero by the Astrologers,
That one day he should be left forlorne. Whereupon this
saying was most rife in his mouth,

Τὸ τεχνίον πᾶσα γαῖα τρέφει,

An Artizane of anie kinde
In every land will living finde,

so that he might the better be excused and borne withall
for studying and practising the art of minstrelsie and singing to the harpe, as a skil delightful unto him now a Prince,
and needfull for him another day a private person. Yet
some there were who promised unto him so forsaken, the
goverment of the East parts: and others by speciall name
the kingdome of Hierusalem: but most of them warranted
him assuredly the restitution of his former estate. And
being inclined rather to rest upon this hope, when he had
lost Britaine and Armenia, and recovered them both againe:
he thought himselfe discharged then and quit from the fatall
calamities destined unto him. But sending one time to the
Oracle of Apollo at Delphi, and hearing this answere from
thence, That hee must beware of the yeare 73[a], as who would
say, He was to dye in that yeare (of his owne age) and not
before; and divining no whit of Galbæs yeeres, with so
assured confidence hee conceived in his heart not onely long
life but also a perpetuall and singular felicity, that when
he had lost by shipwracke things of exceeding price, he
stucke not to say among his familiars: That the fishes

[1] Isidorus.   [2] Of Gaule.

would bring the same againe unto him[1]. At Naples advertised he was of the rebellion in Gaule. Which fell out to be the very same day of the yeare, on which he had killed his mother. But hee tooke this newes so patiently and carelesly, that hee gave suspicion even of joy and contentment: as if occasion had beene offered and presented thereby to make spoyle (by the lawe of armes) of those most rich and wealthy Provinces: and streight waies going forth into the Gymnase[2], he beheld with exceeding great earnestnesse and delight the wrestlers and champions striving for the prise. At supper time also, being interrupted with letters importing more tumults and troubles still: thus farre forth onely he grew into choller and indignation, as that he threatned mischiefe[3] to them who had revolted[4]. To conclude, for eight dayes together he never went about to write backe unto any man nor to give any charge or direction at all, but buried the matter quite in silence.

41

At the last, throughly mooved and netled with the contumelious edicts of Vindex comming so thicke one in the necke of another, he exhorted the Senate, in a letter written unto them, to revenge him and the commonwealth: alleadging for an excuse the Squinsie[5] whereof hee was sicke: and therefore could not himselfe be present in person. But nothing vexed him so much as this, That hee was by him blamed for an unskilfull musician[6], and because in steede of Nero, he called him Ænobarbus[7]. And verely as touching this name appropriate to his house and family, wherewith he was thus in contumelious manner twitted, he professed to resume the same, and to lay away the other that came by adoption[8]. All other reviling taunts and slaunders hee

---

[1] As they did to Polycrates that mighty Tyrant of Samos: but it was not long before his fall and destruction.   [2] Publike place of exercise.
[3] *Malum* an emphaticall and significant word in this place: like as in Livie, lib. 4, *Malum militibus meis nisi quieverint.* As if he had said, A mischiefe take these Rebels: or, Mischiefe will come to them.   [4] *Descissent*, al. *dedissent*, as if mischief wold fall upon the authors heads.   [5] An inflammation or swelling in the throate.   [6] *Cithærædum*, a singer to the Harp.   [7] Which was the name of his family, and so had he been called before his adoption.
[8] Nero Claudius Drusus.

THE HISTORIE OF

confuted as meere false, by no other argument than this,
That unskilfulnesse, forsooth, was objected unto him in that
very art, which he had so painfully studied and brought to
so good perfection: and therewith asked them eftsones one
by one, whether they had ever knowen a more excellent
Musician than himselfe. But when messengers came still
one after another, in great feare he returned to Rome.
And having his hart lightned but a little in the way, with
a vaine and foolish presage by occasion that hee espied
and observed engraven upon a monument, a certaine French
souldiour with a Romane knight overmatched in fight and
trailed along by the haire (of the head): he at this sight
leapt for joy and worshipped the heavens. Neither then
verely, did hee so much as consult in publike with the
Senate, or assemble the people: but onely call forth home
to his house some of the chiefe and principall persons among
them. And having dispatched in great haste this consultation, the rest of that day he led them all about to his
musicall water instruments of a strange devise and fashion,
not before knowen: and shewing every one by it selfe unto
them, discoursing also of the reason and difficult workemanship of each one, he promised even anone to bring
them all forth into the open Theatre, if Vindex would
give him leave [1].

42

After that he understood besides, how Galba likewise and
the provinces of Spaine were revolted, he fell downe at once:
his heart was then daunted and cleane done: and so he lay
a good while speechlesse in a traunce, and ready, as one
would say, to goe out of the world. And so soone as he
came againe to himselfe, he rent his clothes, beat and knockt
his head, saying plainely, That he was utterly undone: yea
and when his nource came about him to comfort his poore
heart, telling him, that the like accidents had befallen to
other princes also before him, hee answered againe, That
hee above all the rest suffred miseries never heard of nor

[1] Which it seems he spake ironically; if simply, he meaneth, in case Vindex
interrupted not his sports and the publike felicitie.

140

TWELVE CÆSARS

knowen before: thus in his life time to forgoe and loose his Empire. Neither yet for all this strucke he saile one whit in laying away or leaving out one jot of his ordinary riot and supine slouthfulnesse. Nay when some little inckling was given of good newes out of the provinces as he sat at a most sumptuous and plentifull supper: hee pronounced even with expresse gesture like a player, certaine ridiculous rimes, and those set to lascivious and wanton measures, against the chiefetaines of rebellion: and what were those? even stale stuffe and commonly knowen already. Being also secretly conveied into the Theatre he sent word unto a certaine Player acting his part with great contentment of them that sawe ánd heard him, That he did but abuse his occupations[1].

43

Immediatly upon the beginning of this feareful tumult[2], it is credibly thought that he intended manie designes and those very cruell and horrible: yet such as agreed well enough with his naturall humour: namely, to sende under hand successours and murderers of all those that were Commanders of armies and regents of Provinces, as if they all had conspired and drawen in one and the selfe same line. Item, to massacre all banished persons where soever, and the Frenchmen every one that were to be found in Rome: those because they should not band and combine with them that revolted: these, as complices with their owne contrie men, and their abbetters. Item, to permit the armies for to make spoyle and havocke of the Provinces in Gaule. Item to poyson all the Senate generally at some appointed feast. Last of all to fire Rome and let wild beasts loose among the people, that thereby there might be more adoe and greater difficulty to save the Citie. But being skared from these designments, not so much upon anie repentance, as despaire of their accomplishment: and perswaded withall, that necessarie it was to make a voyage and warlike expedition; the Consuls then

[1] In that hee plaied without a concurrent, whereas himself but for his Businesses would have put him down.   [2] Occasioned by the Commotions and revolts abroad.

141

in place he deprived of their goverment before the due
time, and himselfe alone entred upon the Consulship in
their roomes, as if forsooth, the destinies had so ordained,
that Gaule could not be subdued but by a (sole) Consul[1].
Having then taken into his hands the knitches of rods[2],
when after meat he withdrew himselfe aside out of his
dining chamber, leaning upon the shoulders of his familiar
friends, hee protested, that so soone as ever he was come
into the Province: he would shew himselfe unarmed before
the armies: and do nothing else but weepe: and after he
had once by that meanes reclaimed the authors of the Revolt
and brought them to repentance, sing merily, the day
following, songs of triumph with them that rejoyced with
him. ' Which songs,' quoth hee, ' ought with all speede even
now to be composed for me.'

44

In the preparation of this warlike voiage, his speciall care
was, to choose forth meete wagons for the cariage of his
musicall instruments; to cut and poll the concubines which
hee caried out with him like men: and to furnish them with
battaile axes and little bucklers after the Amazonian fashion.
This done, he cited the Citie-tribes to take the militarie
oth: and when no serviceable men would answere to their
names, he enjoyned all Masters to set forth a certaine
number of bond-servants, neither admitted he out of the
whole family and houshold of every man, but such only as
were most approved, excepting not so much as their stewards
or clarkes and secretaries. He commanded likewise all
degrees to allow and contribute towards this expedition
part of their estate according as they were valued in the
Censors booke: and more than so, the tenants inhabiting
private messuages and great houses standing by them selves,
to pay out of hand in yearely pension to his exchequer.
Hee exacted also with great skornefulnesse[3] and extremitie,
good money rough and new coyned, silver fine and full of

---

[1] As sometime Cn. Pompeius Magnus was, for the like exploit.   [2] The
Consular authoritie.   [3] Surlinesse.

142

risings: golde pure and red as fire. In so much, as most men openly refused the paiment of all contributions: demanding in a generall consent, that what monies soever promoters had received for their informations, should rather be required backe againe at their hands.

45

By the dearth likewise of corne, looke what hatred was conceived against the gainers [1], the same grewe heavie upon him. For it fell out by chance that in this publicke famine word came of a Ship [2] of Alexandria [a], how it was arrived fraight with a kinde of dust for the wrestlers of Nero his court. Having thus stirred up and kindled the hatred of all the world against him, there was no contumelious despite but he sustained. To one statue of his, just behind the crowne of the heade, was set a chariot [3] with an Imprese in Greeke to this effect, Now in truth, and not before is the combate [b]. And againe, Now or never hale and drawe [c]. To the necke of another, there was tyed a lether-bagge [4], and therewith this title, What could I doe [5][d]? But thou hast deserved a verie lether budge [6][e] indeed. This writing also was fastned upon the Columnes [7], Now with his chaunting hee hath awakened the French [8][f]. And by this time manie there were who in the nigt season making semblance of chiding and brawling with their servants, called often for a Vindex [g].

46

Beside all this, he tooke affrights at the manifest portents [9] as well newe as old, of dreams, of prodigies [a] and of Osses [10]. For where as before time, be was never wont to dreame, when he had murdred his mother [b] once there appeared visions in his sleepe, him thought hee saw the helme of a ship wrested out of his hand as hee steered it: and

---

[1] *i.* Cornemungers *lucrantium.* [2] Or the fleete it selfe, *navis pro classe,* as *classis pro nave* by the figure Synechdoche. [3] Alluding to his Chariot running. [4] A Sachell *ascopera.* [5] *Ego quid potui.* [6] *Culeum.* [7] Pillers. [8] *Gallos et eum cantando excisse.* [9] Presaging foretokens. [10] *Ominum.*

THE HISTORIE OF

that by his wife Octavia hee was haled into a very narrow
and blinde place: one while that he was covered all over
with a multitude of winged ants; another while, that the
images of brave men descended of noble houses dedicated
to Pompeius Theatre, went round about him, and debarred
him from going forward. Also, that his ambling guelding,
wherein hee tooke most delight, was in most parts trans-
figured into the forme of an ape: but having his head only
sound and entier, did set up a lowde and shrill voice neigh-
ing. Out of the Mausoleum[1], when all the dores thereof
flewe of their owne accord open, a voice was heard calling
him by name. Upon the Calends[2] of Januarie, his domesticall gods, garnished and adorned (as they weare), at the
verie time when the sacrifice was in preparing, fell all
downe[3]. And as he was observing the signes by bird flight,
Sporus presented him with a ring for a newe yeares gift: in
the pretious stones whereof, was engraven the ravishing and
carying away of Proserpina. At the solemne nuncapation
of his vowes, when as a great and frequent number of all
degrees were alreadie assembled together, the keyes of the
Capitoll could hardly be found. What time as out of his
invective oration against Vindex these wordes were rehearsed
in the Senate, That such wicked persons should suffer
punishment, they all cryed out with one voice, *Tu facies
Auguste, i.* Thou shalt so doe O Augustus. This also had
beene observed, that the last Tragædie which he acted and
sung in publike place, was *Œdipus the Banished*, and just as
he pronounced this verse,

> Θανεῖν μ' ἄνωγε σύγγαμος, μήτηρ, πάτηρ.
> How can I chuse but death desire, .
> Thus bidden by wife, by mother and sire?'

he fell downe[4].

47

In this meane while, when newes came that all the other
armies also rebelled, the letters delivered unto him, as hee

---

[1] The stately sepulchre of Augustus.   [2] First day.   [3] All this
hapned upon the new-yeares day.   [4] *Decidis* or *desisse, i.* stayed and
gave over.

144

TWELVE CÆSARS

sate at dinner hee tare in peeces, overthrewe the table, and two cuppes (of Chrystall) out of which he tooke the greatest pleasure to drinke, and which he called Homericos, for certaine verses of Homere[1][a] engraven and wrought upon them, he dashed against the paved floure. Then, after he had received a poison of Locusta and put it up in a golden boxe, he went directly into the hortyards of the *Servitii*: where, having sent before his most trusty freed-servants unto Ostia for to rig and prepare a fleet to sea, he sounded the Tribunes and Centurions of the guard, whether they would beare him company and flie with him, or no. But when some of them made it coy and kept some hafting: others in plaine termes refused; and one also cried out aloud,

Usque adeone mori miserum est?[b]

What! is it such a miserie
To leave this life and so to die?

he cast about, and thought of many and sundry shifts. Whether hee should goe as an humble suppliant unto the Parthians or to Galba, or whether it were best for him, arraied all in blacke to come abroad into the Citie, and there in open place before the *Rostra*, with all the rufull and piteous moane that hee could possibly make, crave pardon for all that was past, and unlesse hee could turne the peoples harts unto mercy[2], make suite to have if it were but the Deputy-ship of Ægypt graunted unto him[c]. Certes, found there was afterwards in his Cabinet a Speech of his owne penning, as touching this Argument. But men thinke hee was scared from this enterprise, as fearing least before he thither could come[3], he should be pulled in peeces. Thus, putting off all farther cogitation of this matter unto the next day, and awakened about midnight[4]; when he understood that the guard of his Souldiours was retired and gone, hee leapt forth of his bed, and sent all about to his friends. But because no word was brought back from any of them, himselfe accompanied with a fewe about him went to every one of their lodgings: where finding all dores shut, and no

[1] See the annotation upon this place.   [2] And to suffer him for to injoy the Empire.   [3] To the *Rostra*.   [4] Or starting out of his sleepe.

2 : T   145

THE HISTORIE OF

body to make him answere, he returned to his bed chamber. By which time, his Keepers also and Warders were slipt from thence : but they had stollen away first the hangings and furniture of his chamber, yea and set out of the way the box aforesaid with the poison. Then straightwaies he sought for Spicillus the Sword-fencer[1], or any other common hackster he cared not who, by whose hand he might receive his deaths wound. But finding none, 'Well,' quoth he, 'and have I neither a friend nor a foe?' And so he runnes forth, as if he would have throwne himselfe headlong into Tiberis.

48

But having reclaimed once againe that violent moode, hee desired some more secret retyring place, wherein he might lurke a while and recall his wits together. And when Phaon his freed man made offer unto him of a Farme house of his, that he had by the Citie side, about foure miles off, betweene the high-waies Salaria and Numentana, bare footed as hee was and in his shirt[2], hee cast over it a cloake all sullied and which had lost the colour. And so covering his head, and holding an hand kercheife before his face, to horseback hee went, having not above foure persons in his companie, of which Sporus made one[3]. And being by and by affrighted with an Earthquake and lightning that flashed against his face, he heard withall, as an out-crie and showt (from the Campe hard-by), of the Souldiours ossing all mischiefe at him and all good unto Galba : yea, and one of the passengers that he met, saying, These be they that pursue Nero, as also another asking, What newes in Rome of Nero? Now by occasion that his horse under him senting a dead carkasse that was throwne out in the way, started and flung at on side, his face was discovered, and himselfe knowne of one Missicius a Pretorian Souldiour, who saluted him by his name. When they were come to the next Lane, turning out of the Rodeway, their horses they forsooke and turned them up : and so among thickets of shrubs, rough

[1] *Mirmillonem.* [2] Single wastcoate. [3] The rest were Phaon, Epaphroditus and Neophitus.

146

bushes and briers, with much a-doe through a narrow path within a reed plot, and not without clothes[1] spread under foote, he gat at length as farre as to the wall of the Country house above said over and against him. There, when the said Phaon perswaded him to bestow himselfe the meane while, within a pit, from whence sand had beene cast forth, 'Nay,' quoth he, 'I will never goe quick under ground[2]': and so, after he had staied a little (while there was a secret way a making to let him into the ferme house), he laded up water with his owne hand out of a ditch under him, minding to drink: 'and this,' quoth he, 'is Neroes decocted[3] water.' After this, because his cloake was torne among the bushes and briers aforesaid, he rid it from the pricky sprigs that were runne through and stuck therein, and so creeping upon all foure through a straight and narrow hole digged in the wall for him, received hee was into the next backe roome: where he laid him downe on a pallet made of a simple scant mattrice, and an olde over-worne cloake cast over it for a coverlet. Now when hunger came upon him, and thirst with all the second time, the browne and course bread verily which was offred unto him he refused; but of warme water he dranke a prety draught. .

49

When as each one called then instantly on every side upon him, to deliver him selfe with all speede from the reproachfull contumelies and abuses, whereto hee was hourely subject, he commaunded a grave to be made before his face, and gave a measure therefore according to the just proportion of his body: and therewith, if any peeces of marble stone might be found about the house, to be laid in order: that water also and wood should bee gotten together for his dead body to be washed anone therewith: weeping at every word he spake, and inserting ever and anone this pittifull

[1] For feare either of pricking his feete, or of being heard to goe. [2] Or into my grave. [3] Or sodden. Plinie reporteth, lib. 31, cap. 3: That Nero devised to seeth water first, then within a glasse to let it stand in snow, wherby it became exceeding cold: partly by the snow, and in part by the former decoction. A delicate drinke in the heate of Sommer.

THE HISTORIE OF

speech, *Qualis artifex Pereo!*[1] What an excellent Artisane
am I! and yet nowe must I die[2]. Whiles some stay was
made about these complements, Phaons Courrier[3] brought
certaine letters which hee intercepted and snatcht out of his
hands. And reading therein that hee had his Dome by the
Senate, To be an Enemie to the State: That he was laid
for all about to be punished, *More maiorum.* 'More maiorum!' quoth he, 'what kinde of punishment is that?' and
when he understoode, it implied thus much, That the man
so condemned, should be stript all naked, his head locked[4]
fast in a forke, and his body scourged with rods to death,
he was so terrified therewith, that hee caught up two
daggers[5] which hee had brought with him: and trying the
points of them both how sharpe they were[6], he put them
up againe, making this excuse, That the fatall houre of
his death was not yet come. And one while he exhorted
Sporus to begin for to lament, weepe and waile: another
while he intreated hard, That some one of them would kill
him selfe first, and by his example helpe him to take his
death. Sometime also he checked and blamed his owne
timorousnesse in these wordes, 'I live shamefully': and in
reproach, Οὐ πρέπει Νέρωνι, οὐ πρέπει· νήφειν δεῖ ἐν τοῖς
τοιούτοις· ἄγε ἔγειρε σεαυτόν, i. 'It becomes not Nero; it
becomes him not. In such cases as these hee had neede to
bee wise and sober: goe to man, plucke up thy heart and
rouse thy selfe.' Nowe by this time approached the Horsemen neere at hand, who had a warrant and precept to bring
him alive. Which when hee perceived, after hee had with
trembling and quaking uttered this verse,

ἵππων μ' ὠκυπόδων ἀμφὶ κτύπος οὔατα βάλλει[7],

The trampling noise of horses swift resoundeth in mine eares,

he set a dagger[8] to his throat, whiles Epaphroditus his
Secretarie[9] lent him his hand to dispatch him. When

---

[1] Meaning his singular skill in Musicke, for which pittie it was he should
ever die. [2] Or else, What manner of artisane am I now become, thus to
prepare mine owne funerall? [3] Or Footman. [4] Or set. [5] Or rapiers.
[6] *Acie: pro acumine mucronato.* [7] Homer, *Iliad* x. spoken by Nestor.
[8] Or rapier. [9] Or his Master of requests.

148

TWELVE CÆSARS

he was yet but halfe dead, a Centurion brake in upon him, and putting his cloake upon the wound, made semblance as if hee came to aide and succour him: unto whom he answered nothing but this, 'Too late. And is this your loyaltie and allegeance?' In which very word he yeelded up his breath, with his eyes staring out and set in his head, to the great feare and horrour of all that were present. He had requested of the companie which attended upon him, no one thing more earnestly than this, That no man might have his head severed from the body, but that in any wise he might be burnt whole. And Icelus, a freed man of Galba, who not long before was delivered out of prison (into which he was cast[1] at the beginning of the first tumult[2]) permitted so much[3].

50

His funerals were performed with the charges of 200000 Sesterces: his corps was caried forth (to buriall) enwrapped within white cloathes of Tinsel, woven with gold wire betweene, the very same that hee had worne upon the Calends of Januarie. His reliques, Ecloge and Alexandra his two Nources, together with Acte his Concubine bestowed within the monument belonging to the house of the Domitii his Auncestours: which is to be seene out of Mars field, situate upon the Knap of an hill within their Hortyards. In which Sepulcher his chest[4], made of Porphyrite Marble, with an Altar (as it were) or table of white Marble of Luna standing upon it, was enclosed round about with a fence of Thasian Marble stone.

51

Hee was for stature almost of complet heighth[5]. His body full of specks and freckles, and foule of skinne besides. The haire of his head somewhat yellow: his countenance and visage rather faire, than lovely and well favoured. His eyes gray and somewhat with the dimmest. His neck full

---

[1] By Nero.   [2] Occasioned by the rebellion in Gaule and Spaine.
[3] For he might do all in al with Galba. See Galb. 14.   [4] Or Cophin.
[5] Within a little of sixe foote.

THE HISTORIE OF

and fat. His belly and paunch bearing out: with a paire of passing slender spindle shanks: but withall, he was very healthfull. For, being as he was so untemperate and most royotously given, in 14 yeeres space, he never fell sicke but thrice: yet so, as hee neither forbare drinking of wine, nor any thing else that hee used to doe. About the trimming of his body and wearing of his cloathes so nice, as it was shamefull: in so much as hee would alwaies have the bush of his head laide and plaited by curles in degrees[1]: but what time as he travailed in Achaia, hee drew it backward also from the crowne of his head and wore it long[2]. For the most part, he ware a dainty and effeminate pied garment called Synthesis: and with a fine Lawne neck Kercheif bound about his neck he went abroad in the Streetes, ungirt, untrussed, and unshod.

52

Of all the Liberall Sciences in manner, he had a tast when he was but a child. But from the Studie of Philosophie his mother turned his minde; telling him, It was repugnant to one who another day was to bee a Soveraigne: and from the knowledge of auncient Oratours, his Maister Seneca withdrew him, because hee would hold him the longer in admiration of himselfe. And therefore, being of his owne accord readily enclined to Poetry, he made verses voluntarily and without paine. Neither did he (as some think) set forth other mens Poems as his owne. There have come into mine hands writing tables and bookes containing verses very famous and well knowne abroade, written with his owne hand: so as a man may easily see they were not copied out of other bookes, nor yet taken from the mouth of any other that indited them, but plainely penned, as a man would say, by one that studied for them, and as they came in his head, so put them downe: so many blots and skrapings out, so many dashes and interlinings were in them.

[1] As you may see in the coines and pictures of Otho the Emperour; Statius calleth this *suggestum comæ*, lib. 3, *Sylv.* [2] Haply in imitation of Apollo (who was *Intonsus*, and is called by Homer therefore ἀκερσεκόμης) because there especially he professed Musick, whereof Apollo is the Patrone.

150

TWELVE CÆSARS

53

No small delight he had beside in painting; and most of all in forging and moolding counterfaites. But above all, he was ravished and lifted up with popularity and praise of men: desirous therfore to imitate and equal them, who by any meanes pleased the humours and contented the minds of the common people. There went an opinion and speech of him, that after he had gained the Coronets for his musicall feats performed upon the stage, hee would at the next five yeares revolution, go unto the Olympicke games, and contend for the prise among the Champions there. For, he practised wrestling continually. Neither beheld he the Gymnicke games throughout all Greece otherwise, than sitting below within the Stadium[1], as the manner of the Judges and Umpires of such masteries: and if any paires[2] of them drew to farre backe out of the appointed place, to plucke them with his own hands into the middle againe. He had intended moreover (since he was reputed to have equalled Apollo in singing and matched the Sun in charioting) to imitate also the worthie acts of Hercules. And men say, there was a Lion prepared, which he, all naked, should either with his club braine, or els with streight clasping beetweene his armes throttle and crush to death within the Amphitheatre, in the sight of all the people.

54

Certainely, a little before his ende he had openly made a vowe, That in case he continued stil in good and happie estate, represent he would likewise at the games, in his owne person after victory obtained, an Organist and player upon water instruments, upon the flute also and hautbois, yea and a bagpiper, and on the last day (of the said games) an actor of Enterludes: what time he would daunce and gesture Turnus in Virgill. And some write, that Paris the actor was by him killed, as a concurrent that stood in his way and eclipsed his light.

[1] Or the lists.   [2] Or couples matched.

THE HISTORIE OF

55

A desire he had, (foolish and inconsiderate though it were) of æternity and perpetuall fame. And therefore, abolishing the old names of many things and places, hee did upon them new, after his owne. The moneth Aprill also hee called Neroneus. He ment moreover to have named Rome, Neropolis[1].

56

All Religions whersoever he had in contempt, unlesse it were that onely of the Syrian goddesse[2]. And yet soone after he despised her so farre, that hee polluted her[3] with urine: by occasion that he was wonderfully addicted to an other superstition, wherein alone hee continued and per-severed most constantly. For having received in free gift a little puppet representing a young girle, at the hands of a meane commoner and obscure person[4], as a remedy, forsooth, or defensative against al treacheries and secret practises: and thereupon straight waies chauncing to dis-cover a conspiracie, he held it for the soveraine deity above all, and persisted honoring and worshipping it every day with 3 sacrifices. Nay he would have men beleeve, that he foreknew things to come by advertisement and warning given from her. Some few moneths before he lost his life, he tooke regard also of the Skill in prying into beasts entrailes. Which he observed in deede, but never sped well therewith, nor gained thereby the favour of the Gods.

57

He died in the two and thirtieth yeere of his age; that very day of the yeere, on which in times past he had murdred his wife Octavia: and by his death brought so great joy unto the people generally, that the Commons wore Caps[5], and ranne sporting up and downe throughout the Citie. Yet there wanted not some, who a long time

---

[1] Neroes Citty.   [2] Atergate or Astarte ; the same some think that Juno.
[3] Her image.   [4] Or unknowen to him.   [5] Or Bonets, to testifie freedome recovered.

152

TWELVE CÆSARS

after decked his Tombe with gay flowers that the Spring and Sommer doe affourd : and who, one while brought forth his Images clad in robes embrodred with purple gards before the *Rostra* : otherwhile published his Edicts, as if he had beene yet living and would shortly ,returne to the great mischiefe of his enemies.   Moreover, Vologesus King of the Parthians, when he sent his Embassadours unto the Senate for to treat about the renuing of league and Alliance with them, requested this also very earnestly, That the Memoriall of Nero might be still solemnized.   To conclude, when twenty yeeres after his decease (whiles I my selfe was but a young man) one arose among them (no man knew from whence, nor of what condition) who gave it out, That hee was Nero, (so gracious was his name among the Parthians,) he was mightily upheld and maintained, yea and hardly delivered up againe [1].

NERO CLAUDIUS CÆSAR

[1] Namely, to Calphurnius Asprenas, to be executed for a lying counterfeit.

THE HISTORIE OF

THE HISTORIE OF
SERVIUS SULPITIUS GALBA

1

HE Progenie[1] of the Cæsars ended in Nero. Which, that it would so come to passe, appeared verily by many signes, but by two of all other most evident. As Livia in times past immediatly after her mariage with Augustus, went to see a Mannour house and land of her owne in the Veientane Territorie, it fortuned that an Eagle soaring over her head let fall into her lap a white hen, holding in her bill a Lawrell branch even as she had caught it up. And thinking it good to have both the foule kept, and the said branch set in the ground : behold there came of the one such a goodly broode of chickens[2], that even at this day the very house aforesaid is called *Ad Gallinas* : and sprung of the other so faire a row of Bay trees, that all the Cæsars when they were to ride in triumph gathered from thence their Laurell guirlands[3]. And as the manner was, that when any of them tryumphed, they should pricke downe straight waies others in the same place : so it was observed likewise, that a little before the death of every one the tree by him planted, did mislike and die. In the last yeere therefore of Nero, not onely the whole grove of bay trees withered to the very roote, but all the hens there died every one. And anone after the temple of the Cæsars being strucken with lightning, the heads withall of their

[1] Or line. [2] Which proved white, as also the whole breed of them. Dio.
[3] And branches which they held in their hands. Plin.
154

TWELVE CÆSARS

Statues fell downe all at once, and the Scepter of Augustus was shaken out of his hands[1].

2

After Nero succeeded Galba, in no degree allied unto the house of the Cæsars : but without all question a right noble gentleman of a great and aunciont race[2] : as who in the titles and Inscriptions over his owne Statues wrote himselfe alwaies the Nephew[3] once removooved of Q. Catulus Capitolinus : and being once Emperour did set up also in his Haule[4] the Lineall processe and race of his house, wherein he deriveth his descent by the father side, from Jupiter, and by his mother from Pasiphæ, the wife of King Minos.

A.U.C. 821.

3

To prosecute the Images and Laudatorie testimonials belonging to the whole stocke and linage in generall were a long peece of worke: those onely of his own family wil I briefly touch. The first of all the Sulpitii, why, and wherupon he bare the surname of Galba, there is some doubtfull question. Some thinke it came by occasion of a Towne in Spaine, which after it had beene a long time in vaine assaulted, hee at length set on fire with burning brands besmeered all over with Galbanum[5] : others, for that in a long sickenesse which hee had, hee used continually Galbeum, that is to say, a cure with remedies enwrapped within wooll[6] : some againe because hee seemed to be very fat, and such a one, the French doth name Galba : or contrariwise, in regard that he was as slender, as are those creatures (or wormes)[7] which breede in the trees called Esculi, and be named Galbæ. This familie one Servius Galba who had beene Consul, and in his time most eloquent, ennobled first, and made renowmed, who by report, rulinge

A.U.C. 610.

---

[1] Plin. saith the very same.   [2] Or petigree.   [3] *Pronepotem.*   [4] Or Court yard.   [5] A gumme or hardened juice yssuing out of the roote (when it is wounded) of a plant called *Ferula.*   [6] Like unto those round rols which women in stead of farthingales use under their clothes beneath the wast called in Latine *Galbæi.*   [7] Resembling magots.

THE HISTORIE OF

the province of Spaine as Prætour, having treacherously [1] put to sworde 30000 [2] Lusitanes, was the cause of the Viriatine [3] warre. His Nephew being maliciously bent against Julius Cæsar (whose Lieuetenant he had bin in Gaule) for a repulse that he tooke in suing to be Consul, joyned in the conspiracy with Cassius and Brutus: for which condemned he was by the law Pædia. From this man descended immediately the Grandsire and father of this Galba the Emperour. His Grandfather for his booke and learning was more famous, then for any dignity in common weale that ever he attained unto. For, he arose no higher, than to the degree of a Prætour: but many histories he wrote, and those not slightly nor negligently composed. His father bare the honourable office of Consul: a man very low of stature and withall crowchbacked: and having but a meane gift in Oratory yet used he to plead causes industriously. Two wives he had, Mummia Achaica the neipce of Catulus, and once remooved of Lucius Mummius, who rased and destroyed Corinth: likewise Livia Ocellina, an exceeding welthy Ladie and a beautiful. Of whom for his noble bloud sake, it is thought he was woed [a]: yea, and somewhat the more hotely, after that, (upon her importunate suite) hee stript himselfe once out of his clothes in a secret place before her, and revealed the imperfection of his bodie, because he would not seeme to deceive her, for want of knowledge. By Achaica, he had issew Caius and Servius. Of whome, Caius the elder, having wasted his estate and spent all, left the City of Rome, and was by Tiberius prohibited to put in his lot for to be chosen Proconsull in his yeere [4]: whereupon voluntarilie he killed himselfe.

4

To come now unto Servius Galba the Emperour, borne he was when M. Valerius Messalla, and Cn. Lentulus were Consuls, the ninth day before the Calends of Januarie, in a

---

[1] *Perfidia* according to M. Tullius in *Bruto*. Some expound it otherwise, namelie for their treachery. Livius. [2] 7000 as Valerius Max. saith. [3] Of Viriatus the Captaine thereof. [4] When his time by course came.
156

country house situate under [1] a little hill neere unto Terracina, on the left hand as men goe to Fundie. Being adopted by his stepmother [2], he assumed the name of Livius, and the surname Ocella [3], changing his fore name with all. For, afterwards even unto the time of his Empire, he was forenamed Lucius in steed of Servius. It is for certain knowne, that Augustus (what time as little Galba among other boyes like himselfe saluted him,) tooke him by his pretie cheeke [4] and said, Καὶ σὺ τέκνομ τῆς ἀρχῆς ἡμῶν παραγεύσῃ, i. 'And thou also my child shall have a tast one day of our soveraine rule.' Tiberius likewise, when hee had knowledge once that hee [5] should bee Emperour, but not before old age, 'Go to,' quoth he, 'let him live a Gods name, seeing it is nothing to us.' Also as his Grand-father was sacrificing for the expiation of an adverse flash of lightning [6], (what time an Ægle caught out of his hands the inwards of the beasts, caried them away, and bestowed them in an Oke bearing mast [7]) answere was given unto him by the Soothsayers out of their learning, that thereby was portended and foreshewed unto his house, soveraine government: but it would be late first. Then he againe, by way of Irrision, 'Yee say very true indeed, that will be,' quoth hee, 'when a mule shall bring foorth a fole.' Afterwards when this Galba began to rebell and aspire unto the Empire, nothing hartened him in this dessigne of his so much, as the foling of a mule. For when all men besides, abhorred this foule and monstrous prodigie, he alone tooke it to be most fortunate: calling to remembrance the fore said sacrifice and the speech of his grandfather. When hee had newly put on his virile gowne, he dreamt that fortune spake these words unto him, namely, how she stood before his doore all weary, and unlesse she were let in the sooner she should become a pray unto whom soever shee met. No sooner awakened he, and opened his Port hall doore [8], but he found hard by the entry [9], a brason Image of the said goddesse about a cubit

---

[1] *Supposita*, or rather as some read, *Superposita*, i. upon.   [2] Livia Ocellina.   [3] Or Ocellaris.   [4] As the maner was in kissing young children.   [5] Galba.   [6] For some be fortunate and signifie good.   [7] For some bee fruitlesse.   [8] Or the outward Court-gate.   [9] Or Doore-sill.

157

THE HISTORIE OF

long: which hee caried away with him in his bosome to
Tusculum where he was wont to summer, and having consecrated it in one part of his house there, worshipped the same
from that time forward with monethly supplications, and a
Vigill[1] all night long once every yeere. And albeit he was
not yet come to his middle and staied age, yet retained he
most constantly, this old manner of the Citie (which was
nowe worne out of use, but that it continued still in his
house and linage) that his freed-men and bond servants
should duelie twice a day present themselves all together
before him : and one by one in the morning salute him with
a good morrowe, and in the eveninge take their leave likewise with a farewell and also good night.

5

Among the liberall Sciences he gave himselfe to the
studie of the (Civil) lawe. He entred also into the state of
wedlocke, but having buried his wife Lepida, and two sonnes
that he had by her, he led alwaies after a single life.
Neither could he ever, by any offer or condition be perswaded
to marriage again, no not of Dame Agrippina, who by the
death of Domitius[2] became widdow, and had by all meanes
solicited Galba even whiles he was the husband of a wife,
and not yet a single man, and in so much as at a great meeting of Ladies and Matrones, the mother of his wife Lepida
shooke her uppe roundly, yea and knockt her well for it
with her own fists. He honoured and affected above al
others Livia Augusta the Empresse, through whose grace
and favoure whiles shee lived he became mightie, and by
whose will and testament when she was dead, he had like to
have beene enriched. For wheras among others whom shee
remembred in her will, he had a speciall legacie to the valew
of 50 millians of Sesterces bequeathed unto him[3] : because
the said summe was set downe in figures and cyphres
and not written out at large, her beire Tiberius brought
it downe unto one halfe millian[4] : and yet even that he
never received.

[1] Or wake.   [2] The father of Nero.   [3] *Quingenties* HS., some read
quinquagies rather, *i.* 5 millians.   [4] *Ad quingenta*, sc. *sestertia.*

TWELVE CÆSARS

6

Having entred upon the honourable offices of state before due time by law set downe: when he was Prætour, during the playes and games called Floralia[1], hee shewed a new and strange kind of sight, to wit, Elephants walking uppon Ropes. After that, he governed the province Aquitaine almost one whole yeare. Soone after he bare the ordinarie Consulship in his due time[2] for the space of 6 moneths. And it fell out so, that as himselfe therein succeeded Domitius the father of Nero, so Sylvius the father of Otho followed immediately after him: a very presage of the event ensuing: whereby bee came to bee Emperour just in the middle betweene the sonnes of them both. Being by Caius[3] Cæsar substituted Lord generall for Getulicus, the very next day after he was come to the Legions, when as the soldiers at a solemne shew which happened then to be exhibited, clapped their hands, he restrained them with this Præcept[a], That they should keepe their hands within[4] their Clokes[5]: wherupon, this byword annon ranne rife through the Campe:

Disce miles militare,
Galba est, non Getulicus.

Lerne, soldiers, service Valorous[6]:
Galba is here, and not Getulicus[b].

7

With semblable severitie, he inhibited all petitions for placards[7] and pasports. The old beaten souldiers as well as the new and untrained, hee hardened still with continuall worke and labour: and having soone repressed the Barbarians who by their rodes and incursions had now by this time broken in violently and set foote within Gaule, he quit

[1] Either in honour of Flora the Goddesse of Floures, or else in thankefull memoriall of a famous Curtesan named Flora who made the people of Rome her heire and gave the Citty a great summe of mony: out of the yeerely increase whereof were the charges defraied that went to these licentious plaies. [2] Not substituted in the rowme of another deceased. [3] Caligula. [4] Or under. [5] Or Mandilions. [6] Or Laborious. [7] Licences to be absent from the Camp.

159

THE HISTORIE OF

himselfe so well and shewed such good proofe of his armie
unto Caius [1] also then and there present in proper person as
that among an infinite number of forces levied and assembled
out of all provinces there were none went away with greater
testimonies of proesse nor received larger rewards than he
and his regiments.   Himselfe above them all was most
bravely beseene in this, that marching with his targuet
before him he marshalled the gallants justing and running
at tilt in the plaine field: and for that he ranne also by
the Emperours chariot side, for the space of twentie miles.
When tidings came that Caius [2] was murdered, and many
pricked him forward to take the opportunitie then offered,
hee preferred quietnesse and rest.   For which cause hee
stood in especiall favour with Claudius, and was admitted
into the ranke of his inward friends; a man of that worth
and reputation as that when hee fell sodainely sicke (although
not verie grievously), the day appointed for to set forth in
the Brittish expedition was differred.   He governed Africk
as Proconsul two yeeres: being elected without lots drawing,
for to settle and bring into order that Province farre out of
frame and disquieted as wel with the civil mutinies, among
the soldiers, as tumultuous commotions of the barbarous
inhabitants.   Which commission he discharged with great
regard of severe discipline and execution of Justice even in
very small matters.   A soldier of his there was, who during
the expedition above said, in a great dearth and scarcity of
Corne, was accused to have sold a residue remaining of his
owne allowance, to wit, a Modious [3] of wheat, for one
hundred deniers [4]: whereuppon hee gave straight commandement, that when the said souldier began once to want food,
no man should be so hardy as to relieve him.   And so for
hunger he pined to death.   As for his civill Jurisdiction
and ministring justice: when there grew some question and
debate about the proprietarie and right owner of a labouring
beast [5], and slight evidences and presumptions on both sides
were alledged: as simple witnesses also produced and therefore hard to devine and guesse of the truth, he made this

[1] Caligula.   [2] Caligula.   [3] Much about our peck.   [4] 3l. 2s. 6d.
sterl.   [5] As some horse or mule.

160

TWELVE CÆSARS

decree, That the beast should be led hoodwinked[1] unto the poole where it was wont to be watered: and when it was unhooded againe, he awarded and pronounced the said beast to be his, unto whom of the owne accord he returned directly after he had drunke.

8

For his brave exploits atchieved both in Africke then, and also in Germanie afore time, he received the honour of tryumphall Ornaments and a triple Sacerdotall dignitie, being admitted among the Quindecimvirs[2]; into the guild and confraternitie of the Titii[a]: and the Colledge or societie of the Priests Augustales[b]. And from that time unto the midst well neere of 'Neroes Empire, he lived for the most part private in some retiring place out of the way: yet so as he never went forth any journey (were it but for exercise by way of Gestation[3]) but he tooke forth with him in a wagon going hard by, to the valew of a millian of Sesterces in gold untill such time, as making his abode in a towne called Fundi, the Regencie of a province in Spaine named Tarraconensis, was offered unto him. And it fortuned that when he was newly arrived and entred into that province, as hee sacrificed within a publike temple, a boy among other Ministers holding the Censer[4], sodainely had all the haire of his head turned gray. Now there wanted not some who made this interpretation, That thereby was signified a change in the states, and that an old man should succeede a younge, even himselfe in Neroes steed. And not long after, there fell a Thuntherbolt[5] into a lake[6] of Cantabria: and found there were immediatly twelve axes: a doubtlesse tooken presaging Soveraine Rule.

9

For 8 yeares space he governed that province variably

---

[1] Covered all over the head.   [2] *Sacris faciundis*, or *Sybillinis libris inspiciundis*, *i*. to oversee sacrifices and divine service or to peruse the propheticall books of Sibylla.   They were in number 15.   [3] Carying in a light litter or chaire.   [4] Incence panne.   [5] Or dint of lightening.
[6] *Lacum*, al. *Lucum*, *i*. a grove.

THE HISTORIE OF

and with an uneven hand. At the first, sharpe he was, severe, violent, and in chasticing verily of trespasses beyond all measure extreame. For he caused a Banker, for unfaith-full handling and exchang of mony to leese both his hands, and to have them nailed fast unto his owne shop bourd: a Guardian also he crucified, for poysoning his ward, whose beire he was in remainder. Now, as the partie Delinquent called for the benefit of law, and avouched in his plea, That he was a Romaine Citizen[1], Galba, as if he would alay his punishment with some comfort and honour[2]: commanded the crosse already made to be changed, and another to be reared far higher then the ordinarie: and the same laid over with a white colour. By little and little he grew to be slouthfull, carelesse and Idle, because he would minister no matter unto Nero for to worke uppon: and for that (as himselfe was wont to say) no man was compelled to render an accoumpt of his owne Idlenesse[3]. As hee held the Judiciall Assises at new Carthage, he had intelligence that Gaule[4] was in a tumult. And whiles the Embassadour[5] of Aquitaine besought him earnestly to send aide, the letters of Vindex came in the very nicke: exhorting him to frame and carie himselfe as the deliverer and protectour of Mankinde, even to take upon him to be their generall Captaine. He, making no longer stay upon the point, accepted the offer, partly for feare and in part upon hope. For he had both found out the warrants of Nero sent privily unto his Agents and pro-curatours there, as touching his death: and also much con-firmed and strengthened he was, as well by most luckie Auspices and Osses, as by the prophesie of an honest Virgin: so much the rather, because the very same verses contain-ing the prophesie, the priest of Jupiter at Clunia, had two hundred yeares past (by warning and direction given him in a dreame) fetched out of an inward and secret vault of the Temple, delivered then likewise by a maiden which had the spirit of prophesie. The meaning and effect of which verses was, That one day there should arise

[1] And therefore not to be crucified.   [2] *Solatio et honore,* or comfortable honor: Hen dia duo.   [3] For, they bee stirring spirits, that are looked into in a State.   [4] France.   [5] Or Lieutenant.

TWELVE CÆSARS

out of Spaine the soveraine Prince, and Lord of the whole world.

10

Therefore, when he had mounted the Tribunall, as if hee intended then the manumising[1] of sclaves, and set before him in open sight very many pourtraicts and Images of such as had beene condemned and killed by Nero: whiles there stood also in his presence a boy of noble bloud[2], whom he had sent for of purpose out of one of the Baleare Ilands hard by, where he was exiled[3]: he bewailed the state of those times. Wherupon being with one accord saluted Emperour[4], yet he professed himselfe to be the Lieutenant onely of the Senate and people of Rome. After this, having proclaimed a Cessation of Judicial pleas for the time; out of the Commons verily of that Province, he enrolled both Legions and Auxiliaries, over and above the old armie, which contained on Legion, two cornets of horsemen, and three cohorts: but out of the better sort, to wit, the Nobility and Gentrie, such I meane as for wisdom and age went before the rest, he ordained a body of a Senat: unto whom men shold have recourse touching matters of greater importance, as need required. He chose forth also young gentlemen, for the knights degree, who continuing stil the wearing of (gold) Rings shold be called *Evocati*[5], and kept watch and ward insteede of (sworne) Soldiers[6] about his lodging and bedchamber. Hee sent out his Edicts also in every Province, counselling and perswading all and some to joyne with him in these designements: and (proportionally to the meanes that every one had) to helpe and promote the common cause. Much about the same time, in the fortification of a towne which he had chosen to be the Capitall seate of the warre, a Ring was found of Antique worke, in the Gemm or stone whereof was engraven the expresse resemblance of victorie[a] together with a *Trophee*[b]: and soone after, a ship of Alexandrea, fraight with armour, arrived before

---

[1] Enfraunchesing. [2] Some noble mans sonne of Rome. [3] By Nero.
[4] Or L. General. [5] As if they had served their full time, and were now called forth againe by way of honour. [6] Who usually wore rings of yron.

THE HISTORIE OF

SERVIUS
SULPITIUS
GALBA

Dertosa[1], without pilot, without mariner or passenger: that noe man might make any doubt, but that this warre was just, lawfull, and undertaken with the favour and approbation of the Gods. But lo, sodainely and unlooked for, all in manner was dasht and put out of frame. One of the two Cornets of horsemen above mentioned, as bethinking themselves and repenting that they had changed their military oth was at the point to fall away and forsake him as hee approched the Campe, yea and hardly kept in their alleageance to him: certaine slaves also, whom (being prepared a forehand to doe him a mischiefe) hee had received as a present at the hands of a freed man of Neroes, missed but little of killing him, as he passed through a crosse lane to the Baines for to bath. And surely done the deed they had, but that as they exhorted and incouraged one another not to overslip[2] the opportunitie presented, they were over hearde: who beeing examined and asked, upon what occasion they spake such words, were by torture forced to confesse the truth.

11

Besides these daungers so great, there fel out (to helpe the matter well) the death of Vindex: wherewith being most of all amased, and like to a man utterly forlorne, he went within a little of renouncing this world and forgoing his owne life. But by occasion of messengers comming with newes from the City in the verie instant, no sooner understood he that Nero was slaine, and all men in general had sworne alleageance unto him, but he laide away the name of Lieutenant and tooke upon him the stile of Cæsar. So, he put himselfe on his Journey clad in his Coate armour, with his dagger hanging downe from about his necke just before his breast: neither tooke he to the use of a gown and long robe againe, before they were surprised and suppressed, who made insurrections and rose up in armes against him[3]: namely, at Rome Nymphidius Sabinus Capitaine of

---

[1] *Dertosam appulit:* al. *Decursa appulit, i.* hulled down the tide: or, as the wind did drive it.   [2] *Omitterent,* or *amitterent, i.* to loose.
[3] Notwithstanding that upon the death of Nero, he was declared Emperour at Rome.

164

TWELVE CÆSARS

the Prætorian guard: in Germanie Fonteius Capito, and in Africke Clodius Macer, ij. Lieutenants.

12

There had a rumour beene raised before of his crueltie and covetousnesse both: for punishing the Citties of Spaine which were somewhat slacke in comming to side with him, by laying very heavy tributes and taxes upon them: some of them also by dismanteling and rasing their wals: likewise for putting to death certaine Presidents and Procuratours together with there wives and children: as also for melting a Coronet of gold weighing 15 pound: which the men of Tarracon from out of the old Temple of Jupiter had presented unto him: and commaunding that the three ounces which wanted of the full weight should be exacted and made good [1]. This report was both confirmed and also increased uppon his first entrance into Rome. For when he would have compelled the servitours at Sea (whom Nero had made of mariners and oaremen, full and lawfull souldiers) to returne againe to their former state and condition: when they made refusall, and besides called malapertly for their Ægle and other militarie ensignes: hee not onely sent in among them a troupe of horsemen, and so trode them under foote, but also executed with death every tenth man of them. Semblably, the Cohort of Germaines which in times past had beene by the Cæsars ordained for the guard of their persons, and by many good proofes were found most trustie, hee dissolved: and without any availes and recompence for their service sent them home againe into their Country: pretending that they stood better affected unto Cn. Dolabella (neere unto whose Horthyards and gardens they quartered) than to him. Moreover, these reports also (whether truely or falsely I wote not) went commonly of him by way of mockerie: That when there was a more plentifull supper than usual served up before him, he gave a great grone thereat. His Steward verily in ordinary [2] cast up his bookes and rendred unto him a

[1] Either by wast in melting or by the crafty conveiance of the gold founder.
[2] *Ordinario Dispensatori,* or thus, one Ordinarius his steward.

THE HISTORIE OF

breviary of all reckonings, and accoumpts. For his great
care and serviceable diligence, hee reached unto him a dish
of pulse [1]. But when Caius the minstrill played upon the
Hautbois and pleased him wonderous well, hee bestowed
liberally upon him for his labour five good Deniers [2], and
those he drew with his owne hand out of his privie purse.

13

At his first comming, therefore, he was not so welcome.
And that appeared at the next solemnitie of publick Shewes.[3]
For when as in the Atellane Comædies, some had begun a
most vulgar Canticle with this verse,

> St: *Venit, Io Simus a villa, etc.*
> St: See [4], Our Simus that Country clowne
> Is from his Ferme now come to towne,

the Spectatours all at once with one accord and voice, sung
out the rest in manner of a respond: and repeating withall
the said verse oft, as the fore-burden of the Song, acted (and
with gesture) noted him.

14

Thus verily with farre greater favour and aucthoritie
obtained hee the Empire than menaged it when he was
therein; notwithstanding, hee gave many proofes of an
excellent Prince: but nothing so acceptable were his good
Acts, as those were odious and displeasant wherein he faulted
and did amisse. Ruled he was according to the will and
pleasure of three persons: whom dwelling as they did
together and that within the Palatium (readie evermore
at his elbow and in his eare), men commonly called his
Pædagogues. These were, Titus Junius [5], his Lieutenant in
Spaine; a man infinitely covetous: Cornelius Laco, who
being of his Counsell and assistance was advanced by him to
be Capitaine of the guard; one for his arrogancie and lusk-
ishnesse [6] intollerable: and a freed man of his, Icelus, who
but a little before, being honoured with the golden ring [7],

---

[1] As of peasen or beanes, etc.   [2] Or pence, 3s. 1d. *ob*. English.
[3] See Turneb. *Advers.* 5, cap. 2.   [4] Husht or whist, an Interjection of
silence.   [5] Or Vinius.   [6] *Socordia*, or sottishnes.   [7] Knighthood.

TWELVE CÆSARS

and endowed with the surname Martianus, looked now for to bee the Provost and Captaine of the Pretorian Gentlemen and Knights Degree [1]. Unto these men, I say, playing their parts and committing outrages correspondent to their vices in divers kinds, hee yeelded and wholly gave himselfe to be abused so much, as that scarcely he was like himselfe, but alwaies variable: one while precise and neere, otherwhiles as remisse and carelesse; more, ywis, than became a Prince elected, and a man of these yeeres [2]. Some honourable persons of both degrees [3] he condemned upon the least suspition, before their cause was heard. The Freedome of Rome Citie he seldome graunted to any. The priviledge and Immunitie due to those who had three children, hee gave to one or two at most with much a-doe: not to them verily, but for a certaine time limitted and set downe. The Judges making suite for to have a sixth Decurie adjoyned unto them, he not onely denied flatly, but also this benefite of vacation graunted unto them by Claudius, That they should not be called forth to sit in the Winter season [a], and at the beginning of the yeere, he tooke from them.

SERVIUS
SULPITIUS
GALBA

15

It was thought also, that hee purposed to determine and limit the Offices belonging to Senatours and Gentlemen, within the compasse of two yeeres: and not to bestow the same but upon such as were unwilling and refused to take them. The Liberalities and bountifull Donations of Nero [4], hee tooke order by a Commission directed unto fiftie Gentlemen of Rome [5], for to bee revoked: yea, and the same to bee exacted for his behoofe, allowing out thereof not above the tenth part: with this straight condition moreover, That if Actours upon the Stage, or Wrestlers and Champions otherwise, had sold any such donation given unto them aforetime, the same should be taken from the Buiers, since that the parties who had sold the same had spent the money,

---

[1] *Summæ æquestris gradus,* or *summi equestris ordinis.* [2] 73. [3] Gentlemen and Senatours. [4] Which amounted according to Tacitus into *bis et vicies millies,* 2200 millians. [5] Tacitus saith 30.

and were not sufficient to repay it. Contrariwise, there was
not any thing, but by the meanes of his followers, Favorites
and freed men, he suffred either to bee purchased for money,
or graunted freely for favour: as for example, Customes,
Imposts, Immunities, Punishments of the Innocent, and
Impunitie of Malefactours. Moreover, when as the people
of Rome called upon him for Justice, and namely to have
Halotus and Tigellinus executed, the onely men of all the
bloud-hounds and instruments of Nero that wrought most
mischiefe, he saved them from daunger: and besides, advaunced Halotus to a most honourable Procuratorship: and
in the behalfe of Tigellinus rebuked the people by an Edict
for their crueltie unto him.

16

Having heereby given offence and discontentment[1] to the
States and Degrees in manner all, yet he incurred the
displeasure and ill will most of the Souldiours. For, when
his Provosts had promised and pronounced unto them, (what
time they sware alleageance unto him), a greater Donative
than usually had beene given, hee would not make good and
ratifie the same; but eft-soones gave it out, That his manner
had ever beene to choose and not buy his Souldiours. And
as, upon that occasion verily hee angred all his Souldiours
wheresoever: so, the Pretorians and those of his guard he
provoked moreover with feare, and netled with offring them
indignities; namely, by removing and displacing most of
them one after another, as suspected persons, and the adhærents of Nymphidius. But the forces of higher Germanie
grumbled and fumed most of all, for being defrauded of
their rewards for service performed against the French and
Vindex. They were the first therefore that durst breake out
into open disobedience: and upon the Newyeeres day refused
to take an oath and binde themselves in alleageance unto any
other than the Senate of Rome. They intended also to
dispatch forthwith an Embassie unto the Pretorian guard,
with these advertisements and messages from them, namely,
That they were displeased with an Emperour made in

---

[1] *Propt universis ordinibus offensis.*

TWELVE CÆSARS

Spaine: and therefore themselves should elect one, whom all the Armies in Generall might allow and approve.

17

No sooner heard he this newes, but supposing that hee was become contemptible, not so much for his olde age, as his childlesse estate, hee presently out of the thick throng and middle multitude that came to salute him, caught hold of Piso Frugi Licinianus, a noble young Gentleman and of excellent parts, one whom in times past he had made right great account of, and alwaies[1] in his will remembred as Inheritour to succeede in his goods and name: him he now called Sonne, him he presented unto the Pretorian Campe, and there before a publick assembly, adopted. But of the fore-saide Donative not a word all this while, no not at that very time. Whereby he ministred unto M. Salvius Otho better occasion and readier meanes to accomplish his enterprises within six daies after his Adoption.

18

Manie prodigious sights and those presented continuallie even from the verie first beginning, had portended unto him such an end as ensued. When all the way as hee journeyed, beasts were sacrificed to doe him honour in everie towne on both sides, it chaunced that a Bull astonied with the stroke of the Butchers axe, brake the bond wherewith hee stoode tied and ranne full upon his Chariot; and rising up with his (fore) feete, all to bespreinct and drenched it with bloud. As he alight out of it, one of the guard and Pensioners about him, with the thrusting of the throng had like with his speare to have wounded him. As he entred also the Citie of Rome and so passed forward up to the Palatium, hee was welcomed with an Earthquake, and a certaine noise resembling the lowing of a beast. But there followed after these, greater Prodigies still and more fearefull. He had selected and layed by it selfe out of all his Treasure, a jewell set thick with pearle and pretious stones, for to beautifie and adorne his Goddesse Fortune at Tusculum. This Jewell (as if it had

---

[1] *Semper*, or *super*, i. beside.

2 : Y   169

THE HISTORIE OF

beene worthy of a more stately and sacred place), all of a
suddaine hee dedicated to Venus in the Capitoll, and the next
night following he dreamt, that he saw Fortune making her
moane and complaining, how shee was defrauded of the gift
intended and meant unto her : threatning withall, that shee
her selfe also would take away what shee had given him.
Now, being affrighted with this vision, when in great hast
hee was gone apace to Tusculum, and had by breake of day
sent certaine before of purpose to provide an expiatorie
sacrifice for this dreame [1], he found nothing there but warme
embers upon the altar herth, and an olde man all in blacke [2]
sitting hard by, holding in a dish of glasse, Frankincense, and
in an earthen cup, wine [3]. Observed also it was, that upon the
Kalends of Januarie while hee sacrificed, his coronet fell from
his head.   As he tooke his Auspices, the pullets flew away.
And upon the Solemne day of the fore-said Adoption, when
hee should make a Speech unto the Souldiours, the Camp-
Throne [4] stoode not, (as the manner was) before his Tribunall ; (such was the forgetfulnesse of his Ministers) and in
the Senate, his Curule chaire was placed wrong, with the
back toward him.

19

But before he was slaine, as he sacrificed that morning,
the Southsayer oftentimes warned him to beware of daunger:
for murderers were not farre off.   And not long after hee
tooke knowledge that Otho was possessed of the Campe [5].
And when most of those about his person perswaded him
still to make what speed hee could and goe forward thither
(for why ? by his authority and presence hee might beare
sway and prevaile) hee resolved to doe no more but keepe
close within house : to stand upon his guard, and to fortifie
himselfe with the strength of his legionarie Souldiours, in
many and divers places quartered.   Howbeit, hee put on a
good linen Jack [6a]: although hee seemed to acknowledge, that
in small steed it would stand him, against so many sword-

---

[1] To avert the harme prognosticated thereby.   [2] Like a mourner.
[3] Ominous tokens presaging his brittle state.   [4] Or chaire of Estate.
[5] Prætorian.   [6] Cuirace.

170

TWELVE CÆSARS

points. But being borne in hand and seduced with rumours which the Conspiratours had of purpose spread abroad to traine him out into the open street : whiles some few rashly affirmed, That all was dispatched : the rebels and seditious persons defaited : and the rest comming in great frequencie with joy and gratulation, ready to do him all the obsequious service they could : hee to meete them went forth ; and that with so great confidence as that unto a Souldiour who made his boast, He had slaine Otho, he answered, ' And by whose warrant ^b? ' Thus advaunced he as farre as into the Market-place. There, the Horsemen having commission and commaundement to kill him : when they had voided the common people out of the way, and put their horses forward through the streetes, and espied him a farre off, staied a while : but afterwards, setting spurres to againe, fell upon him and slew him outright, forsaken as he was of all his traine and followers.

20

There be that report, how at the first uprore, hee cried aloud : ' What meane yee my fellow Souldiours ? I am yours, and yee are mine ': and withall promised (to pay) the Donative. But, many more have left in writing, that of himselfe he offred them his throat, and willed them (since they thought so good) to mind that onely which they came for, even to strike and spare not. A strange and wonderfull thing it was, that of those who were there present not one went about to helpe their Emperour : and all that were sent for, rejected the messenger, saving onely a guidon of Germane Horsemen. These in regard of his fresh demerite (in that hee had tenderly cherished and made much of them being sicke and feeble) hastned to the rescue : howbeit they came too late, by occasion, that beeing ignorant of the streetes and places they tooke a wrong way and were hindered. Killed hee was at the Lake Curtius[1], and there left lying even as hee was; untill such time as a common Souldiour as he returned from foraging and providing of corne, threw downe his load and cut his head off. Now, because hee could not catch hold of

---

[1] The place where somtime that lake was.

171

THE HISTORIE OF

the haire of his head (so bald hee was) hee hid it in his lap:
and anone thrust his thumbe into his mouth and so brought
it to Otho: who gave it to the Scullians, Lackies, and
Varlets[1] that follow the Campe. These sticking it upon a
speare caried it, not without reproachfull scorne all about
the Campe setting up ever and anone this Note, 'Galba, thou
lovely Cupid take thy time, and make use of thy fresh and
youthfull yeeres[2]': provoked they were, especially to such
malapert frumps and floutes, because some daies before there
ranne a rife report abroad, that unto one who commended
that visage and person of his, as continuing still fresh, faire,
and vigorous, he made this answere,

ἔτι μοι μένος ἔμπεδόν ἐστιν.
I have yet still
My strength at will[3]

At their hands, a freed man of Patrobius Neronianus, bought
the same for one hundred peeces of gold[a], and flung it into
that very place[b], where, before time his Patron[4] by the
commaundement of Galba, had been executed. At length
(late though it was) his Steward Argius buried both it and
the trunk of his body within his owne private Hortyards in
the way Aurelia.

21

Of full stature he was: his head bald: his eyes gray, and
his nose hooked: his hands and feete by reason of the gout
growne exceeding crooked; in so much as uneth he was able
either to abide shooes on the one, or to turne over, or so much
as hold his bookes with the other. There was an excrescence[5] also of flesh in the right side of his body: and the
same hung downward so much, as hardly it could be tied up
with a trusse[6].

22

A great feeder and meate-man by report, he was. For in
Winter time hee used to eate before day light: and at supper

---

[1] Or water-bearers and wood purveiers for the Souldiours.   [2] *Galba,
Cupido*, etc.   [3] Homer, *Iliad* 5, Diomedes to Sthenelus.   [4] Patrobius.
[5] Or bunch.   [6] Or swathing band.

172

TWELVE CÆSARS

to bee served so plentifully, that the reliques and reversion of the bourd being gathered together into heapes, hee commaunded to be caried round about and distributed among those that stoode waiting at his feete. Given he was over much to the unnaturall lust of Male-kind : but such chose he (and none else) for his Dearlings, as were stale-thick-skins and past growth. It was reported that in Spaine when Icelus one of his olde Catamites brought him word of Neroes end, he not onely received him in open sight with most kinde kisses, but intreated him without delay to be plucked[1], and so led him at one side out of the way.

23

He died in the 73 yeere of his age, and seventh moneth of his Empire. The Senate as soone as lawfully they might, had decreed for him a Statue standing upon a Columne adorned with the Stemmes and beake-heads of ships[2], in that part of the Mercate-steed of Rome where hee lost his life : but Vespasian repealed that Decree : as being thus conceited of him, That he had suborned and sent under hand out of Spaine into Jurie, certaine of purpose to murder him.

[1] Made smooth. [2] *Rostratæ.*

173

THE HISTORIE OF

THE HISTORIE OF
MARCUS SALVIUS OTHO

1

HE Auncestors of Otho had their begin-
ning in a towne called Ferentinum;
extract out of an auncient and honourable family, even from the Princes of
Hetruria. His grandfather M. Salvius
Otho having for his Father a Gentleman
of Rome, and for his mother a woman
of base condition (and whether shee was
free-borne or no, it is uncertaine) through the favour of
Livia Augusta, in whose house he had his rising and growth,
was made a Senatour, and exceeded not the degree of a
Pretour. His Father, L. Otho, by his mothers side of right
noble bloud descended, and thereby allied to many great
kinreds, was so deere and in face so like unto Tiberius the
Emperour, that most men beleeved verily, hee was his owne
sonne. The Honourable Offices within the Citie: the
Proconsulship of Asia, and other extraordinarie places of
Conduct and Commaund, hee managed most severely. Hee
adventured also in Illyricum to proceed so far, as to put
certaine soldiers to death, for that in the commotion of
Camillus upon a touch of conscience they had killed their
Captaines and provosts[1], as authors of the revolt and
rebellion against Claudius, and verily this execution himselfe in person saw performed in the Campe even before
the Principia[a] : notwithstanding that he knew they were for
that service advanced to higher places by Claudius. By

---

[1] Or his, *i.* Camillus.

TWELVE CÆSARS

which act of his as he grew in glory so hee decreased in favour. And yet the same he soone recovered againe, by detecting the perfidious plot of a Romaine Knight, whom by the appeachment of his own servants he found to have attempted the death of Claudius. For, both the Senate endowed him with an honour most rare and seldome seene, to wit his owne statue erected in the Palatium; and also Claudius when he ranged him among the Patritians, and in most honourable tearmes praised him added these words withall, ' Hee is a man, than whom I would not wish I assure you to have better Children of mine owne.' Of Albia Terentia a right noble and gallant Lady he begat two sonnes, Lucius Titianus, and a younger forenamed Marcus, and carying the surname of his father [1]: a daughter also hee had by her, whom as yet not mariageable, he affianced unto Drusus the sonne of Germanicus.

2

This Otho the Emperour, was borne the 4 day before the Kalends of May [2], when Camillus Arruntius and Domitius Ænobarbus were Consuls. From the very prime of his youth, hee was roiotous, wild and wanton: in so much as his father swindged him well and soundly for it: reported also to use night walking; and as he met any one either feeble or cupshotten or overcome with drinke, to catch hold of him, lay him upon a soldiers gaberdine, and so to tosse and hoist him up into the aire [a]. Afterwardes, uppon his fathers death, a certaine Libertine woman of the Court, a dame very gratious (because hee would make the more benefit by following and courting her as his mistrisse) he pretended love unto: albeit an old trot shee was in manner doting for age. By her meanes winding himselfe into the favour of Nero, he easily obtained the cheife place among his minions and favorites (such was the congruence of their humours and dispositions) and as some write by mutuall abusing also of one anothers bodie against kind. But so mightie hee waxed and bare such a side, as that in con-

[1] i. Otho. [2] 28 Aprill.

THE HISTORIE OF

sideration of a great peece of money agreed upon, he presumed to bring into the Senate house for to give thankes[1], a man of Consular degree, who stood condemned for extortion, even before hee had fully obtained his restitution[2].

3

Being now, as he was, privie and partie to all the counsels and secret dessignes of Nero : he to avert all manner of suspicion, that very day which Nero had appointed for the murdering of his mother, entertained them both at supper with most exquisite, and the kindest welcome that might be. Semblably, Dame Poppæa Sabina, being as yet but the paramour of Nero, whom he had newly taken from her husband[3], and committed in the meane while unto himselfe upon trust for to keepe[4], under a colour of mariage[5] hee received : and not content herewith that he alienated her hart from Nero and used her body, hee loved her so entirely, that he could not endure Nero himselfe to be his Corrivall[6]. Certes, it is thought of a truth, that not onely the messengers who were sent to fetch her, came againe without her : but also that one time he kept Nero himselfe without dores standing there and cooling his heeles, with threates also and prayers intermingled, demanding his pawne[7] which hee had left with him but all in vaine. Whereupon after the said mariage broken and dissolved, sent out of the way hee was under a pretence of an Embassage into Portugal. Which course was thought sufficient for feare least his proceeding to any sharper punishment might have told tales[8] abroad and marred all the play : howbeit as secretly conveied as it was, out it came and was made knowne by this Distichon[9].

> *Cur Otho mentito sit quæritis exul honore?*
> *Uxoris Mœchus cœperat esse suæ.*
> Exil'd in shew of Embassage was Otho. Aske yee, why?
> With his owne wife begon he had to act adulterie[a].

---

[1] For pardon.   [2] Restoring to his former state.   [3] Rufus Crispus. [4] Untill he could put awaie Octavia.   [5] So writeth Plutarch. But Tacitus differeth from this Narration.   [6] Partner with him in love of that Mistris. [7] Pledge or gage, to wit Poppæa.   [8] How Nero had beene excluded and shut out of doores, etc.   [9] ij. Verses.

TWELVE CÆSARS

Having beene afore time in no higher place then Questour, yet governed hee a province for the space of x. yeeres with singular moderation [1] and abstinence [2].

4

As occasion at length and opportunitie of revenge [3] was offred, he was the first that combined with Galba in his attempts. At which very instant himself also conceived hope of the Empire: and great the same was, no doubt, considering the condition and state of those times, but greater somewhat by reason of Seleucus the Astrologers words: who having long before warranted him that he should survive Nero, was then of his owne accord come unlooked for, and promised againe that shortly also he should be Emperour. Omitting therfore no kind of obsequious office and ambitious popularity even to the very meanest: looke how often he invited the Emperour [4] to supper, he wold deale throughout the Cohort that then warded, to every man a peece of gold [5]: and no lesse carefull was he to oblige unto him one way or other, the rest of the soldiers. And when one of them went to law with his neighbour about a parcell of ground in the skirts and confines of both their lands, he being chosen Arbitratour, bought the whole land for the said souldier and enfeoffed him in it. So as now by this time there was scarce one, but both thought and said that he alone was worthy to succeede in the Empire.

5

Moreover he had fed himselfe with hopes to have been adopted by Galba, and that looked hee for daily: but after that Piso was preferred and himselfe disappointed of his hope, he turned to plaine violence: pricked therto, over and besides the discontentment of his mind, by occasion that he was so deepely indebted. For he stucke not to professe, He was not able to stand, unlesse he were Emperour: and it skilled not whether he were overthrowne by his

---

[1] Without rigour.   [2] Without pillaging, polling and extortion.   [3] Of Nero.   [4] Galba.   [5] 15s. 7d. *ob.* English.

THE HISTORIE OF

enemie in the field, or fell under his creditours hands at the Barre. Some few daies before, he had fetch over one of Cæsars servants in a millene of Sesterces for the obtaining of a Stewardship: and with the helpe of this sum of mony, enterprised he so great a project. At the first he committed the matter to 5 souldiers emploied in Espiall[1]: then to x. others whom they had brought forth with them, to wit every man twaine. To ech one of these he payd in hand x. thousand sesterces[2], and promised 50000 more. By these were the rest solicited, and those not very many: as making no doubt but presuming confidently of this that a number besides would be ready in the very action to second it.

6

He had minded once, presently after the adoption (of Piso) to seize their campe into his owne hands, and so to set uppon Galba as hee sat at supper in the Pallace: but the respective regarde hee had of the Cohort, which then kept watch and warde, hee checked this intent of his: for feare least the same should incurre the intolerable hatred of the world: considering, by the guard of that very Cohort, Caius had beene slaine before, and Nero perfidiouslie betrayed afterwards. Moreover, exception was taken against the middle time betweene, partly upon a superstition[3] that hee had, and in part by direction from Seleucus. Well then, upon a day[4] appointed, after warning given aforehand unto those that were privie to the conspiracie, for to attend him in the market place at the golden Milliarum[a] under the Temple of Saturne, hee saluted Galba in the morning, and (as the manner was) beeing received with a kisse, was present also as hee sacrificed and heard the Soothsayers predictions. Which done, a freed man of his brought him word that the Architects were come (this was the watchword agreed upon between them) wherupon as if forsooth he were to look upon an house that was to be sold, he departed, gat him quickly away through the backe side of the Palace, and hied a pace toward the place appointed. Others say, that

---

[1] *Speculat oribus.*   [2] 100 Aurei: every Aureus being 15s. 7d. *ob.*
[3] Scrupulosity.   [4] 15 Januarii.

178

TWELVE CÆSARS

he feigned himselfe to have an ague, and willed those that stood next to him to make that excuse in case he were asked for. Then lying hidden within a womans Licter [1], he hastened to the Campe: and for that the Licter bearers were tired and faint, hee allighted on the ground and beganne to runne a foote: but by occasion that his shooes latchet was slacke, he stayed behinde, untill such time as without any further delay, he was taken up on mens shoulders, and by the traine and Company there present saluted Emperour; and so with lucky acclamations among drawen swords, came as farre as to the Principia [2], whiles every one all the way hee went adhæred unto him, as if they had beene all privie and party in the conspiracy. There, after he had dispatched certaine away to kill both Galba and Piso, he to win the soldiers hearts by faire promises, protested before them all assembled together, That himselfe would have and hold no more, then just that which they would leave for him.

7

This done, as the day drewe toward evening, he entred into the Senate: and briefely laying before them a reason of his proceeding, as if he had been caried away perforce out of the market place and compelled to take the Empire upon him (which he would administer according to the generall will and pleasure of them al), to the pallace he goeth. Now when as beside other sweet and plausible words delivered by such as did congratulate and flatter him, he was by the base common people called Nero, he gave no token at al that he refused it: nay rather, as some have reported, ever in his patents, graunts and missives which he first wrote unto certaine presidents and governours of Provinces, he added unto his stile the surname of Nero. This is certen, he both suffered his images [3] and Statues [4] to be erected againe in their own places: and also restored his Procuratours and freed men to the same offices that they had enjoyed before.

---

[1] Or close chaire, wherein women use to be carried.   [2] A principall place within the Camp.   [3] Which either were of wax, or peincted.
[4] Commonly of brasse, stoone or such solid matter.

THE HISTORIE OF

Neither, by his imperiall prerogative and absolute power subscribed he any thing, before a warrant for fiftie millians of Sesterces [1] to the finishing of (Neroes) golden house. It is said that the same night being affrighted in his sleepe hee groned very sore, and was by his servitours that ran thick into the chamber found lying on the bare floore before his bed : also that he assaied by all kind of propitiatorie sacrifices and peace offrings to appease the spirit [2] of Galba, whome hee had seene in his sleepe, to thrust and drive him foorth : semblably, the morrow after as he was taking his Auspices [3], there arose a sodaine tempest, whereupon hee caught a grievous fall, and oftentimes hee mumbled this to himselfe :

Τί γὰρ μοι καὶ μακροῖς αὐλοῖς.

For, how can I (whose blast is short)
With these long hautboies fitly sort [a]?

8

And verily about the same time, the forces and Armies in Germanie [a] had sworne fealtie and alleageance unto Vitellius, which when he understood, hee propounded unto the Senate, That an Embassage might be sent thither, to advertise them that there was an Emperour chosen alreadie, and advise them with all to peace and concord : yet, by entercourse of messengers and letters between, he made offer unto Vitellius to pertake equally with him in the Empire, and accept of a marriage with his daughter : but when there was no way but one and that by open warre : seeing that now alreadie the Capitaines and forces which Vitellius had sent before, approched [4], hee had good proofe what loyall and faithfull harts, the pretorian souldiers caried towards him, even to the utter ruine and destruction well neere of the most honourable degree of Senatours.   Nowe decreed it had beene [5], that by the Sea servitours the armour [6] should be

---

[1] *Quingenties* HS. or *Sestertium*.   [2] Or Ghost.   [3] By observing the sacred Birds.   [4] For Fabius Valens and Aulus Cæcina were come with a power out of Germanie into Italie.   [5] By Otho and the Senate.   [6] With which the 17th cohort, sent for out of the Colonie Ostia before to Rome, should be armed.

180

TWELVE CÆSARS

conveied over and sent backe (to Ostia) by shipping. And as the said armour was in taking foorth out of the armorie in the Campe, at the shutting of the Evening, some (souldiers) suspecting treacherie and treason, raised a tumult and gave an Alarum: wherewith sodainely all of them [1] without any certaine leader to conduct them, ranne to the Palace, calling hard to have the Senate [2] massacred: and when they had repelled some of the Tribunes who assaied to represse their violence, and killed other of them, all embreued in bloud as they were, and askinge still where the Emperour was, they rushed in as farre as into his banquetting rowme, and never rested untill they had seene him. Then set he forward his expedition lustilie: and beganne with more hast then good speed ; without any care at all of religion and the will of God : as having onely stirred and taken those sacred shields [3] called *Ancilia* [b], and not bestowed them quietly againe in their due place (a thing in olde time held ominous and ever presaging ill lucke): besides, the very same day it was upon which the priest and ministers [4] of (Cybele) the mother of the Gods, beginne to lament, weepe and waile : to conclude, when all signes and tokens, were as crosse as possibly they might be. For not onely in the beast killed for sacrifice unto Father Dis [5], he found the Inwards propitious (whereas in such a sacrifice as that the contrarie had beene more acceptable) but also at his first setting out, staied he was by the inundation and swelling of the river Tiberis. At the twentie miles ende likewise, he found the highway choaked and stopped up against him with the ruines of certaine houses fallen downe.

9

With like inconsiderate rashnes, albeit no man doubted but that in good pollicy, the warre ought to have beene protracted, because the enimie was distressed as wel with famine,

[1] The Pretorian or gaurd Souldiers. [2] Who to the number of four score, with many Ladies were at supper that night with Otho, and by the souldiers suspected to have plotted his death. [3] Of Mars. [4] Galli. [5] The infernall God so named *quasi dives*, *i.* rich as Pluto, of Ploutose riches, because all things arise out of the earth and fall into it againe.

THE HISTORIE OF

as the streight wherein he was pent, yet resolved hee with all
speed, to hazard the fortune of the field and to trie it out by
fight; as one, either impatient of longer thought and pen-
sivenesse hoping that before the comming of Vitellius most
part of the businesse might be dispatched, or else because
hee could not rule his souldiers calling so hotely upon him
to give battaile. Yet was not he present in that conflict
but staied behind at Bryxellum. And verily in three several
skirmishes, which were not great, to wit, upon the Alpes,
about Placentia and at Castoris[1], (a place so called) he wan
the victorie: but in the last battaile of all, (which was the
greatest) he lost the day, and was by a treacherous practise
vanquished, namely, when upon hope of a parly pretended,
as if the soldiers had been brought out of the Campe to treat
of conditions of peace: sodainely and unlooked for, even as
they saluted one another[2], there was no remedie but fight it
out they must. And straight wayes in a melancholy, he
conceived a resolution to make him selfe away (as many are
of opinion and not without cause) rather for shame, that he
would not be thought to persevere in the maintenance of his
soveraine dominion with so great jeopardie of the State and
losse of men, than upon any dispaire or distrust of his forces.
For still there remained a puissant armie whole and entier,
which he had detained with him for tryall of better fortune:
and another poure was comming out of Dalmatia, Pannonia
and Mæsia. Neither verily were they discomfited, so much
daunted and dejected, but that, for to be revenged of this
disgrace and shamefull foile, ready they were of themselves,
and alone without helpe of others, to undergoe any hard
adventure whatsoever.

10

In this warre served mine own father Suetonius Lenis, in
qualitie of a Tribune[3] of the thirteenth Legion, and by
degree a Senatour of the seconde rancke[4]. He was wont

---

[1] Tacitus calleth it *Castrorum*, or rather *Castorum*, of Castor and Pollux.
[2] By the name of *Commilitones*: *in ipsa consalutatione*. Some read *in ipsa
consultatione, i.* as they were in consultation.   [3] Or Colonel.   [4] *Angusti-
clavius.*

TWELVE CÆSARS

afterwards very often to report that Otho, even when hee lived a private person, detested all civile warres so farre foorth, that as one related at the table the ende of Cassius and Brutus, he fell a quaking and trembling therat. Also, that he never would have beene Galbæs concurrent, but that he confidently thought, the quarrell might have ended without warre. Well then, upon a new accident incited he was to the contempt of this present life, even by the example of a common and ordinary souldier: who reporting this overthrowe of the armie, when he could of no man have credite, but was charged one while with the lie, another while for his feare and cowardise (as who was run away out of the battaile) fell upon his owne sworde at Othoes feete. At which sight, hee cryed out alowd and said, That he would no more cast so brave men and of so good desert into danger. Having exhorted therefore his owne brother, his brothers sonne and every one of his freinds severally, to make what shift they could for themselves, after hee had embraced and kissed them ech one, he sent them all away: and retyring himselfe into a secret rowm, two letters he wrot ful of consolation to his sister, as also to Messallina, Neroes widow, whom he had purposed to wed, recommending the reliques of his bodie and his memoriall. And looke what Epistles soever hee had in his custody, he burnt them al, because they should breed no man any danger, losse, or displeasure with the conquerour. And out of that store of treasure which hee had about him, he dealt monie to his domestical servitours.

11

Being now thus prepared and fully bent to die, perceiving by occasion of some hurliburly, which while he made delay, arose, that those who began to slip away and depart[1], were (by his souldiers) rebuked as traytors and perforce detained: 'Let us,' quoth he, 'prolong our life yet this one night.' Upon which words and no more, hee charged that no violence should be offred to any; but suffering his bedchamber

---

[1] *i.* The Senatours.

(doore) to stand wide open untill it was late in the evening, he permitted al that wold to have accesse unto him. After this, having allayed his thirst with a draught of cold water he caught up two daggers [1], and when he had tryed how sharpe the points of them both were, and layed one of them under his pillow [2]; and so the dores being fast shut he tooke his rest and slept most soundly. Wakening then at last about day light and not before, with one onely thrust under his left pap he stabbed himselfe. And when at the first grone that he gave, his servants brake in, hee one while concealing and another while discovering the wound, yeelded up his vitall breath, and quicklye (as he had given charge before) was brought to his funerall fire [3]: in the yeere of his age 38, and the 95 day of his Empire.

12

Unto so great a mind and generous courage of Otho, neither was his person nor habite answerable: for he was by report of a meane and low stature: feeble feet he had besides, and as crooked shanks. As for his manner of attire, as fine and nice he was well neere as any woman: his bodie plucked and made smooth: wearing by reason of thin haire a perrucke [4], so fitted and fastened to his head, that no man there was, but would have taken it for his owne. Nay his very face he was wont every day to shave and besmeere all over with soked bread [a]. Which devise he tooke to at first, when the downe began to bud forth, because he would never have a beard. It is said moreover, that many a time hee openlie celebrated the divine service and sacred rights of Isis, in a religious vestiment of linnen. Whereby, I would thinke it came to passe, that his death nothing at all consonant to his life was the more wondered at. Manie of his souldiers who were present about him, when with plentifull teares they had kissed his hands and feete dead as he lay, and commended him with all for a most valiant man, and the onely Emperour that ever was, presently in the place,

---

[1] Or rapiers. [2] Or beds-head. [3] For feare his head should be severed from his bodie, etc. [4] Or counterfeit cap of false haire.

TWELVE CÆSARS

and not farre from his funerall fire, killed themselves. Many of them also, who were absent, hearing of the newes of his end, for very greife of heart ran with their weapons one at another to death. Finally most men who in his life time cursed and .detested him, now when he was dead highly praised him : so as it came to be a common and rife speech abroad, That Galba was by him slaine, not so much for that he affected to be Soveraine Ruler as because he desired to restore the State of the Republike, and recover the freedome that was lost.

THE HISTORIE OF
AULUS VITELLIUS

1

S touching the Originall and beginning of the Vitellii, some write this, others that; and all as contrary as may be: reporting it partly to be auncient and noble, and in part new start up and obscure, and very base and beggerly. Which I would suppose to have hapned by meanes of the flatterers and backbiters both, of Vitellius the Emperour: but that I see there is sometime variance and diversity about the very condition of that family. A little booke there is extant of one Q. Eulogius[1a] his making, written unto Q. Vitellius, Questor to Augustus Cæsar of sacred memorie: wherein is contained thus much, That the Vitellii descended from Faunus K. of the Aborigines, and Lady Vitellia (who in many places was worshipped for a Goddesse) raigned over all Latium: that the of-spring remaining of them, remooved out of the Sabines Country to Rome, and were taken into the ranke of the Patritii: that many monuments giving testimonie of this race, continued a long time, to wit, the high way[2] Vitellia reaching from Janiculum[3] to the sea: likewise a Colonie of the same name, the defence and keeping whereof against the Æquiculi, they in times past required, with the strength onely and puissance of their owne family: moreover, that afterwards in the time of the Samnites warre, when a garrison was sent into Apulia[4],

---

[1] *Extat Q. Eulogii,* etc.   [2] Or causey.   [3] An hill on the other side of Tiberis, adjoyning to Rome by a bridge.   [4] By the Romaines.

TWELVE CÆSARS

some of the Vitellii remained behind at Nuceria: and their progenie many a yeere after returned to Rome and recovered their Senatours degree.

2

Contrariwise, more Authors there be, who have left upon record, that their Stock-father was a Libertine. Cassius Severus, and others as well as hee, doe write, That the same man was also a very Cobler[1a]; whose sonne having gotten more by chaffering[2] at a price for the confiscate goods of men condemned[3], and by gaines arising of undertaking mens suites[b], of a common naughty pack, the daughter of one Antiochus a Baker, begat a sonne, who proved afterwards a Gentleman of Rome. This dissonance of opinions I leave indifferent for men to beleeve which they will. But, to the purpose; Publius Vitellius borne in Nuceria, (whether he were of that auncient linage, or descended from base parents and Grandfathers) a Romaine Gentleman doubtlesse, and a Procuratour under Augustus of his affaires, left behind him foure sonnes, men of qualitie all and right honourable persons; bearing also their Fathers surname[4]: and distinguished onely by their forenames, Aulus, Quintus, Publius and Lucius. Aulus died even when he was Consull: which dignity he had entred upon with Domitius the Father of Nero Cæsar: a man very sumpteous otherwise in his house and much spoken of for his magnificent suppers. Quintus was displaced from his Senatours estate, what time as by the motion and perswasion of Tiberius there passed an Act: That such Senatours as were thought insufficient should be culled out and removed. Publius a Companion and Dependant of Germanicus, accused and convicted Cn. Piso his mortall enemie[5], and the man who murdred him: and after the honourable place of Prætour, being apprehended among the Complices of Sejanus Conspiracie and committed to the keeping of his brother[6], with a penknife cut his owne veines: and after that, not so much repenting that hee

A.U.C. 785.

A.U.C. 773.

A.U.C. 788.

---

[1] *Sutorem veteramentarium.*   [2] *Sectionibus et cognituris.*   [3] Or proscribed and outlawed.   [4] Which as Onuphrius saith, was Nepos.   [5] Of Germanicus Cæsar.   [6] Aulus.

187

THE HISTORIE OF

sought his owne death, as overcome with the earnest intreatie of his friends about him, suffred his wounds to be
bound up and cured: but in the same imprisonment[1] hee
died of sicknesse. Lucius, after his Consulship being Provost[2] of Syria, with passing fine slights and cunning devises
trained and entised forth Artabanus King of the Parthians,
not onely to parly with him, but also to worship and adore
the Standard of the Romaine Legions. Soone after, together with Claudius the Emperour, he bare two ordinarie
Consulates, one immediatly upon another, and the Censureship also: likewise the charge of the whole Empire,
whiles Claudius was absent in the expedition of Britaine,
he sustained: an harmlesse person; active and industrious:
howbeit blemished with a very bad name, for the love he
bare unto a Libertine woman[b]: whose spettle mixed with
honey he used as a remedie[3] (and that not closely and seldome but every day and openly) washing therewith his
pipes[4] and throat. He was besides of a wonderfull glaver-
ing nature and given to flatteries. He it was, that first by
his example brought up the order to adore[5] Caius Cæsar[6] as
a God what time as being returned out of Syria, he durst
not come into his presence otherwise than with his head
covered[7], turning himselfe about, and then falling downe
prostrate before him at his feete. And because he would
omit no artificiall meanes to curry favour with Claudius,
a Prince so addicted to his wife and freed men, he made
suit unto Messallina, as if it had beene for the greatest gift
shee could bestow upon him, to doe him the grace that he
might have the D'offing of her shoes: and the right foote
pumpe[c] which he had drawne off, hee caried in his bosome
continually betweene his gowne and inward clothes; yea,
and many times would kisse the same. The golden images
also of Narcissus and Pallas hee reverently honoured among
his domesticall Gods. This was a word likewise of his,
when he did congratulate Claudius at the exhibiting of the

---

[1] Or restraint of liberty and duresse.   [2] Or Præsident.   [3] A Collution.
[4] *Arterias.*   [5] Or salute after a devout manner.   [6] Caligula.   [7] Which
be the reverent gestures used in worshipping the Gods. See Plin., lib. 28
cap. 2.

TWELVE CÆSARS

Secular plaies[1], *Sæpe facias, i.* Many a time may you this
doe. He died of a palsey[d], the very next day after it tooke
him : leaving behind him two sonnes, whom Sextilia his
wife a woman for her vertue highly approved, and of no
meane parentage descended, bare unto him. Them he saw
both, Consuls, and that in one ˙yeere, yea and the same
throughout; for that the younger succeeded the elder for
sixe moneths. When hee was departed this life, the Senate
graunted unto him the honour of a publick funerall : a statue
likewise before the *Rostra* with this Inscription, *Pietatis
immobilis erga principem, i.* [2]Of constant devotion and irre-
moveable pietie to his Prince.

.   3

Aulus Vitellius the sonne of Lucius, and Emperour, was
borne the eighth day before the Calends of October[3] : or,
as some will have it, the seventh day before the Ides of
September[4], when Drusus Cæsar and Norbanus Flaccus were
Consuls. His Nativity[5] foretold by the Astrologers, his
parents had in such horrour, that his father endevoured
alwaies what he could, that no Province whiles he lived
should be committed unto him : and his mother, what time
he was both sent unto the Legions and saluted Lord
Generall[6], straight-waies lamented as if then he had beene
undone for ever. His childhood and flower of youth hee
spent at Capreæ among the Strumpets and Catamites that
Tiberius kept there : himselfe noted alwaies with the surname of Spintria[7], was thought also by suffring the abuse
of his owne body to have beene the cause of his fathers
rising and advauncement.

4

All the time also of his age ensuing stained as he was
with all manner of reproachable villanies, for hee caried
a principall sway above others in the Court, growen into

---

[1] So called, because they were solemnized but once in an hundred, or an
hundred and x. yeeres.   [2] *Subaudi* (A man).   [3] 24 September.   [4] 7th
of September.   [5] Or fortune by the Horoscope of his Nativity.   [6] Or
Emperour.   [7] A deviser of new fashions and formes of filthy uncleannes.

189

THE HISTORIE OF

familiar acquaintance with Caius for his love to chariot
running, and with Claudius for his affection to dice-play:
but in greater favour he was a good deale with Nero, both
in the selfe same regards afore-said, as also for this especiall
demerite, in that being president at the solemnity called
Neroneum, when Nero was desirous to strive for the prise
among the Harpers and Musicians, but yet durst not promise so to do, (notwithstanding all the people called
instantly upon him) and thereupon went out of the Theater:
hee pretending that hee was sent Embassadour unto him
from the people persisting still in their earnest request,
had called him back, and so brought him in the end to
be entreated.

5

Through the favourable indulgence therefore of three
Emperours, being advaunced not onely to right honourable
offices of State, but also to as high Sacerdotall dignities,
he managed after all these the Proconsulate of Africk, and
executed the charge of surveying and supravising the publick
works: but with mind and reputation both, far unlike.
For in his Province he demeaned himselfe for two yeeres
together with singular innocencie and integrity; as who
after his brother succeeded in his stead, staied there still
in quality of his Lieutenant. But in his office within the
Citie, he was reported to have secretly stollen away, the
oblations, gifts and ornaments of the Temples; to have
embecilled and chaunged some of them; yea, and in lieu of
gold and silver to have foisted in Tinn and Copper.

6

Hee tooke to wife Petronia the daughter of one that had
beene Consull, by whom hee had a sonne with one eye
named Petronianus, him being by his mother [1] ordained her
beire upon condition that he were freed once out of his
fathers power, he manumised indeede: but soone after (as
it was thought) killed: having charged him besides with
parricidie, and pretending withall, that the poison which

[1] Deceased.

TWELVE CÆSARS

was provided to worke that mischiefe, hee upon remorse of conscience had drunke himselfe. After this, he wedded Galeria Fundana, whose father had beene Pretour: and of her body also begat children of both sexes: but the male child had such an impediment of stutting and stammering, that little better he was than dumbe and tonguelesse.

AULUS
VITELLIUS

7

By Galba, sent he was contrary to all expectation into the Low-Countries of Germanie: furthered as it is thought by the voice and favour of T. Vinius a man in those daies most mighty; and unto whom long before, he had been wonne by favourizing the faction [1a] unto which they both were equally affected: but that Galba professed plainly, that none were lesse to be feared than those who thought of nothing but their victuals onely, and that his greedy appetite and hungry belly might bee satisfied and filled with the plenteous store that the Province did yeeld. So that evident it was to every man, that he chose him in contempt rather, than upon any speciall grace. This is for certaine knowne, that when he was to goe forth, he wanted provision for his journey by the way; and for the maintenance of his family was driven to those hard shifts and extremities, that muing up his wife and children (whom he left at Rome) in a little upper lodging [2] that he rented [3]; and let out his owne dwelling house for the rest of the yeere: yea, and tooke from his mothers eare a pearle, which he laid to gage: and all for to defray the charges of that voiage. As for a number verily of his Creditours, who waited for him as ready to stay his passage: and among them, the Sinnessanes and Formians, whose publick imposts, tollage, and revenewes he had intercepted and converted to his owne use, he could not be rid of, but by terrifying them with an action of the case: serving one of them, and namely a Libertine (who very eagerly demaunded a debt) with processe upon an action of batterie, as if he had stricken him with his heele; and

A.U.C. 821.

---

[1] *Venetæ*, which Galba likewise with them favoured.   [2] For in such, tenants dwelt, whereas the Lord himselfe kept beneath.   [3] Tooke for rent.

191

THE HISTORIE OF

AULUS
VITELLIUS would not withdraw the suit before he had extorted from
him fiftie thousand Sesterces. In his comming toward the
Campe, the armie maliciously bent against the Emperour,
and ready to intertaine any revolt and chaunge of State,
willingly and with open armes received him, as a gift of the
Gods presented unto them from heaven above; the sonne
of one thrice Consull; a man in the vigour and strength of
his yeeres; of a gentle disposition besides, and of a frank
and prodigall heart. Which opinion and perswasion, being
of old conceived and settled in mens heads, Vitellius had
augmented by some fresh proofes lately given of himselfe:
kissing all the way as hee went along every meane common
Souldiour that hee met: so courteous and affable above all
measure, to the very mulitiers and wayfaring passengers, in
every Inn and baiting place, that he would in a morning
betimes aske them one by one, whether they had yet broken
their fast, and shew unto them even by his belching, that
hee had beene at his breakfast already.

8

Now when hee was entred once into the Camp, no suit
denied he to any man: nay, of his owne accord hee tooke off
their marks of ignominie who stoode in disgrace; dispensed
with those that were obnoxious to the Lawes for wearing poore
and sullied garments; and forgave condemned persons their
A.U.C. 822. punishments. Whereupon, before one moneth was fully come
and gone, without all respect either of day or time, when
the very evening was now shooting in, suddainly by the
Souldiours called forth he was out of his bed-chamber: and
clad as he was in his domesticall and home apparrell, saluted
by the name of *Imperator*, and caried round about the most
frequented and populous townes[1], holding in his hand the
naked sword of Julius (Dictator) of famous memorie: which
beeing taken out of the Temple of Mars, was at the first
gratulation presented by one unto him. Neither returned
he into the Pretorium[2], before the dining roome was on a
light fire, by occasion of the chimney there, where it first

---

[1] *Vicos*, or street: of Colonia Agrippinæ where all this was done, as some
write.   [2] The L. Generals lodging.

TWELVE CÆSARS

caught. And then verily, when all besides were amazed and in great perplexity upon this adverse and ominous accident; 'Be of good cheere,' quoth hee, 'it hath shined faire upon us': and no other speech at all made hee unto his Souldiours. After this, when the armie also of the higher Province, consented now by this time with the other, (that armie I meane which had revolted before from Galba and sided with the Senate) the surname of Germanicus generallie offred unto him hee gladly accepted; the addition of Augustus he put off; and the stile of Cæsar hee utterly for ever refused.

9

And soone after, when newes came unto him that Galba was slaine, having settled the State of Germanie, he divided his forces thus: sending one part thereof before[1], against Otho, and minding to leade the rest himselfe. Unto the armie which was sent before, there hapned a fortunate and luckie signe: for on the right hand, all on a suddaine flew an Eagle toward them: and when shee had fetched a compasse round about the Standerds and Ensignes, hovered softly before them as they marched on the way. Contrariwise, as himselfe removed and set forward, the Statues on horseback, erected in many places for him, all at once suddainly brake their legges and tumbled downe: and the guirland of Lawrell, which most devoutly he had done about (his head) fell from it into a running river. Within a while after, as he sate judicially upon the Tribunall to minister Justice at Vienna[2], a Cock first settled upon his shoulder, and anone perched upon his very head. Upon which prodigious sights, ensued an event correspondent thereto. For the Empire which by his Lieutenants was confirmed and established unto him, he by himselfe was not able to hold.

10

Of the victorie before Bebriacum and the death of Otho, he heard whiles he was yet in Gaule: and without delay,

---

[1] Under the conduct of Fabius Valens by the Alpes, and of Cæcina, over the Apennine.   [2] In Fraunce within the province Narbonensis.

2 : BB   193

THE HISTORIE OF

whosoever belonged to the Pretorian Cohorts, hee by vertue of
one edict cassed and discharged all, for the most daungerous
precedent and example that they had given [1], commaunding
them to yeeld up their armour into the Marshals [2] hands. As
for those hundred and twenty, whose Supplications exhibited
unto Otho hee had found, such I meane as claimed rewards
for their good service in killing Galba, hee gave commaundement they should be sought out and executed every one. A
worthy beginning I assure you, and a magnificent: such as
might give good hope of an excellent Prinče, had hee not
menaged all matters else, according to his owne naturall
disposition and the course of his former life, rather than
respecting the majestie of an Emperour. For no sooner put
he himselfe in his journey, but he rode through the midst
of Cities in Triumphant wise: and passed along the great
rivers in most delicate barges, garnished and adorned with
Coronets of sundry sorts: faring at his table most sumptuously and served with all manner of dainty Viands: observing
no discipline either of houshold servitour or of Souldiour:
but turning the outrages, villanies and licentious prankes of
them all to a jest: who, not content with their ordinary diet
allowed and provided for them in every place where they
came at the common charges of the State; looke what slaves
or Aliens it pleased them, they manumised and made free:
but paied as many as withstoode them with whipping cheere,
blowes, knocks, bloudie wounds oftentimes, yea and otherwhiles with present death. When hee came into the fields
where the battaile [3] was fought: and some of his traine
loathed and abhorred the putrified corruption of the dead
bodies, he stuck not to harten and encourage them with this
cursed speech: That an Enemie slaine had a very good smell,
but a Citizen farre better. Howbeit to qualifie and allay the
strong savour and sent that they cast, hee poured downe his
throat before them all, exceeding great store of strong wine,
and dealt the same plentifully about [4], with as much vanity
as insolent pride. When he beheld the Stone, under which

---

[1] In betraying Galba their Soveraigne.   [2] Or Tribunes.   [3] Before
Bebriacum, or Betriacum.   [4] Some conclude the former periode heare, and
begin a new sentence thus, *Pari vanitate*, etc., With like vanitie, etc.

TWELVE CÆSARS

Otho lay interred, with an Inscription[1] in his memoriall: ' Worthy was he of such a monument[2],' quoth hee. And the very same dagger wherewith he had killed himselfe, he sent to Colein for to be dedicated unto Mars. Certes, upon the top of the Apennine Hill, hee celebrated a sacrifice, with a Vigil[3] all night long.

11

At length hee entred the Citie with warlike sound of trumpet, in his coate-armour, and with a sword girt unto him, among Ensignes, Banners and Flags[4]: his followers and dependants clad in militarie cassocks, and the armour of all his fellow Souldiours discovered in open view. Thus neglecting more and more from time to time, all Law of God and man, upon the very disasterous day *Alliensis*[a], he was enstalled in the Sacerdotall dignity of High Priest. Hee ordained, that the solemne assembly[5] for Election of Magistrates should be held every tenth yeere, and himselfe bee perpetuall dictatour. And to the end that no man might doubt what patterne hee chose to follow for government of Common-weale, calling a frequent number of the publick Priests about him in the middle of Mars field, hee sacrificed to the Spirit and ghost of Nero: and at a solemne feast openly put the Harper in minde singing as he did to his great contentment, for to say somewhat also of Domitius[6][b]: and as he began to chaunt Neroes Canticles, he was the first that leapt for joy and clapped his hands withall.

12

Having in this manner begun his Empire, a great part thereof he administred no otherwise, than according to the advise and pleasure of the basest Stage-plaiers and chariotiers that could be found: but especially of Asiaticus, a freed man of his owne. This Asiaticus when he was a very youth had in mutuall filthines with him abused his owne bodie: and afterwards lothing that abominable sinne, runne his way. Now,

---

[1] 'M. Othonis.' Plutarch.   [2] Or Mausoleum.   [3] Or wake.   [4] Or among the Standards and other Ensignes, *inter signa et vexilla*.   [5] Or Folk mote.   [6] *i.* Nero.

THE HISTORIE OF

finding him once at Puteoli selling of a certaine drinke made
of water and Vineger [1], first he laied him by the heeles, and
hung a paire of fetters at his feete: but foorthwith loosened
him [2] and intertained him as his derling againe. After which
a second time being offended with his contumacy and malapert stubbornnesse [3]: he sold him to one of these common
fencers that went from market to market [4], and by occasion
that he was upon a time put of to the last place in a sword
fight for to play his prises: at unwares he privily stole him
away: and no sooner was hee gone into his province but he
manumised him. The first day of his Empire, as he sat at
supper, hee dubbed him knight of Rome: and gave him the
golden Ring: notwithstanding that the very morning before,
when all the souldiers intreated in his behalfe, he detested
so foule a blot to disteine and discredite the worshipfull
degree of knighthood.

13

But being given most of all to excessive bellie cheere and
crueltie, he devided his repast into three meales every day at
the least, and sometime into foure, to wit, Breakefast, Dinner,
Supper and rere-bankets [5], able to beare them all very well,
hee used to vomit so ordinarily [a]. Now his manner was to
send word that hee would breake his fast with one (freind)
dine with another, etc., and all in one day. And everie one
of these refections, when it stood them in least, cost 40000
Sesterces [6]. But the most notorious and memorable supper
above all other was that, which his brother made for a welcome at his first comming (to Rome) at which by report
were served up to the Table before him, two thousand
severall dishes of fish the most daintie and choisest that
could be had, and seven thousand of foule. And yet, even
this (as sumptuous as it was) himselfe surpassed at the dedication of that platter [7], which for the huge capacitie therof he
used to call the targuet of Minerva, and αἰγίδα Πολιούχου, i.
the sheild of the Cities protectresse [8]. In this he hudled and

---

[1] *Poscam, oxycraton.*   [2] *Statimque solvit.*   [3] *Ferocitatem* or *furacitatem*,
i. theeverie.   [4] In manner of mountbankes.   [5] After supper.   [6] 3125l.
sterling.   [7] Or charger.   [8] Minerva.

TWELVE CÆSARS

blended together the livers of Giltheads [1][b]: the delicate braines of Phesants and Peacockes: the tongues of the Birds Phœnicopterie: the tender small guts of Sea-lampries fet as farre as from the Carpathian sea and the straights of Spaine, by his Captaines over Gallies [2]. And, as a man that had not onely a wide throat of his owne to devour much, but also as greedie a stomach to feede both unseasonably and also grossly of what ever came next hand, he could not so much as at anie sacrifice whensoever, or in any journy wheresoever forbeare but amonge the altars snatch up by and by the flesh, the parched corne also and meale even from the very hearth, and eate the same: yea and at every victualling house by the way side, fall to viands piping hote, yet reaking and not cooled one jote; and not spare so much as meats dressed the day before and halfe eaten alreadie.

14

Being forward enough to put to death and punish any man, what cause soever was pretended: noble men, his schoole fellowes, and play-feeres in time past, (whom by al faire meanes and flattering allurements he had enticed and drawn to the societie as it were of the Empire with him) by sundrie sorts of fraud and trechery, he killed, and one above the rest he made away with poyson, which he raught unto him with his owne hand in a draught of cold water, that he called for lying in a fit of an ague. Of Usurers, takers of bonds and obligations [3], and publicanes, who ever at any time had demanded of him either at Rome debt, or by the way as he travailed toll and custome, hee hardly spared one. And one of them, whom even as he came to salute him and doe his dutie, he had delivered over to the executioner for to suffer death, he called straightwaies backe againe: and when all that were by praised him for his clemencie, he commanded the said partie to bee killed before his face, saying with all, That he would feede his eyes. At the execution of another, he caused two of his sonnes to beare him companie, for nothing in the world, but because they presumed to intreat

[1] *Scarorum.*   [2] *Per nauarchos ac triremes:* Hen dio duo.   [3] As our Scrivenars and Atturneyes do, for other men.

197

AULUS
VITELLIUS

for their fathers life. Ther was besides a gentleman of Rome who being haled away to take his death, cryed alowd unto him, 'Sir I have made you my heire.' Him he compelled to bring foorth the writing tables containing his last will: and so soone as he red therein that a freed man of the Testatours was nominated fellow heire with him, he commanded both Maister and man to be killed. Certaine Commoners also, for this onely that they had railed alowd uppon the faction of the watchet liverie[1], he slew: being thus conceited, that in daring so to doe, they had him in contempt and hoped for a day. Yet was he to none more spitefully bent than to the wiseards and Astrologers[a]. Was any of them presented and enformed against? he made no more a do, but without hearing what he could say for himselfe, bereaved him of his life. Netled he was and exasperate against them, for that after an edict of his, wherein he gave commandement that all judiciall Astrologers should depart out of Rome and Italie before the first of October: presently, there was a writing or libell set up in open place to this effect, that the Chaldeans[2] made this Edict, as followeth, 'Bonum factum[b], etc. We give warning by these presents, unto Vitellius Germanicus, that by the Calends[3] of the said October, he be not extant[4] in any place wheresoever[5].' Suspected also hee was to be consenting unto his owne mothers death, as if hee had straightly forbidden that any food should be ministred unto her lying sicke: induced thereto by one Catta[6], a wise woman, (in whom hee rested as in an Oracle): That then and not before, hee should sit sure in his Emperiall Throne and continue very long, in case he overlived his mother. And others report, how his mother her selfe wery of the present state, and fearing what evill dayes were toward, obtained at her sonnes hand poison, and that without any great intreatie.

15

In the eight moneth of his Empire, the armies of Mæsia[7]

---

[1] Of Chariot runners: *venetæ factionis.*   [2] *i.* Astrologers.   [3] Or first day.   [4] Or to bee seene.   [5] Not in Rome and Italy onely, as before he denounced unto them.   [6] Or by a wise woman of that country where the people Catti inhabit, in Germanie.   [7] *Mæsiarum:* because there was the high and the low.

TWELVE CÆSARS

both the one and the other, as also at Pannonia revolted
from him : likewise, of the forces beyond sea, those of Jurie
and of Syria, and some of them sware alleageance unto
Vespasian who was present among them.   To retaine therefore the love and favour of all other men, he cared not what
largesses he made both in publike and private, beyond all
measure.   Hee mustred also and levied souldiers within the
City, with this covenant and faire condition [1], That all volun-
taries should by vertue of his promise, have not onelie their
discharge from service after victorie, but also the availes and
fees due unto olde souldiers for serving out their full time.
But afterwardes, as the enemie came hotely uppon him both
by land and sea, on the one side he opposed his brother with
the fleete and young untrained souldiers, together with a
crewe of sworde fencers ; on the other, what forces hee had
about Bebriacum and the Captaines there: and in everie
place, being their discomfited in open feild or privily betrayed,
he capitulated and covenanted with Flavius Sabinus brother
of Vespasian, (to give up all) reserving his owne life, and a
100 millians of sesterces.   And foorthwith upon the verie
staires of the Palace professing openly before a frequent
assemblie of his souldiers, how willing he was to resigne up
that emperiall dignity which hee had received against his will,
when they all gaine said it, hee put of the matter for that
instant ; and but one night beetweene, even the next morning
by breake of day, hee came downe in poore and simple array
to the *Rostra*, where, with many a teare, he recited the same
words out of a little written skrow.   Now, as the souldiers
and people both, interrupted him a second time and exhorted
him not to cast downe his heart, promising also with their
utmost endeavour, and striving a vie who should do best to
assist him, hee tooke courage againe and pluckt up his spirits:
so that now fearing nothing [2] at all hee came with a sodaine
power and violently chased Sabinus and the rest of the
Flavians [3] into the Capitoll : and there having set on fire the
Temple of Jupiter Optimus Maximus, vanquished and slew

AULUS
VITELLIUS

[1] Or offer.   [2] *Nihil iam metuens,* some read *metuentes,* to this sense,
that he chased them fearing no such thing.   [3] The faction of Flavius
Vespatianus.

them: whiles himself beheld both the fight and the fire out
of Tiberius his house, sitting ther at meat and making
good cheere[1]. Not long after repenting what he had done,
and laying all the fault upon others, hee called a publicke
assembly: where hee sware and compelled all the rest to take
the same oth, That he and they would respect nothing
in the world before the common peace. Then loosened
he his dagger[2] from his side[a], and raught it first to the
Consul, then upon his refusal to the other Magistrates;
and anon to the Senatours one after another. But when
none of them all would receive it, hee departed, as if hee
ment to bestow it in the Chappell of Concord. Now
when some cryed out unto him: That himselfe was Concord, hee came backe againe, and protested, that hee not
onely retained still the blade with him, but also accepted
the surname of Concord.

16

Hereupon hee mooved and advised the Senate, to send
Embassadours together with the vestall virgins to crave
peace, or else some longer time to consult uppon the point.
The next morrow, as he stood expecting an answere, word
was brought unto him by his espiall, that the enemie
approched. Immediatly therfore shutting himselfe close
within a bearing chaire[3], accompanied with two persons
onely, his baker and his Cooke[4], secretly hee tooke his way
to the Aventine (hill) and his fathers house: minding from
thence to make an escape into Campania. Soone after,
uppon a flying and headlesse rumour, That peace was
obtained, he suffred him selfe to be brought backe to the
Palace. Where, finding all places solitary and abandoned:
seeing those also to slinke from him and slip away who were
with him, he did about him a girdle[5] full of golden peeces of
coine[6], and fled into the Porters lodge, having first tied a

[1] For yee must remember how much hee was given to gourmandise.
[2] *Pugionem* or rapier, *a pungendo quia punctim potius quam cæsim vulnerat.*
[3] Or Licter.   [4] That made his deinty pastry works and sweet meates:
meete grooms to accompanie such a glutton.   [5] Or bandelier.   [6] 15
Shilling peeces and better.

TWELVE CÆSARS

ban-dog[a] at the doore and set against it the bedsteed and
bedding thereto.

17

By this time had the Avantcurriers[1] of the (Flavians)
maine armie broken into the Palace: and meeting noe
bodie searched as the manner is, everie blind corner. By
them was hee plucked out of his lurking hole: and when
they asked who he was, (for they knewe him not) and where,
upon his knowledge Vitellius was, he shifted them of with
a lie: after this, beeing once knowen, hee intreated hard
(as if he had somewhat to deliver concerning the life and
safetie of Vespasian) to be kept sure in the mean season,
though it were in some prison: and desisted not untill such
time as having his hands pinnioned fast at his backe, an
halter cast about his necke, and his apparell torne from his
bodie, he was haled halfe naked into the Forum[2]. Among
many skornefull indignities offred unto him both in deede
and word throughout the spatious street *sacra via*[3] from
one end to the other, whiles they drew his head backward
by the bush of his haire (as condemned malefactours are
wont to be served) and set a swordes point under his chinne[4],
and all to the end he might shew his face and not holde it
down: whiles some pelted him with dung and durtie mire,
others called him with open mouth Incendiarie[5] and Patin-
arium[6]: and some of the common sort twitted him also
with faults and deformities of his bodie: (for, of stature hee
was beyond measure tall: a red face he had, occasioned for
the most part by swilling in wine, and a grand fat paunch
besides: hee limped somewhat also by reason that one of
his thighes was enfeebled withe the rush of a chariot against
it, what time he served Caius[7] as his henxman at a Chariot
running) and at the last upon the staires Gemoniæ with
many a small stroke all to mangled he was and killed in
the end: and so from thence drawne with a drag into the
River Tiberis.

---

[1] Or the vaward.   [2] Or market place.   [3] *Sacra via* reacheth from the
palace to the Forum.   [4] As a gag.   [5] Or firebrand, because he burnt the
Capitoll.   [6] Or Platter Knight, for his gormandize and huge platter aforesaid.   [7] Caligula.

THE HISTORIE OF

Thus perished he with his brother and sonne togither, in the 57 yeere of his age. Neither falsified he their conjecture who had foretold him, that by the prodigious signe which befell unto him (as we have said) at Vienna, nothing else was portended, but that he should fall into the hands of some Frenchman [a]. For, dispatched he was by one Antonius Primus a Capitaine of the adverse part : who being borne at Tolosa, was in his childhood surnamed Beccus [1] which in the French tongue signifieth a Cockes-bill.

---

[1] Or *Becco* a beak in English, which may somewhat confirme the learned conjecture of him, who guesseth that both our auncient nation and language were extract from Gaule.

THE HISTORIE OF
FLAVIUS VESPASIANUS
AUGUSTUS

. 1

HE Empire standing thus a long time in doubtfull termes, unsetled and wandering (as it were) by occasion of the rebellious broils and bloudy slaughter of three princes[1], the Flavii at length tooke into their hands and established: a house I must needs say, of obscure descent and not able to shew any pedigree and images of auncestours to commend their race; howbeit, such as the common weale had no cause to dislike and bee ashamed of; although it be well knowne that Domitian abidd condigne punishment for his avarice and crueltie. Titus Flavius Petronianus, a burgesse of the free borrough Reate, and a Centurion, siding in time of the civill warre, with Pompeius (but whether he served voluntarie or was called foorth and prest it is uncertaine) fledde out of the battaile[2] in Pharsalia and went home to his house. Where afterwardes, having obteined his pardon and discharge from warrefare, he became a bailife under the Bankers and mony changers to gather up their monies. This mans sonne surnamed Sabinus, nothing martiall nor skilfull in feates of armes (although some write, that he had beene a principall leader of the formost Cohorts: and others that whilest he led certaine companies, hee was acquit from his militarie oth by occasion

---

[1] Galba, Otho, Vitellius.   [2] Or, after the battaile, fled from him.

THE HISTORIE OF

of sicklinesse [1]) came to be a Publicane [2] in Asia, and gathered the custome or impost Quadragesima [a] for the state. And there remained certaine Images which the Cities in that province erected for him with this title and superscription, Καλῶς τελωνήσαντι, i. For him that was a good and faithfull Publicane [3]. After this he put foorth mony to usurie among the Helvetians, where he ended his life, leaving behinde him his wife Polla Vespasia, and two children which he had by her. The elder of which, named Sabinus, was advanced to the provostship of the Cittie: the younger called Vespasianus, attained to the dignitie Imperiall. This dame Polla, borne at Nursia and descended of worshipfull parentage, was the daughter of Vespasius Pollio, one that had beene a militarie Tribune [4] thrice, and provost Marshal [5] of the Campe besides: and sister to a man of Senatours degree, and promoted to the dignitie of Prætour. There is a place moreover even at this day sixe miles from Rome, (as men goe to Spoletum from Nursia) upon the hill top, bearing the name of Vespasiæ: where many monuments of the Vespasii are to be seene: a great evidence to prove the Noblenesse and antiquitie of that family. I cannot deny, that some have given out, how the father of that Petrojanus came out of the Transpadane region [6], and was an undertaker by the great, to hire those labourers and hines which were wont yeerely to repaire out of Umbria into the Sabines Countrie for to till their grounds: how hee planted himselfe and stayed in the Towne Reate aforesaid, and there maried a wife. But my selfe could never finde (make what search I could) any signe or trace to lead me thereto.

2

Vespasian [7] was borne in the Sabines territorie beyond Reate within a smal village named Phalacrine, the fifteenth day before the Calends of December [8], in the evening, when Q. Camerinus and Caius Poppæus Sabinus were consuls: five yeeres before that Augustus departed out of this world.

[1] Such be called *Causarii*.   [2] *Publicanum*, or *Publcium*, both to the same effect.   [3] Or customer.   [4] Or Colonel.   [5] Or camp maister.   [6] Beyond the river Po in respect of Rome.   [7] The Emperour.   [8] 17th of November.

TWELVE CÆSARS

His bringing up he had under Tertulla his grandmother by
the fathers side, in the land and living that she had about
Cosa. Whereupon, when hee was Emperour hee both frequented continually the place of his birth and breeding, the
Capitall house and manour remaining still as it had beene
in former times, nothing altered (because forsooth, his eyes
should have no losse nor misse of that which they were wont
to see there) and loved also the memoriall of his grandmother so deerely, that on all solemne and festivall, and
high daies, hee continued ever drinking out of a silver pot
that was hers and out of none other. After he had put on
his virile gowne[1], he refused a long time the Senatours
robe[a], although his brother had attained therto: neither
could he be forced to seeke for it at last but by his owne
mother. Shee in the end wrought perforce so much from
him, by way of reprochful taunts more than by faire intreatie or reverent authoritie: whiles, ever and anone, shee
called him in taunting wise, his brothers huisher. He served
as Tribune military in Thracia: and in quality of Questor had
the government of Crete and Cyrene, provinces by lot fallen
unto him. When he sued to be Ædile, and afterwards
Pretour, he hardly attained to the former Offices (and not
without some repulse) even in the sixth place: but presently
at his first suit and with the formost being chosen Pretour,
and upon displeasure taken, maliciously affected against the
Senate, because he would by all maner of demerite win the
favour of Caius the Emperor, he earnestly demanded extraordinary playes and games in honor of him for his victory
in Germanie: and gave opinion in the Senate house, that
to augment the p n   n of certeine conspiratours (against
him), their dead bodies should bee cast forth and left un-
buried. Hee gave him also solemne thankes before that
right honorable degree, for vouchsafing him the honor to be
a guest of his at a supper.

3

Amid these occurrents, he espoused Flavia Domitilla, the
freed woman of Statilius Capella, a Romane gentleman of

[1] In 17th yeere of his age.

THE HISTORIE OF

Sabraca, and an Africane borne, committed unto him sometime upon trust, and enfranchised in the freedom of Latium :
but afterwards pronounced a gentlewoman born and natural-
ized a Citizen of Rome, in the Court of Judges delegate,
upon claime made by her father Flavius Liberalis borne
at Ferentinum, (a man that never rose higher than to be
a Scribe[1] to a Questour) who vouched her freedome. By
her he had issew, Titus, Domitianus, and Domitilla. His
wife and daughter he overlived, and buried them whiles he
was yet in state of a private person. After his foresaid
wives decease, he called home againe to cohabite with him
in his house Cænis a freed-woman of Antonia, and her
Secretarie[2], whom he had fansied in former time : and
her he kept when he was Emperour, insteede of his true
and lawfull wife.

4

Under the Emperour Claudius, by especiall favour of
Narcissus, sent he was into Germanie as Lieutenant of a
legion : from thence being removed into Britaine, he fought
thirtie battailes with the enemie: two most mightie nations,
and above twentie towns, togither with the Isle of Wight
lying next to the said Britaine, he subdued, under the conduct partly of A. Plautius Lieutenant to the consul, and in
part of Claudius himselfe, for which worthy acts he received
triumphall ornaments, and in short space two sacerdotall
dignities with a consulship besides which he bare the two
last moneths of the yeere. For the middle time between,
even until he was Proconsul, he led a private life in a retyring place out of the way, for feare of Agrippina, who as
yet bare a great stroke with her sonne[3], and hated to the
heart all the friends of Narcissus, although deceased. After
this, having the province of Africk allotted unto him, hee
governed the same with singular integritie, and not without
much honor and reputation : but that in a seditious commotion at Adrumetum, there were Rape-rootes[4a] flung at his
head. Certaine it is, that from thence he returned nothing

---

[1] Or notarie.   [2] Or Keeper of her books and accompts.   [3] Nero.
[4] Or turneps.

206

TWELVE CÆSARS

richer than he was; as who not able to keepe credit, but
growen almost bankrupt, was driven to mortgage all his
houses and lands unto his brother: and of necessitie, for
the maintenance of his estate and dignity, went so low as
to make gaines by hucksters trade [1] pampering beastes [2] for
better sale. Whereupon he was commonly named Mulio,
i. Mulitier. It is said also that convicted he was for ex-
torting from a young man 200 thousand sesterces, in consideration that by his meanes hee had obteined a Senators
dignitie even against his owne fathers will, for which hee had
a sore rebuke. Whiles he travailed through Achaia in the
traine and inward companie of Nero, he incurred his heavie
displeasure in the highest degree, for that whiles he was
chaunting, either he made many starts away out of the
place, or else slept, if he staied there still. And being forbidden not only to converse in the same lodging with him,
but also to salute him publikely with others, he withdrew
himselfe aside into a small cittie, and which stood out of
the way: untill such time, as lying close there and fearing
the worst, the goverment of a province [3] with the commaund of an armie was offred unto him. There had been
spred throughout all the East parts an opinion of olde, and
the same setled in mens heades and constantly beleeved,
That by the appointment of the destinies about such a
time there should come out of Jury those, who were to be
Lords of the whole World [b]: which being a prophesie (as
afterwards the event shewed) foretelling of the Romane
Emperour, the Jewes [4] drawing to themselves, rebelled: and
having slaine the President [5] there, put to flight also the
Lieutenant generall of Syria [6] (a man of consular degree)
comming in to ayde; and tooke from him the Ægle [7]. To
represse this insurrection, because there was neede of a
greater armie and a valiant Captaine, yet such an one, as
to whom a matter of so great consequence might safely be
committed, himselfe was chosen above all others, as a man
of approved valour and industrie; howbeit no way to be

---

[1] *Mangonicos quæstus.*   [2] Which extendeth also to slaves and old wares or
thripperie.   [3] Jurie.   [4] Who then looked for their Messias and doe so
still.   [5] Or governour, Sabinus.   [6] Gallus.   [7] i. The maine standerd.

feared for the meannesse of his birth, linage and name. Having therefore under his hand an addition to the former poure, of two legions[1], eight cornets of horse and tenne cohorts[2] (of foote): taking also unto him among other Lieutenants, his elder son[3], no sooner arrived he in that province, but the other states[4] likewise next adjoyning, he brought into admiration of him, for reforming immediatly at his first comming the discipline of the campe, and giving the charge in one or two battailes with such resolution, as that in the assault of a castle, he caught a rap with a stone upon his knee, and received in his targuete some shot of arrowes.

5

After Nero and Galba, whiles Otho and Vitellius strove for Soveraintie, hee had good hope of the Empire, conceived long before, by these presaging tokens (which I wil now relate): within a countrey ferme by the Citie side, belonging to the Flavii, there stood an olde Oke consecrated unto Mars, which at 3 childbirths of Vespasia sodainly did put forth every time a several bough from the stock: undoubted signes fore-shewing the destinie and fortune of each one. The first was small and slender, which quickly withered (and therefore the girle at that time borne lived not one yeere to an end): the second grewe very stiffe and long withall, which pretended great felicitie: but the third, came to the bignesse of a tree. Whereupon Sabinus the father (of Vespasian) beeing confirmed beside by the answere of a Southsayer[5], brought word backe (by report) unto his owne Mother[6], that she had a Nephew borne who should be Cæsar[7]: whereat, shee did nothing else but set up a laughter, mervailing that her sonne should have a cracked braine and fall a doting now, since that his Mother had her wittes still whole and sound. Soone after, when Caius Cæsar, offended and angrie with him, for that beeing Ædile hee

---

[1] Romaine. [2] These cornets and cohorts seeme to bee Auxiliaries.
[3] Titus. [4] Or Provinces rather in the East part. [5] One of these that prie into heastes bowels. [6] Tertulla the Grandmother of Vespasian.
[7] Emperour.

TWELVE CÆSARS

had not beene carefull about sweeping and clensing the streetes, had commanded hee should bee all bedawbed with mire that the Souldiours gathered up and threw into the lap of his embrodred robe, some were ready to make this interpretation thereof, That the common weale trodden one day under foote and forlorne by some civill troubles, should fall into his protection and as it were into his bosome. As hee was at his dinner upon a time, a strange dog brought into his dining roome a mans hand and layed it under the boarde. Againe, as hee sate another time at supper, an Oxe having beene at plough and shaken of his yoke, rushed into the parlour where hee was at meate: and when hee had driven the waiters and servitours out, as if all on a sodaine hee had beene wearie, layed him downe along at his feete where hee sate, and gently put his necke under him. A Cypresse tree likewise in his Grand-fathers land without anie force of tempest plucked up by the roote and layed along, the very next day following rose up againe greener and stronger than before. But in Achaia hee dreamed, That hee and his, should beginne to prosper so soone as Nero had a tooth drawn out of his head. Now it fortuned, that the morrow following, a Chirurgion that came forth into the court-yeard shewed unto him a tooth of Neroes newly drawen. In Jurie, when hee consulted with the Oracle of the god Carmelus[a], the answere which was given, assured him in these tearmes, That whatsoever he thought upon and cast in his minde (were it never so great) it should so come to passe. And one of the Noble men of that Countrey taken captive, named Josephus[1], when hee was cast into prison, avouched and sayde unto him most constantly, that hee should shortly be set at liberty even by him, but hee should be Emperour first. There were moreover significant tokens presaging no lesse reported unto him out of the very Citie of Rome: and namely, that Nero in his latter dayes, a little before his death, was warned in a dreame to take the sacred Chariot of Jupiter Optimus Maximus forth of the Chappel where it stoode, into Vespasians house, and so from thence into the Cirque[2]. Also, not long after, as

---

[1] Who wrote the Jewish historie.   [2] *Inde in Circum.*

2 : DD

209

THE HISTORIE OF

Galba held the solemne election for his[1] second Consulship, the statue of Julius, late Cæsar of famous memorie, turned of it selfe into the East [b]. And at the field fought before Bebriacum, ere the battailes joyned, two Ægles had a conflict and bickered together in all their sights: and when the one of them was foyled and overcome, a third came at the very instant from the sunne rising and chased the Victresse away.

6

Yet for all this attempted he no enterprise (notwithstanding his friends and souldiours were most prest and forward yea and urgent upon him) before that hee was sollicited by the unexpected favour, of some, who as it fell out were both unknowen to him and also absent. Two thousand drawen out of the three legions of the Mæsian armie and sent to ayde Otho, when they were upon the way marching (albeit newes came unto them that hee was vanquished and had layed violent hands upon himselfe), held on their journey neverthelesse as farre as to Aquileia, as giving small credit to that rumour: where after they had by vantage of opportunities offred, and uncontrolled libertie, committed all manner of robberies and outrageous villanies, fearing least if they returned backe againe, they should answere for their misdemeanours, and abide condigne punishment therefore; layed their heades togither, and consulted about the chusing and creating of an Emperour. For, worse they tooke not themselves nor inferiour, eyther to the armie in Spaine that had set up Galba: or to the Pretorian bands, which had made Otho: or to the Germanician forces who had elected Vitellius, Emperours. Having purposed therefore and nominated of the Consular Lieutenants as manie, as they coulde in anie place thinke upon: when they misliked all the rest, taking exceptions against one for this cause and another for that: whiles some againe of that third Legion, which a little before the death of Nero had been translated out of Syria into Mesia, highly praysed and extolled Vespasian, they all accorded

[1] Vespasians.

TWELVE CÆSARS

thereto, and without delay, wrote his name upon their
flagges and banners. And verily, for that time this project
was smuddred, the companies for a while reclaimed, and all
brought into good order. But when the sayde fact was
once divulged: Tiberius Alexander Provost[1] of Ægypt
was the first that forced the Legions to sweare allegeance
unto Vespasian, upon the kalends[2] of July, which ever after
was celebrated for the first day and beginning of his Empire.
After them, the armie in Jurie tooke the same oath before
Vespasian himselfe, the fifth day before the Ides of Julie[3].
These enterprises were very much farthered, by the copie of
a letter that went commonly through mens hands (true or
false I wote not) of Otho now deceased, to Vespasian, charging
and willing him now at the last cast, of all love to revenge
his death, and wishing him withall, to relieve the distressed
state of the Common-wealth: by a rumour also spred
abroad, That Vitellius upon his victorie ment fully to make
an exchange of the legions winter harbours: namely, to
remove those that wintered in Germanie into the East
Provinces[4], as to a more secure service and easier warfare.
Moreover, among the Governours of Provinces, Lucinius
Mucianus, and of the Kings, Vologesus of Parthia, had
promised, the one[5] (laying downe all grudge and enmitie
which unto that time he openly professed[6] upon a humour
of æmulation) the Syrian armie: and the other[7] fortie
thousand archers.

7

Vespasian therefore having undertaken a civill warre, and
sent before him his Capitaines and forces into Italie, passed
over in the meane time to Alexandria, for to be possessed of
the frontier streights and Avenues of Ægypt. Heere when
he had voided all companie from him and was entred alone
into the Temple of Serapis, after he had, upon much propitious favour of that god obtained, devoutly at length
turned him selfe about, him thought hee sawe Basilides[a],

[1] Or Governour.   [2] The first day.   [3] The 11 of July.   [4] No
marvaile then, if the armies there inclined to Vespasian.   [5] Mucianus.
[6] Unto Vespasian.   [7] K. Vologesus.

THE HISTORIE OF

one who was knowen to have had accesse unto no man, and long since for the infirmitie of his sinewes[1], scarce able to set one foote before another, and withall to bee absent a great way of[2], to present unto him Vervaine and sacred herbes, guirlands also and loaves of bread (as the manner is in that place). And heereupon immediately letters came unto him, emporting thus much, that the forces of Vitellius were discomfited before Cremona: reporting besides, that himselfe was killed at Rome. The onely thing that hee wanted (being as one would say, a Prince unlooked for, and as yet new come to the Empire) was Countenance, authoritie, and a kinde as it were of royall majestie. But even that also came on apace (by this occasion). It fortuned that a certaine meane commoner starke blind, another likewise with a feeble and lame leg, came both togither unto him as hee sat upon the tribunall, craving that helpe and remedie for their infirmities which had beene shewed unto them by Serapis in their dreames: That hee[3] should restore the one to his sight, if he did but spit into his eyes: and strengthen the others legge, if hee vouchsafed onely to touch it with his heele. Now when as hee could hardly beleeve, that the thing anie way would finde successe and speede accordingly, and therefore durst not so much as put it to the venture: at the last through the perswasion of friends, openly before the whole assembly, hee assayed both meanes, neither missed hee of the effect. About the same time, at Tegea in Arcadia, by the Instinct and motion of Prophets, there were digged out of the ground in a consecrated place, manufactures and vessels of antique worke: and among the same an Image, resembling for all the World Vespasian.

8

Thus qualified as hee was and graced with so great fame, hee returned to Rome: and after his triumph over the Jewes, hee added eight Consulships more to that which of olde hee had borne. He tooke upon him also the Censureship: and all the time of his Empire esteemed nothing more

[1] The Palsey.   [2] 80 Miles; happily, the same whom Tacitus reporteth to have been the Priest of Carmelus.   [3] Vespasian.

TWELVE CÆSARS

deare, than first to establish and afterwards to adorne the Common weale, brought almost to utter decay, and at the point to fall downe. The souldiours, some presuming boldly of their victories, others in griefe for their shamefull disgrace[1] were growen to all manner of licentiousnesse and audacitie. The Provinces likewise and free states, yea and some kingdomes, fell to discord and seditious tumults among them selves. And therefore of the Vitellians be both cassed and also chasticed very many. As for the partners with him in victorie: so farre was hee from allowing them any extraordinary indulgence, that their very due and lawfull rewardes hee payed not but slackely. And because hee would not let slip anie occasion of reforming militarie discipline, when a certain gallant youth smelling hote of sweet balmes and perfumes came unto him, to give thanks for an Office[2] obtained at his hands, after a strange countenance shewing his dislike of him, hee gave him also in words, a most bitter and grievous checke, saying, 'I would rather thou haddest stunke of garlicke,' and so revoked his letters patents for the graunt. As touching the mariners and sea servitours, such of them as are wont to passe to and fro on foote, by turnes[3] from Ostia and Puteoli to Rome, who were petitioners unto him that some certaine allowance might bee set downe for to finde them shoes: hee thought it not sufficient to sende them away without answere, but commanded that for ever after they should runne up and downe betweene unshod[4]. And so, from that time they use to doe. Achaia, Lycia, Rhodes, Bizantium and Samos, first diffranchised[5]: likewise Thracia, Cilicia and Comagene, subject untill that time to Kings, hee reduced all into the forme of a province. Into Cappadocia, for the continuall rodes and incursions that the Barbarians made, he brought a poure besides, of Legions, and in lieu of a Romane knight, he placed there for Ruler, a man who had beene Consul. The Citie of Rome by reason of olde skarefires and ruines was much blemished and disfigured. Hee permitted there-

---

[1] In taking part against him.   [2] Or charge.   [3] *Per vices*, some reade *per vicos, i.* along the townes and villages.   [4] Barefoote.   [5] Whereas they had been free States.

THE HISTORIE OF

fore any man to seize as his owne all vacant plots of ground, and to builde thereupon, in case the owners and Land-lords were slacke in that behalfe. Him selfe tooke upon him the reedifying of the Capitoll, and was the first man that· did set his hand to the ridding of the rubbish and rammell, yea and upon his owne necke caried some of it awaye: three thousand tables of brasse also which were burnt with the sayd Temple, hee undertooke to make and set up againe, having searched and sought out from all places the pattrons and copies thereof[1]. A most bewtifull instrument and right auncient record of the whole Empire hee compiled and finished, wherein were contained from the first beginning well neere of the Citie, all actes of Senate, all deedes passed by the Communalty as concerning Leagues, Alliances and priviledges granted to any whatsoever.

9

Hee built also newe workes: the temple of peace, situate next unto the Forum: that likewise of Claudius, late Emperour of sacred memorie, seated upon the mount Cælius, which verily had beene begun by Agrippina[2] but almost from the very foundation destroyed by Nero. Item, a most stately Amphitheatre in the heart of the Citie, according as hee understood that Augustus intended such an one[3]. The two degrees[4] wasted by sundry massacres and disteined through the negligence of former times, he cleansed and supplyed, by a review and visitation of Senate and gentry both: wherein he remooved the unworthiest persons and tooke in the most honest that were to bee found, either of Italians or provinciall inhabitants. And to the ende it might be knowne, that both the said degrees differed one from another not so much in libertie as in dignitie, hee pronounced in the case of a certaine braule betweene a Senatour and a knight of Rome, That Senatours might not be provoked first with foule language: mary to aunswere them

---

[1] For in them were engraven the publike evidences and records, etc.
[2] Claudius his wife.   [3] *Ut destinasse compererat Augustum, amplissimum.*
[4] Of Senatours and gentlemen.

214

TWELVE CÆSARS

with evill words agaіne, was but Civilitie and a matter allowed.

10

Suites in law depending one uppon another were growen in everie Court exceeding much: whiles the old Actions by the Intervall of Jurisdiction[1], hung still undecided, and new quarrels arose to encrease them, occasioned by the tumultuous troubles of those times. Hee chose therefore certaine commissioners by lot, some by whome the goods taken and caried away perforce during the warres might be restored; and others, who extraordinarily should determine and judge betweene partie and partie in Centumvirall cases[2][a] (which were so many, as that the parties[3] themselves, as it was thought, could hardly by course of nature live to see an end of them), and reduce them all to as small a number as possiblie might be.

11

Wanton lust and wastfull expense, without restraint of any man, had gotten a mightie head. Hee mooved the Senate therefore to make a decree: That, what woman soever joyned her selfe in wedlocke[4] unto another mans bondservant, should be reputed a bondwoman. Item, that it might not bee lawfull for Usurers to demaund any debt of young men whiles they were under their fathers tuition for mony credited out unto them: I mean, not so much as after their decease. In all other matters, from the very first beginning of his Empire unto the end, hee was curteous enough and full of Clemencie.

12

His former meane estate and condition, hee dissimuled not at anie time: nay hee would often of himselfe professe the same and make it knowen openly: yea and when some went

---

[1] The vacation during the Civil troubles. [2] Which pertained to the Centumvirs Court: to wit, Civile causes between private persons, as probates of Testaments, etc. *Vide* Cicer. i. *de Oratore*. [3] Plantifes and defendants. [4] *Si iunxisset*, as Sabellicus expoundeth it: or, at large, carnally.

about to fetch the originall of the Flavian Linage, from as farre as the founders of Reate, and the companion of Hercules, whose monument is to bee seene in the way Salaria [1], hee mocked and laughed them to skorne for their labours. And so farre was he from desiring anie outward ornaments [2] in shew of the World, that upon his triumph day, being wearied with the slow march and tædious traine of the pompe, he could not hold but say plainely, that hee was well enough served and justly punished, who beeing an aged man had so foolishly longed for a triumph : as if forsooth it had of right beene due unto his forefathers [3], or ever hoped for by himselfe [4]. Neither accepted he so much, as the tribunes authority and addition, of *Pater patriæ* in his stile, but it was long first. For hee had forlet altogether the custome of searching those that came in duty to salute him even whiles yet the Civill warre continued.

13

The franke-speech [5] of his friendes: the figurative tearmes and quips of Lawyers pleading at the barre, and the unmannerly rudenesse of Philosophers hee tooke most mildely. Licinius Mucianus [6], a man notorious for preposterous wantonnesse but (presuming confidently of his good deserts [7]) not so respective of him as reverent duty would, hee could never finde in his heart to gird and nip againe but secretly : and thus farre forth onely as in complaining of him unto some good friend of them both to knit up all with these words for a conclusion, 'Yet am I a man [8].' When Salvius Liberalis [9], pleading in the defence of a rich client was so bolde as to say, 'What is that to Cæsar [10], if Hipparchus be worth an hundred millians of Sesterces?' him selfe also commended and thanked him for it. Demetrius the Cynicke [11] meeting

---

[1] By which salt was brought out of the Sabines countrey to Rome. [2] *Extrinsecus.* [3] Who were but of meane calling. [4] Being three-score of age, and therefore past the ambitious desire of such glory. [5] *Libertatem,* which the Greekes call Parrhesian. [6] His friend. [7] For he was the chiefe helper of him to the Empire. [8] Whatsoever you are : noting him for that he was *Pathicus.* [9] A Lawyer. [10] Noting Vespasian, as if he had a longing eye after his wealth and therefore sought his condemnation. [11] A philosopher.

TWELVE CÆSARS

him in the way after hee was come to his Soveraigne dignitie[1], and not deigning once to rise up nor to salute him,
but rather barking at him I wote not what, he thought
it enough to call Cur-dogge[a].

14

Displeasures to him done, and enmities, he never caried
in mind nor revenged. The daughter of Vitellius his enemie
he maried into a most noble house: he gave unto her a rich
dowry withall, and furniture accordingly. Whenas, by
reason that he was forbidden the Court under Nero, hee
stood in great feare, and was to seeke what to do or whether
to goe: one of the gentlemen huishers, whose office it was
to admit men into the presence, in thrusting him out, had
bidden him *abire Morboniam*[2], *i.* to be gone in a mischiefe.
When this fellow afterwards came to aske forgivenesse, he
proceeded no further in heat of anger but to wordes onely,
and to quite him with just as many and almost the very
same. For, so farre was he from working the overthrowe
and death of anye person, upon anye suspicion or feare conceived: that when his friendes admonished him to beware of
Mætius Pomposianus, because it was generally believed that
the Astrologers had by the horoscope of his nativitie assured
him to bee Emperour another day, hee advanced the same
Metius to the Consulship, presuming and promising in the
mans behalfe, that hee would be one day mindfull of this
benefit and good turne of his.

15

There is not lightly found an innocent person to have
beene punished, but when hee was absent and not ware
thereof: or at leastwise unwilling thereto and deceived.
With Helvidius Priscus, who onely had saluted him after
his returne out of Syria, by his private name, plaine Ves-

---

[1] *Post dominationem alias damnationem*, *i.* after he was condemned, for
Vespasian had banished al Philosophers out of Rome and confined this
Demetrius to an Iland. Xiphilin.   [2] Or *Morboviam*, according to which
phrase we say, The foule ill take thee. The Greekes *Eis Choracas*, *i.* The
Crowes eate thee. The Latines *in malam crucem*, *i.* Go hang.

THE HISTORIE OF

pasian[1]: and being pretour in all his Edicts and Proclamations passed him over without any honour at all, or once
naming him, hee was not angry and displeased, before that
he had, with his most insolent altercations made him in
manner contemptible and little better than an ordinarie
person. Him also, notwithstanding he was first confined
to a place and afterwards commanded to bee killed, hee
would have given a great deale to have saved by all meanes
possible: as who sent certein of purpose to call backe the
murderers: and saved his life hee had, but that false word
came backe that he was dispatched alreadie. Otherwise he
never rejoyced in the death of any, but rather when malefactours were justly punished and executed hee would weepe
and groane againe.

16

The onely thing for which hee might worthily bee blamed
was covetousnesse. For, not content with this, to have
revived the taxes and payments omitted by Galba: to have
laied unto them other newe and heavie impositions: to
have enhaunsed also the Tributes of the provinces, yea and
of some dupled the same: he fell openly to negotiate and
deale in certaine trades, which, even for a private person
were a shame to use: buying up and engrossing some commodities for this purpose, onely to put the same of afterwardes at an higher price. Neither made hee it straung
to sell either honourable places unto suiters for them: or
absolutions and pardons, to men in trouble, whether they
were innocent or gultie it skilled not. Furthermore, it is
verily thought that of his Procuratours, if any were greedy
and given to extortion more than other, his manner was to
promote such for the nonce to higher offices: to the ende,
that when they were more enriched, hee might soone after
condemne them. And commonly it was sayd, that those hee
used as spunges, for that hee did wet them well when they
were drie, and presse them hard when they were wette.
Some write that hee was by nature most covetous, and that
an old Neat heard upbraided him once therwith, who being

[1] Not Cæsar nor Augustus nor Imperator.

TWELVE CÆSARS

at his bandes denied freedome without paying for it (which
hee humblie craved of him now invested in the Empire),
cried out with a lowd voice and said, The Wolfe might
change his haire, but not his qualities. Contrariwise there
bee againe who are of opinion, that hee was driven to spoyle,
to pill and poll of necessitie, even for extreame want both
in the common treasurie and also in his owne exchequer :
whereof he gave some testimonie in the beginning immediately of his Empire, professing that there was neede of
fortie thousand Millenes to set the State upright againe.
Which also seemeth to sounde more neere unto the truth,
because the monie by him ill gotten, hee used and bestowed
passing well. To all sorts of men hee was most liberall.
The Estate and wealth of Senatours ᵃ he made up to the
full. To decaied men that had beene Consuls, hee allowed
for their maintenance 500 thousand Sesterces by the yeere.
Very many Cities throughout the World by Earth quake or
fire ruinate, hee reedified better then they were before.

17

Fine wits and cunning Artisanes hee set much store by,
and cherished them above all others. Hee was the first,
that out of his owne coffers appointed for professed Rhetori-
cians, as well in Latine as in Greeke, an yeerely Salarie of an
hundred thousand Sesterces a peece. Excellent Poets, as
also Actours [1] he bought up [2]. Semblably, upon the workeman who had repaired and set up againe, the Geantlike
Image called Colossus ᵃ, hee bestowed a notable congiarie [3],
and endewed him with a great stipend beside : to an En-
giner also, who promised to bring into the Capitoll huge
Columnes with small charges, hee gave for his devise onely
no meane reward, and released him his labour in perform-
ing that worke, saying withall by way of preface, That he
should suffer him to feed the poore commons [4].

---

[1] Artificers, for so Livie termeth *Ludios et histriones, i.* stage players.
[2] Or hyred.   [3] Or reward.   [4] To allow them wages for their painefull
labor in such works rather then to have the same done without them : and
as we say, to keep poore people at worke.

THE HISTORIE OF

18

At those playes during which the stage of Marcellus Theatre newly reedified, was dedicated : he had brought into request and use againe even the olde Acroames [1] [a]. To Apollinaris the Tragœdian hee gave foure hundred thousand sesterces. To Terpnus and Diodorus two harpers, two hundred thousand a peece : to some one hundred : and to whom hee gave least fortie thousand, over and above a great number of golden Coronets. Hee feasted continually : and for the most part by making full suppers, and those very plentifull [2] : for why ? His meaning was to helpe the Butchers and such as solde victuals. As hee delivered foorth giftes unto men at the *Saturnalia*, so hee did to Women upon the Kalends of March [b]. Yet verely for all this, coulde hee not avoide the infamous name of his former avarice. The men of Alexandria termed him still Cybiosastes after the surname of one of their Kings, given to most base and beggerly gayne. And even at his very funerals, Favor the Arch-counterfaict representing his person, and imitating (as the manner is) his deeds and wordes whiles hee lived, when hee asked the Procuratours openly, what the charges might bee of his funerall and the pompe thereto belonging, no sooner hearde that it would arise to tenne Millenes of Sesterces, but hee cried, ' Give mee one hundred thousand, and make no more adoe but throw mee into Tiber.'

19

Of a middle stature hee was : well set : his limmes compact and strongly made : with a countenance as if he streined hard for a stoole. Whereupon one of these plaisants came out with a pretie conceit. For when Vespasian seemed to request the fellow for to breake a jest upon him also, as well as upon others, ' That I will,' quoth he, ' if you had .done your businesse once upon the seege.' His health hee had, no man better : although for the preservation thereof hee

[1] Eare delights, as Players, Musicians, etc.   [2] *Recta :* in opposition to *sportulæ*.

TWELVE CÆSARS

did no more, but rub his owne chawes and other parts of the bodie to a certeine just number within the *Sphæristerium* [2][a]: and withall, monethly interpose abstinence from all foode one whole day [2].

20

This course and order of life for the most part he held. Whiles hee was Emperour he waked alwayes very early, and late in the night [3]. Then, having red through all missives, and the Breviaries of everie office, hee admitted his friends: and whiles hee was saluted, he both put on his own shooes, and also apparailled and made himselfe ready. After dispatch of all occurrent businesses, hee tooke himselfe to gestation [a], and so to rest: having one of his Concubines lying by his side: of whom hee had appointed a great number in steede of Cænis deceassed. From his privie closet [4], hee passed into his Baine and so to his refection roume. Neyther was he, by report, at any time fuller of humanitie, or redier to doe a pleasure. And such oportunities of time as these, his domesticall servants waited for especially, to preferre their petitions in.

21

At his suppers, and otherwise at all times with his friends being most pleasant and courteous [5][a], hee dispatched many matters by way of mirth. For given exceedingly hee was to skoffs, and those so skurrile and filthy, that he could not so much as forbeare words of ribaudrie [b]. And yet there bee many right pleasant conceited jests of his extant. Among which this also goes for one. Being advertised by Menstrius Florus, a man of Consuls degree, to pronounce *Plaustra* [6], rather than *Plostra*, hee saluted him the next morrow by

---

[1] A round place of exercise belonging to the baines. Some would have it to be a tennis court. [2] Naturall, *i.* 24 houres. [3] Or arose before day, *de nocte vigilabat.* Sextus Aurelius writeth of him that he watched al night. Plinie also saith *Nocte uti solitum: ut dierum actus noctibus, et nocturnos diebus traiiceret.* [4] A Secrete, or retiring place. [5] *Et semper alias Cum amicis,* etc. Others read, *et super aleas Communissimus, i.* and whiles he plaied at hazard, etc. [6] A word in Latine that signifieth Cartes or waines.

the name of Flaurus[1c]. Having yeelded at length to a certaine woman enamoured of him, and readie as it were to dye for pure love, when she was brought to his bed[2], and had given him fortie thousand sesterces for lying with her[3], his Steward comes to put him in minde in what manner and forme hee would have this summe of money to bee set downe in his booke of accompts[4]. 'Marie thus,' quoth he, ' *Vespasiano adamato*,' i. Item, given to Vespasian beloved[d].

22

Hee used Greeke Verses also in good season and aptly applyed: as namely of a certaine fellow, tall and high of stature, but shrewde and testie withall[a], in this manner,

Μακρὰ βιβὰς κραδάων δολιχόσκιον ἔγχος[b],

and especially of Cerylus, his freed-man: upon whom, for that being exceeding rich, yet to avoyde a payment sometime to his Exchequer, hee began to give it out that hee was free borne, and so changed his name and called himselfe Laches, Vespasian played in these tearmes:

ὦ λάχης, λάχης, ἐπὰν ἀποθάνῃς,
αὖθις ἐξ ὑπαρχῆς εἰρήσῃ κήρυλος.

O Laches, Laches, wert thou once dead in grave :
Thine olde name Cerylus, againe thou shalt have.

Howbeit, most of all hee affected a kinde of dicacitie in his unseemely gayne and filthy lucre : to the end, that by some skoffing cavill, hee might put by and doe awaie the envie of the thing, turning all to merrie jests. A Minister and servitour about him, whom hee loved deerely, made suite in the behalfe of one as his brother, for a Stewardship. When hee had put him off to a farther day, hee called unto him the partie himselfe, that made meanes for the thing : and having exacted[5] so much monie at his hands, as hee had agreed for with the Mediatour aforesayd, without more

---

[1] And not Florus.   [2] *Cum perducta*, etc., not *perductæ*, in a quite contrarie sense, as if he had given her so much.   [3] *Quadraginta Sestertia, alias quadringenta sestertia, i.* 400 thousand.   [4] To wit, in the page of receits.
[5] Or received.

TWELVE CÆSARS

delay, he ordained him Steward. Soone after when the Servitour interposed him selfe, 'Goe your wayes,' quoth he, 'seeke you another to be your brother: for, this fellow whom you think to be yours is become mine.' Suspecting that his mulitier who drave his carroch alighted one time, as it were to shoo his Mules, thereby to winne some advantage of time and delay, for one that had a matter in lawe and was comming unto him: hee asked the Mulitier what might the shooing of his mules cost [1], and so covenanted with him to have part of his gaines. When his sonne Titus seemed to finde fault with him for devising a kinde of tribute, even out of urine [c]: the monie that came unto his hand of the first paiment, hee put unto his sonnes nose: asking withall, whether he was offended with the smell, or no, and when he answered No: 'And yet,' quoth he, 'it commeth of Urine.' Certaine Embassadours brought him word, that there was decreed for him at the common charges of the States a geantlike image, that would cost no meane summe of money. He commanded them to reare the same immediately, shewing therewith his hand Hallow [2]. 'Here is the base,' quoth he, 'and piedstall [3] for it, ready.' And not so much as in the feare and extreame perill of death forbare he skoffing. For when as among other prodigious signes the Mausoleum [4] of the Cæsars opened sodainely, and a blazing starre appeared: the one [5] of them, he sayde, did concerne Junia Calvina a gentlewoman of Augustus (Cæsars) race [6]: the other [7] had reference to the King of the Parthians, who ware his haire long [8]. In the very first accesse also and fit of his disease, 'Me thinkes,' quoth he, 'I am a deifying [9].'

23

In his ninth Consulship, after he had been assayled in Campania with some light motions and grudgings of his sicknesse, and thereupon returned forthwith to the Citie,

---

[1] The partie that came to sollicite his owne cause. [2] For to receive the money. [3] Meaning his hand. [4] Monument or Sepulchre. [5] The Mausoleum. [6] Wheras himself was not of that line. [7] A blazing starre. [8] Whereupon is called *Stella Crinita* and *Cometes* in Greeke. [9] Am a dying, and so, grow to be a god.

THE HISTORIE OF

hee went from thence to Catiliæ and the lands he had about Reate, where every yeere hee was wont to summer. Heere, having (besides the maladie still growing upon him) hurt also his guttes and bowels with the use of colde water[1a], and yet neverthelesse executed the functions of an Emperour, after his accustomed manner, in so much as lying upon his bed, hee gave audience to Embassadours: when all of a sodaine he fell into a loosenesse of the bellic, that hee fainted and was ready to swound therewith. 'An Emperour,'
quoth he, 'ought to dye standing.' As he was arising therfore and streining still to ease his bodie[2], he dyed in their hands that helped to lift him up, the 8th day before the Calends of July[3]: when he had lived threescore yeeres and nine, seven moneths and seven dayes over[4].

24

All writers agree in this, that so confident he was alwayes of his owne Horoscope[5] and his childrens, that after so many conspiracies continually plotted against him hee durst warrant and assure the Senate that either his owne Sonnes should succeede him or none. It is sayde moreover, that hee dreamed upon a time, how hee sawe a paire of skales hanging in the midst of the porch and entrie of his house palatine, with the beame thereof even ballanced, so as in the one ballance stoode Claudius and Nero: in the other, himselfe and his sonnes. And it fell out so indeede: for they ruled the Empire of both sides so many yeers, and the like space of time just.

---

[1] These waters of Catiliæ as Plinie writeth were exceeding cold.   [2] To avoid the ordure of the guttes.   [3] 24 June.   [4] *Superque mensem ac diem septimum.*   [5] Or nativitie.

224

THE HISTORIE OF
TITUS FLAVIUS VESPASIANUS
AUGUSTUS

· 1

ITUS, surnamed as his Father was, Vespasi-
anus, the lovely dearling and delightfull
joy of Mankinde (so fully was he, either
endued with good nature and disposition,
or enriched with skilfull cunning, or else
graced with fortunes favour; and that
(which is hardest of all) in his Imperiall
State, considering that whiles hee lived
as a private person under the Emperour his Father, he could
not avoid the very hatred and much lesse the reproofe of the
world). This Titus, I say, was borne the third day before
the Calends of Januarie[1]: in that yeere which was remarke-   <inline-section>A.U.C. 794.</inline-section>
able for the death of Caius the Emperour, neere unto the
Septizonium[a], within a poore ill-favoured house, in a very
little Chamber and darke withall: for it remaineth yet to
bee seene. His Education hee had in the Court together
with Britannicus, trained up in the like Arts and Disciplines,
under the same teachers. At which time verily, men say,
that a Fortune-teller[2][b], whom Narcissus the freed man of
Claudius brought to see Britannicus, after Inspection affirmed
most constantly, that by no meanes hee[3], but Titus who
then stoode hard by, should surely bee Emperour. Now
were these two so familiar, that (as it is verily thought) of
the same cup of poison whereof Britannicus drank and died,

---

[1] 30 of December.   [2] *Metoposcopum.*   [3] Britannicus.

THE HISTORIE OF

Titus also sitting neere unto him, tasted : whereupon he fell
into a grievous disease, that held him long and put him to
great paine. In memoriall of all which premisses, he erected
afterwards for him [1] one Statue of gold in the Palatium ; as
also another of Ivorie on horsebacke (which at the Circeian
Games is even at this day caried before in the Solemne pomp)
he dedicated, and accompanied accordingly.

2

At the very first, even in his child-hood, there shone forth
in him, the gifts both of body and minde : and the same
more and more still by degrees as hee grew in yeeres : a
goodly presence and countenance, wherein was seated no
lesse majestie [2] than favour and beauty : a speciall cleane
strength, albeit his stature was not tall : but his belly bare
out somewhat with the most. A singular memorie : and
aptnesse to learne all the Arts, in manner, as well of warre
as of peace. Most skilfull he was in handling his weapon,
and withall a passing good horsman : for his Latine and
Greeke tongue, whether it were in making Orations or composing Poemes, prompt and ready even to the performance
thereof *ex tempore*. Neither was he unseene in Musick as
who could both sing and also play upon instruments sweetly
and with knowledge. I have heard also many men say, That
he was wont to write with Cyphers and Characters most
swiftly, striving by way of sport and mirth with his owne
Clerks, whether he or they could write fastest, to expresse
likewise and imitate what hand so ever hee had seene : yea,
and to professe many a time, that he would have made a
notable forger and counterfaiter of writings.

3

In quality of Tribune Militare, he served in the warres
both in Germanie and also in Britaine, with exceeding commendation for his industrie and no lesse report of modestie [3],

---

[1] Britannicus.   [2] *Aucthoritatis*, which Tacitus calleth *maiestatem*.
[3] Temperate behaviour.

226

as appeareth by a number of his images and titles to them annexed [a], throughout both Provinces. After this warfare of his, hee pleaded causes in Court, which he did rather to winne credite and reputation [1], than to make it an ordinarie practise [2]. At which very time, he wedded Arricidia, the daughter of Tertullus a Gentleman of Rome, but Capitaine sometime of the Prætorian Bands: and in the roome of her deceased, he tooke to wife Martia Flavia: and from her when she had borne unto him a daughter, he divorsed him-selfe. After this, upon his Questureship, being Colonell and Commaunder of a whole Legion, he brought under his sub-jection Tarichea [3] and Gamala two most puissant Cities of Jurie: where, in a certaine battaile having lost his horse under him (by a deadly wound) within his flankes, hee mounted another whose rider in fight against him had beene slaine and was fallen.

TITUS
FLAVIUS
VESPA-
SIANUS
AUGUSTUS

A.U.C. 820.

4

Afterwards, when Galba was possessed of the State, being sent to congratulate his advauncement: what way so ever he went, he turned all mens eyes upon him, as if he had beene singled forth to be adopted. But so soone as he per-ceived all to be full of troubles againe, hee returned back out of his very journey, and visited the Oracle of Venus Paphia [4]: where, whilst he asked counsell, about his pas-sage at sea, he was confirmed withall in his hope of the Empire. Having attained thereto within short time, and being left behind to subdue Jurie throughly in the last assault of Hierusalem, he slew twelve enemies that defended the wall [5], with just so many arrowes shot: and wonne the Citie upon the very birth-day of his daughter [6], with so great joy and favourable applause of all his Souldiours: that in their gratulation they saluted him Emperour: and soone after, when he was to depart out of that Province, deteined him: in humble manner, yea and eft-soones in threatning

A.U.C. 821.

---

[1] In undertaking causes of greatest importance. [2] In entertaining al matters whatsoever. [3] Neere to the Lake Genezareth. [4] In Paphos a citie within the Isle Cyprus. [5] 12 Propugnatores. [6] 8th of September, Joseph. lib. 7: *De Bello Judaico*.

THE HISTORIE OF

wise instantly calling upon him, to stay, or else to take them all away together with him. Whereupon arose the first suspition, that he revolted from his father, and had attempted to chalenge the kingdome of the East parts for him selfe. Which surmise himselfe made the more, after that in his way to Alexandrea, as he consecrated at Memphis the Ox Apis, he wore a Diademe [a]: which he did in deed according to the custome and rites of the auncient religion there. But there wanted not some, who construed it otherwise. Making hast therefore into Italie; after hee was arrived first at Rhegium and from thence at Puteoli, embarqued in a Merchants ship of burden; to Rome he goes directly with all speed and most lightly appointed: and unto his father looking for nothing lesse, 'I am come,' quoth he, 'father, I am come': checking thereby the rash and inconsiderate rumors raised of him.

5

From that time forward hee ceased not to carie himselfe as partner with his Father, yea and Protectour also of the Empire: with him hee triumphed: with him hee jointly administred the Censureship: his Colleague hee was in the Tribunes authority: his Companion likewise in seven Consulships. And having taken to himselfe the charge well-neere of all Offices, whiles hee both endited letters and penned Edicts in his Fathers name: yea, and read Orations [1] in Senate, and that in the Questours turne, he assumed also the Captainship of the Guard, an Office never to that time executed but by a Gentleman of Rome. In this place hee demeaned himselfe nothing civilly, but proceeded with much violence: for ever as he had any in most jelousie and suspition, he, by sending secretly and under-hand certaine of purpose, who in the Theaters and Campe should require for to have them punished (as it were with his Fathers consent) made no more a-doe but brought them all to their end. As for example, among these, hee commaunded Aulus Cæcina, a man of Consular Degree, and a guest by him invited to supper, when hee was scarce gone out of the

[1] Missives.

228

TWELVE CÆSARS

Banquetting parlor to bee stabbed. I must needes say, that driven he was to this violent proceeding upon an extremity of daunger: considering that he had found out his handwriting bearing evidence of a conspiracie that he plotted with the Souldiours. By which courses, as he provided well and sufficiently for his owne security another day: so, for the present time he incurred very much displeasure and hatred of the world: in so much, as no man lightly, when so adverse a rumor was on foote, and that which more is, against the wills of all men, would have stepped to the Imperiall throne.

6

Beside his cruelty, suspected he was also for roiotous life: in that he continued banquetting untill midnight with the most profuse and wastfull spend-thrifts of his familiar minions: for wanton lust likewise, by reason of a sort of stale Catamites and guelded Eunuchs that he kept about him; and the affectionate love that hee was noted to beare to Queene Berenice [1], unto whom also, as it was said he promised mariage. Suspition there was moreover of his pilling and polling. For certain it was, that in the commissions and hearing of causes [2] which his father held, he was wont to sel the decision of matters, and to make a gaine thereby. After this, men both reputed and also reported him to be even another Nero. But this name that went of him proved good for him and turned to his greatest commendation: considering that no grosse vice could bee found in him, but contrariwise many excellent vertues. The feasts that he made were pleasant meriments, rather than lavish and sumpteous. He chose for his friends such, as in whom the Emperours also his successours reposed themselves, and whom they used especially as necessarie members both for them and also for the Common-wealth. As for Queene Berenice, he sent her quickly away from the Citie of Rome; but full loath they were both of them to part a sunder. Certaine of his minions and dearlings whom hee favoured

---

[1] The sister as some thinke of Agrippa, and wife for a while of Polemon King of Lycia: others say, she was the wife first of Aristobulus, afterwards of Antipater.   [2] *Agnitionibus.*

THE HISTORIE OF

TITUS
FLAVIUS
VESPA-
SIANUS
AUGUSTUS

and fansied most, albeit they were such artificiall Dauncers, that within a while after they caried the greatest praise and prise upon the stage, he forbare quite not onely to huggle and embrace long together, but to behold so much as once in any publick meeting and assembly. From no Citizen tooke he ought: and from aliens goods he abstained, if ever any did. Nay, he received not the very contributions graunted and usually paied. And yet, being inferiour to none of his predecessours in munificence, as having dedicated an Amphitheatre[1], and built the Baines hard-by, with great expedition[2a], he exhibited a Spectacle of Sword-fencers, with all kindes of furniture thereto belonging in most plentifull manner. Hee represented also a navall fight in the old *Naumachia* ; in which very place he brought forth likewise his sword-fencers to play their prises: and in that one day he put out to be baited 5000 wilde beasts of all sorts.

7

Furthermore, being of his owne nature most kinde and gracious ; whereas by a constitution and order that Tiberius began, all the Cæsars his Successours held not the Benefits graunted by former Princes good and in force, unlesse they also themselves made new graunts of the same againe : hee was the first, that by vertue of one sole edict, ratified and confirmed all that had passed before : neither suffred he any petition to be made unto him for them. In all other Suits and Requests, hee ever more held most constantly mens mindes at this passe, that hee would send none away without hope. And when his Domesticall Ministers about his person would seeme to tell him, That he promised more than he was able to performe : ' What !' quoth he, ' there ought no man to depart from the speech of a Prince, sad and discontented.' Calling to minde one time as he sat at supper, that he had done nothing for any man that day, hee uttered this memorable and praise-worthy Apophthegme, ' My friends, I have lost a day.' The people especially in generall he intreated in all occasions, with so great courtesie, that

[1] At which solemnity 5000 wilde beasts were killed. As Eusebius Chronographus and Eutropius write. [2] *Celeriter.*

230

TWELVE CÆSARS

having proposed a solemne Sword-fight, he made open profession, that he would set it forth, not to please him selfe
but to content the beholders. And verily, even so hee did:
for, neither denied he ought to them that would call for it:
and of his owne accord, willed them to aske what their
mindes stoode to. Moreover, shewing plainly, that hee
stoode well affected to the manner of the Thracian sword-
fencers[1]-fight and their Armature, hee would many times
even with the rest of the people both in word and gesture
(as a favourer of that kinde) jest and make sport: yet so, as
hee kept still the majestie of an Emperour: and withall
judged with equitie indifferently. And because hee would
pretermit no point of popularity, sometime as hee bathed in
his owne baines hee admitted the Commons thither unto
him. There fell out in his daies certaine mischaunces and
heavie accidents: as, the burning of the mountaine Vesævus
in Campania: a Skar-fire at Rome, which lasted three daies
and three nights; as also a pestilence[2], the like whereof had
not lightly beene knowne else where at any other time. In
these calamities so many and so grievous, he shewed not
onely a Princely care, but also a singular fatherly affection:
sometime comforting (his people) by his Edicts, otherwhiles
helping them so farre forth as his power would extend.
For repairing the losses in Campania[3], he chose by lot
certaine Commissioners to looke thereto, even out of the
ranke of those that had beene Consuls. The goods of such
as perished in the said mount, whose heires could not be
found, hee awarded to the reedification of the ruinate Cities
adjoyning. And having made publick protestation, that
in the said skare-fire of the Citie, there was no losse at all
but to himselfe: looke what ornaments were in any of his
owne Palaces and royall houses[4], the same he appointed to
the Citie buildings and the Temples: for which purpose
hee made divers of Knights degree Supravisors, to the end
that every thing might be dispatched with greater expedi-

TITUS FLAVIUS VESPASIANUS AUGUSTUS

---

[1] Who were opposite to the *Mirmillones*, that were armed after the French
fashion.   [2] Wherin there died ten thousand a day. Euseb.   [3] By the
burning of Vesevus which consumed many towns and much people.   [4] In
the Country, as Columnes, statues, painted tables, etc.

231

THE HISTORIE OF

tion. To cure the sicknesse and mitigate the furie of those contagious Diseases, hee used all helpe of God and man, having sought out what soever kindes of Sacrifices and remedies might bee found : among the adversities of those times, may bee reckoned these Promoters and Informers, with such as under hand set them a worke, occasioned all by old licentiousnesse and impunitie. And those he commaunded to be whipped and beaten with cudgels ordinarily in the open Market place : and last of all, when they had beene brought in a Shew through the Amphitheatre, partly to be solde in port-sale for slaves : and in part to be caried away into the roughest and bleakest Ilands that were. And because hee would for ever restraine such, as at any time should dare to doe the like : hee made an Acte among many others, prohibiting, one and the same matter to bee sued by vertue of many Statutes and Lawes enacted in that behalfe ; or to make inquisition as touching the estate of any man deceased, after the terme of certaine yeeres limited.

8

Having professed that he tooke upon him the High-Priesthood in this regard, because hee would keepe his hands pure and innocent, hee made good his word. For, after that time, never was hee the principall Author of any mans death, nor privie and accessarie thereto (albeit hee wanted not sometimes just cause of revenge), but sware devoutly, That hee would rather die himselfe, than doe others to death. Two noble men of the Patritian ranke, convicted for affecting and aspiring to the Empire, he proceeded against no farther than to admonish them to desist and give over, saying, That Soveraigne power was the gift of Destinie and Divine providence. If they were Petitioners for any thing else, he promised to give it unto them. And verily, out of hand, to the mother of the one, who was then farre of (wofull and pensive woman as shee was) he dispatched his owne coursitours and foote-men to carie word that her sonne was safe : as for themselves hee not onely invited them to a familiar and friendly supper that night : but also the next day following, at the fight of Sword-
232

TWELVE CÆSARS

fencers placing them of purpose neere about his owne person, the Ornaments[1] of the Champions that were to fight, presented unto him, hee reached unto them for to view and peruse[a]. It is said, moreover, that having knowledge of both their Horoscopes[2], he avouched that daunger was toward them both and would light upon their heads one day, but from some other ; as it fell out in deede. His owne brother[3] never ceasing to lay waite for his life, but professedly in manner soliciting the armies against him : plotting also and intending thereupon to flie and be gone, hee could never endure either to kill or to sequester and confine, no nor so much as to abridge of any honour : but, as hee had alwaies done from þe first day of his imperiall dignity, persevered to testifie and declare, that Partner he was with him in the Soveraigne government, and his heire apparent to succeede him : otherwhiles secretly with teares and praiers beseeching, That he would vouchsafe him yet at length, mutuall love and affection.

9

Amid this blessed course of life, cut short he was and prevented by death, to the greater losse of mankinde than of himselfe. After he had finished the solemne Shewes and Games exhibited to the people, in the end and upshot whereof, hee had shed teares abundantly : he went toward the Sabines territorie somwhat more sad than usually he had beene : by occasion, that as hee sacrificed, the beast brake loose and gat away : as also because in faire and cleare weather it had thundered[a]. Hereupon, having gotten an ague at his first lodging and baiting place, when he was removing from thence in his Licter, it is said that putting by the Curtaines of the windowe, hee looked up to heaven, and complained very piteously, that his life should be taken from him who had not deserved to die : for there was no fact of his extant, of which hee was to repent, save onely one. Now what that one should be, neither uttered he himselfe at that instant, neither is any man able readily to

[1] As their armour, weapons, etc.   [2] Ascendents of their Nativity.
[3] Domitian.

2 : GG   233

guesse thereat. Some thinke, he called to minde the over-familiar acquaintance that he had with his brothers wife[1]. But Domitia devoutly sware, That he never had such dealing with her: who no doubt would not have denied it, if there had beene any folly at all betweene them: nay, shee would rather have made her vaunt thereof: so ordinary a thing it was with her to glory in all naughtinesse and shamefull deedes.

10

He departed this world [a], in the very same Country-house wherein his father died before him: upon the Ides of September[2], two yeeres, two moneths and twenty dayes after that he succeeded his father, and in the two and fortieth yeere of his age. Which being once notified and knowen abroade, when all men throughout the Citie mourned no lesse than in some domesticall occasion of Sorow and Lamentation: the Senate before they were summoned and called together by any Edict, ranne to the *Curia*, finding as yet the dores fast locked: but when they were set open, they rendred unto him now dead so much thanks, and heaped upon him so great a measure of praises, as they never did before, at any time, whiles he was living and present among them.

[1] Domitia.   [2] 13th of September.

TWELVE CÆSARS

THE HISTORIE OF
FLAVIUS DOMITIANUS

1

OMITIAN was borne the ninth day before the Calends of November[1] what time his father was Consul Elect, and to enter upon that honorable place the moneth ensuing[2], within the sixt region of Rome Citty, at the Pomegranate[3]: and in that house which afterwards he converted into the temple of the Flavian familie. The floure of his tender yeeres and the verie prime of youth, he passed by report, in so great povertie and infamy[4] withall, that he had not one peece of plate or vessel of silver to be served with. And ful well it is knowen, that Clodius Pollio, a man of Pretours degree (against whome there is a Poem of Neroes extant, entituled *Luscio*[a]) kept by him a skro[5] of his owne hand writing, yea and other whiles brought the same foorth to bee seene, wherein he promised him the use[6] of his bodie one night. Neither wanted some who constantly avouched, that Domitian was in that sort abused, even by Nerva, who soone after succeeded him. In the Vitellian troubles[7] he fled into the Capitol with his Unkle Sabinus, and part of the forces which were then present. But when the adverse faction brake in, and while the Temple was on fire, hee lay close all night in the Sextaines lodging: and

---

[1] 24 Octobris. [2] Januarie. [3] A place so called like as before, *ad capita Bubula* and *ad Gallinas*. [4] For his impure life. [5] Or Bil. [6] Or abuse rather. [7] Betweene Vitellius and his father Vespasian: and their factions.

THE HISTORIE OF

early in the morning, disguised in the habit of a priest of
Isis[b], and among the sacrificers belonging to that vaine
superstition, after hee had passed over Tiberis, accompanied
with one onely person, to the mother of a schoole fellow of
his, hee lurked there so secretly, that albeit the serchers
traced him by his footing, yet could hee not be found. At
last after victory obtained hee went foorth and shewed himselfe; and being generally saluted by the name of Cæsar[1],
the honourable dignitie of the Citi Prætour in the consular
authoritie, hee tooke uppon him in name and title onely:
the jurisdiction whereof hee made over to his next Colleague.
But in all power of Lordly rule[2], he caried himself so
licentiously and without controlment that hee shewed even
then betimes, what a one hee would prove hereafter. And
not to handle every particular: having with uncleane hands
offred dishonour to many mens wives, hee fled away and
maried also Domitia Longina the wedded wife of Ælius Longinus: and in one day gave and dealt above twentie offices,
within the Citie and abroad in foraine provinces: in so
much as Vespasian commonly said, That hee marvailed why
he sent not one also to succeed in his place.

2

Hee enterprised moreover a voiage into Gaule and Germanie, notwithstanding the same was needlesse, and his
fathers freinds diswaded him from it; onely, because hee
would equallize his brother both in workes[3] and reputation.
For these prankes of his rebuked he was: and to the end he
might the rather be put in mind of his young yeeres and
private condition, hee dwelt together with his father: in a
licter hee attended the (Curule) chaire of father and brother,
whensoever they went foorth of doores: and being mounted
upon a white Courser accompanied them both in their
tryumph over Jurie. Of 6 Consulships hee bare but one
ordinary[4]; and the same by occasion that his brother Titus

[1] The Emperours sonne and heire apparant of the Empire.　[2] As being
a young Prince and a Cæsar.　[3] *Operibus, i.* deeds and exploits.　[4] Which
began the first of January, in his owne right, and not in the vacant roome of
others.

236

TWELVE CÆSARS

yeelded unto him his own place and furthered him in his
suite.   Himselfe likewise made wonderfull semblance of
modestie.   But above all, hee seemed outwardly to affect
Poetrie, (a studie which he was not so much unacquainted
with before time, but he despised and rejected it as much
afterwards) and recited his owne verses even in publike place.
Yet netherthelesse, when Vologesus King of the Parthians
required aide against the Alanes, and one of Vespasians
two sonnes to be the Generall of those forces, he laboured
with might and maine, that himselfe before all others should
be sent: and beecause the quarrel was dispatched alreadie
to his hand[1], hee assaied by gifts and large promises to
solicite other Kings of the East, to make the same request.
When his father was dead, standing in doubtfull tearmes
with himselfe a longe time, whether hee should offer unto the
souldiers a donative duple to that of his brother Titus, hee
never stucke to give out and make his boast, That left hee
was to bee partner with him in the Empire, but that his
fathers will was verie much abused.   Neither would hee give
over from that time forwarde both to lay wait secretly for
his brother, and also to practise openly against 'him, untill
such time as he gave commandement when hee was stricken
with greivous sickenesse, that he should be left for dead
before the breath was out of his bodie: and after he was
departed indeed, vouchsafing him no other honour but his
consecration[2], he carped also at him many a time as well in
glauncing figurative speeches as in open Edicts.

3

In the beginning of his Empire his manner was, to retire
himselfe daily into a secret place for one houre[3], and there
to do nothing else but to catch flies, and with the sharp
point of a bodkin or writing steele pricke them through :
in so much, as when one enquired, whether any bodie were
with Cæsar within, Vibius Crispus made answer not imper-
tinently, 'No, not so much as a flie.'   After this, Domitia
his owne wife, who in his second Consulship had borne him

[1] Peace concluded between the 2 nations.   [2] Canonization for a God.
[3] *Horarium* or for a certaine time of the day : some say three houres.

THE HISTORIE OF

a sonne, and whome two yeeres after he had saluted as
Empresse, by the name of Augusta, her I say, falling in
fansie with Paris the stage player and ready to die for his
love, hee put away: but within a smal while after (as impatient of this breach and divorse) tooke her home, and
maried her againe, as if the people had instantly called uppon
him so to do. In the administration of the Empire hee
behaved him selfe for a good while variablie, as one made of
an equall mixture and temper of vices and vertues, untill
at length hee turned his vertues also into vices: being, (so
far as we may conjecture) over and above his naturall inclination, for want covetous and greedie; for feare bloudy
and cruell.

4

Hee exhibited ordinarily magnificent and sumpteous
shewes not onely in the Amphitheatre, but in the Cirque
also. In which, beside the usuall running of Chariots,
drawen as well with two steedes as foure, hee represented
likewise two battailes of horsemen and foote men both: and
in the Amphitheatre a Navall fight. For, baitings of wild
beasts, and sword fencers, he shewed in the very night by
cresset and torch lights; and hee brought into the place not
men onely to fight, but women also to encounter wild beasts.
Furthermore, at the games of swordfight set out by the
Questours (which having in times past been discontinued and
forlet, hee brought into use againe) hee was alwaies present
in person, so as he gave the people leave to choose two
paire of swordfencers out of his owne schoole, and those
hee brought in, royally, and courtlike appointed in the last
place. And at all sights of sword players, there stood ever
at his feet a little dwarfe arraied in skarlet with a small
head that it was wonderfull: with whome hee used to talke
and conferre otherwhiles of serious matters. Certes, over
heard he was, when hee demanded him of what he knew,
and what he thoght, of the last dispose of the Provinces,
and namely of ordaining Metius Rufus Lieutenant generall
of Ægypt. Hee exhibited navall battailes performed in
manner, by full fleetes and compleat navies: having digged

238

TWELVE CÆSARS

out a great pit for a lake, and built a stone wall round about it [1], neere unto Tiberis: and those he would behold in the greatest stormes and showers that were. Hee set forth also the Secular plaies and games making his computation from the yeere, not wherein Claudius, but Augustus longe before had made them. During these, upon the daie of the Circentian solemnities, to the end there might be an hundred courses [2] the sooner runne, hee abridged the races of every one, to wit, from 7 to 4. He ordained moreover, in the honour of Jupiter Capitolinus, Quinquennall Games of three fold Maisteries, musicke, horse-riding, and Gymnicke exercises: and in the same, rewarding victours with Coronets, more by a good many then now they be. Herein the concurrents strove also for the prise in Prose, both Greeke and Latin: and besides single harpers, there were Setts of those also that played uppon the harpe, yea and consorts of such as sung therto, in a quire. In the running place, Virgins also ran for the best games. At all these masteries and solemnities, he sat as president in his Pantofles [3], clad in a robe of purple after the Greekish fashion [3], wearing on his head a golden Coronet, with the Image of Jupiter, Juno and Minerva: having the priest of Jupiter and the Colledge of the religious, called Flaviales, sitting by him in like habit; saving that in their Coronets there was his Image also. Semblably, hee celebrated everie yeere uppon the Albane mount, the Quinquatria of Minerva, in whose honor he had instituted a Societie, out of which there should be chosen by lot, Maisters and Wardens of that solemnitie who were to exhibite peculier and especiall Beastbaitings and stage playes, yea and contentions for the prise, of Oratours and Poets besides. He gave a largesse [4] to the people thrice: to wit, three hundred sesterces a peece: and at the shew of the swordfight a most plenteous dinner [5]. At the solemne Septimontiall [6] sacrifice, hee made a dole of Viands, allowing to the Senatours and gentlemen faire large paniars: to the commons, smal maunds [7] with Cates in them: and was the

---

[1] *Circumstructo.*   [2] *Missus,* every of which ordinarily consists of 7 races.
[3] Or slippers.   [4] *Congiarium.*   [5] Xiphilin.   [6] So called of the seaven hils, whereupon the Citie stood.   [7] Or Baskets.

239

THE HISTORIE OF

first himselfe that fell to his meat. The next day after he skattered[1] among them, Missils[2] of al sorts : and because the greater part thereof, fell to the rankes of the common people, he pronounced by word of mouth for every skaffold of Senatours and gentlemen, 50 tickets or talies.

5

Manie buildings, and those most stately, which had beene consumed with fire, hee reedified: and among them the Capitoll which had been fired again[3]: but all under the title of his owne name, without any memoriall of the former founders. Mary, he founded a new Temple in the Capitoll to the honour of Jupiter Custos: also the Forum, which is now called Nervæ Forum: likewise the Temple of the Flavian familie: a shew place for running and wrestling: another for Poets and Musicians to contend in, and a Naumachie for ships to encounter. Of the stone that was about which, the greatest Cirque of al was afterwards built, by occasion that both sides thereof had been burnt downe.

6

Expeditions hee made, some voluntarie, some uppon necessitie: of his owne accord that against the Catti: uppon constreint one, against the Sarmatians; by occasion that one whole Legion together with their Lieutenant fell upon the sword: two against the Daci, the former, because Oppius Sabinus a man of Consuls degree was defaited and slaine; and the second, for that Cornelius Fuscus, Capitaine of the Prætorian bands (unto whom he had committed the whole conduct of that war) lost his life. Over the Catti and Daci (after sundry feilds fought with varietie of fortune) he triumphed twice. For his victory of the Sarmatians, hee presented only Jupiter Capitolinus with his Lawrel guirland. The civill warre stirred up by Lucius Antonius gòverner of the higher Germanie, hee dispatched and ended in his absence[4]: and that by a wonderfull good hap: when, as at the very houre of conflict, the Rhene swelling and overflowing

[1] Or sent. [2] Gifts or favours. [3] In Vespasians dayes. [4] By Norbanus Appius who slew the said Antonius.

TWELVE CÆSARS

sodainly staied the Barbarians forces as they wold have passed over to Antonius. Of which victorie hee had intelligence by presages, before the newes by messengers came. For uppon that very day when the battaile was fought, an Eagle after a straung manner having overspred his statue at Rome and clasped it about with her wings, made a great flapping noise in token of much joy ; and within a little after, the bruit was blowen abroade so rife and common, of Antonies death, that many avouched confidently, they had seene his head also brought home (to Rome).

7

Many new orders besides in matters of common use, hee brought uppe. The dole of Viands given and distributed in little baskets in lieu of a publike supper, he abolished : and reduced the auncient custome of compleat and formall suppers[1]. Unto the 4 factions[2] in former time, of severall crewes running with Chariots at Circean games, hee added twaine ; to wit the golden and purple livery. Players and Actours of enterludes hee forbad the open stage : but within house verily, he granted free and lawfull exercise of their Art. Hee gave commandement that no males should be guelded : and of such Eunuchs as remained in the hands of Hucksters[3], hee abated the price and brought it downe to a meaner. By reason one time of an exceeding plentiful vintage, and as much scarcity of Corne, supposing that by the immoderate care imployed upon Vineyards tillage was neglected, hee made an Edict, That no man in all Italie should plant any newe young Vineyardes : and that in foraine Provinces they should cut them all downe, reserving at the most but the one halfe[a]. Howbeit, hee continued not in the full execution of this Act: some of the greatest offices he communicated indifferently between Libertines and souldiers. He prohibited, that there should be two Camps of the legions[4][b]. Item that any man should lay up more than a thousand Sesterces about the Camp-ensignes[c]. For that L. Antonius

---

[1] Whereas contrariwise under Nero, *publicæ cænæ ad sportulas reductæ.*
[2] White, Blew, Red, Greene. [3] Who guelded, pampered and set them out to sale. [4] *Geminari castra,* the greater and the lesse as we read in Livie, etc.

THE HISTORIE OF

intending rebellion in the wintering harbour of two Legions, was thought to have taken heart and presumed more confidently, upon the great summes of monie there bestowed in stocke. Hee added a fourth stipend also for souldiers, to wit, 3 peeces of gold by the poll[1].

8

In ministring justice precise he was and industrious. Many a time, even in the common place, sitting extraordinarily upon the Tribunal he reversed the definitive sentences of the Centumvirs, given for favour and obtained by flattery. He warned eftsoones the commissioners and Judges delegate, not to accommodate themselves and give eare unto perswasive and Rhetoricall Assertions[2]. The judges that were bribed and corrupted with monie hee noted and disgraced every one, together with their Assessours upon the bench. Hee mooved also and perswaded the Tribunes of the Commons to accuse Judicially for extortion, and to force unto restitution, a base and corrupt Ædile[3]: yea and to call unto the Senate, for to have a Jurie empannelled upon him. Moreover, so carefull was hee to chastise as well the magistrates within Rome, as the Rulers of Provinces abroad of their misdemeanours, that never at any time, they were either more temperate or just in their places. The most part of whome after his dayes, we our selves have seene culpable, yea and brought into question for all manner of crimes. Having taken uppon him the censuring and reformation of manners, he inhibited that licentious libertie taken up in Theatres, of beholding the playes and games pell-mell one with another in the quarter and rankes appointed for gentlemen. Diffamatorie libels written and divulged, wherin men and women of good marke were touched and taxed, hee abolished not without shame and ignominie of the Authors. A man of Questours degree, because he took pleasure in Puppet-like gesturing and dauncing, hee remooved out of the Senate. From women of dishonest cariage, he tooke away the priviledge and use

[1] Every one about 15s. 7d. *ob.* sterling. [2] Of such bond men, as against their Lordes and Masters right claimed freedome, and used therein the plea of Oratours. [3] Who by taking money exercised his office otherwise then he ought.

242

of their Licters: hee made them uncapable also of Legacies and inheritances. A gentleman of Rome hee rased out of the Roll and Tables of Judges, for receiving his wife againe into Wedlocke, whome hee had before put away and sued in an action of adulterie. Some of both degrees, as well Senatours as Gentlemen, hee condemned, by vertue of the law Scantinia[1]. The Incestuous whoredomes committed by vestall votaries, negligently passed over, by his father and brother both, hee punished after sundrie sorts: the former delinquents in that kinde, with simple death[2]: the later sort according to the auncient manner[a]: for, having given libertie unto the sisters Ocellatæ[3] as also to Varomilla, for to chuse their owne deaths, and banished•those who had defloured them, hee afterwardes commanded, that Cornelia Maximilla[4], who in times past had beene acquit, and a long time after was called into question againe and convicted, shold be buried quicke: and the parties who had committed incest with her, beaten with rods to death in the *Comitium*: except on alone a man of Prætours degree; unto whome whiles the matter remained yet doubtful, and because he had confessed and bewraied himselfe (upon his examination by torture which was uncertaine) he granted the favour of Exile. And that no religious service of the Gods should bee contaminated and polluted without condigne punishment, the monument or Tombe, which his freedman had built for a sonne of his with the stones appointed for the Temple of Jupiter Capitolinus, hee caused his souldiers to demolish: and the bones and reliques therein hee drowned in the Sea.

9

At the first hee abhorred all bloudshed and slaughter, so farre foorth, as that (while his father was yet absent) callinge to remembraunce this Verse of Virgil,

> *Impia quam[5] cæsis gens est epulata iuvencis,*
> Ere godlesse people made their feasts,
> With Oxen slaine (poore harmlesse beasts),

---

[1] Against the filthy sin of Pæderastie or Sodomie. [2] As to loose their heads. [3] Surnamed so of a familie in Rome. [4] Or Maxima, sc. *Vestalis, i.* the chiefe of those Nunns, as Lady Prioresse or Abbatesse. [5] 2 *Georgicorum.* This hath relation to the last word (*Ante*) in the verse præcedent.

THE HISTORIE OF

FLAVIUS DOMI-TIANUS hee purposed fully to publish an Edict, forbiddinge to kill and sacrifice any Oxe. Of Covetousnesse also and avarice [1], hee gave scarcely the least suspition, either at any time when hee led a private life, or a good while after hee was Emperour: but contrariwise rather, he shewed great proufes oftentimes, not of abstinence onely but also of liberalitie. And whensoever he had bestowed gifts most bountifully upon those that were about him, hee laied uppon them no charge before this nor with more earnestnesse, than to do nothing basely and beggerly. Moreover, one Legacie put downe in the last Will of Ruscius Cæpio who had provided therin, That his heire should give yeerely unto every one of the Senatours, as they went into the *Curia*, a certaine summe of monie, he made voide. Al those likewise, whose suits had hung and depended in the Chamber of the Citie, from before five yeeres last past, hee discharged and delivered from trouble. Neither suffered hee them to be sued and molested againe, but within the compasse of one yeare and with this condition, that the accuser [2] (unlesse hee overthrew his adversarie [3] by that time) should be banished for his labour. The Scribes and Notaries beelonging to the Questours, who by an olde custome, (but yet against the Law Clodia) used to negotiate and trade, he pardoned onely for the time past. The od ends and cantels of grounds, which after the division of lands by the Veteran Souldiours [4], remained heere and there cut out, as it were, from the rest, hee graunted unto the olde owners and Landlords as in the right of Prescription. The false information of matters, whereof the penaltie came to the Exchequer, he repressed: and sharplie punished such Informers. And this (by mens saying) was a speech of his, 'The Prince that chastneth not Promoters, setteth them on to promote.'

10

But long continued he not in this traine, either of

---

[1] *Cupiditatis quoque atque avaritiæ.* By covetousnesse hee meaneth the greedy desire of other mens goods: by avarice, in this place the pinching expense of his owne.   [2] Plaintife.   [3] Defendant.   [4] Old souldiers who had served out their full time.

TWELVE CÆSARS

clemencie or of abstinence. And yet fell hee somewhat sooner to crueltie than to covetousnesse. A Schollar of the cunning player and counterfeit Paris, being as yet of tender yeeres, and at that time very sicke, hee murdered: for that, both in skill and also in countenance and feature of body he seemed to resemble his Maister. Semblably dealt he with Hermogenes of Tarsus, for certaine figures of Rhetorick[1] interlaced in his Historie: and withall, crucified the Scrivenars and Writers that had copied it out. An Housholder[a], for saying these words, That the Thracian Fencer[2] was equall to the Mirmillon[b], but inferiour to the setter forth of the Game[3], he caused to bee plucked downe from the scaffold in the Theater, into the plaine beneath, and there to be cast before the greedy Mastives, with this title, *Impie locutus Parmularius, i.* The Parmularius[4c] hath blasphemed. Many Senatours, and some of them which had beene Consuls, hee killed. Among whom Civicus Cerealis, in the very time when he was Proconsull in Asia, Salvidienus Orfitus and Acilius Glabrio during their exile, he put to death, pretending that they practised Innovation in the State: all the rest every one for most slight causes. As for example, Ælius Lamia, for certaine suspitious jests (I must needs say) but such as were stale and harmlesse: namely, because unto Domitian when (after he had taken from him his wife[5]) he fell a praising of her voice[6], he said, ' I hold my peace[7], Helas[d].' As also, for that unto Titus, moving him to a second mariage,·he made answer, *Me kai su Gamesai Theleis?* ' What! (and if I should wed another) would not you also marie her?' Salvius Coccejanus[8], because he had celebrated the Birth-dayes-minde, of Otho the Emperour, his Unkle[9]. Metius Pomposianus[10], for that it was commonly said, He had the Horoscope in his Nativity of an Emperour; and caried about him the Map or Geo-

[1] As *Ironia* and *Antiphrasis*, etc., whereby he seemed to glaunce at him. [2] Who was armed with a buckeler. [3] Of swordfight. [4] The favourer of the armed fenser Thrax, above saide. [5] Domitia Longina. [6] *Vocem suam*, or Lamia his voice, as some expound it. [7] As if he had uttered these words: This is meere injury but I must say nothing. [8] Understand here, and in the other following (he slew or put to death). [9] For his father L. Salvius Titianus was Othoes brother. [10] See Vespasian, cap. 14.

THE HISTORIE OF

graphical description of the world[1] in certaine parchments,
and withall, the Orations of Kings and brave Capitaines
written out of Titus Livius, for imposing likewise the
names of Mago and Annibal[2] upon some of his slaves.
Sallustius Lucullus Lieutenant generall of Britaine, for
suffring certaine speares of a new fashion to be called
Lucullecæ[3]. Junius Rusticus, for publishing the praises of
Pætus Thrasea[4] and Helvidius Priscus[5]; and calling them
most holy and upright persons. By occasion of which
criminous imputation (charged upon Rusticus) hee packed
away all Philosophers out of the Citie of Rome and Italie.
Hee slewe also Helvidius the sonne[6], for that in an Enterlude (as it were), and by way of an *Exodium* upon the
Stage, hee had under the persons of Paris and Œnone
acted[7] the Divorse betweene him[8] and his wife. Flavius
Sabinus, one of his cousin germaines, because upon the
Election day of the Consuls, the Crier chaunced to mistake
a little, and before the people to pronounce him (being
Consul Elect) not Consull, but Emperour. And yet, after
his victorie in the Civill warre[9], hee became much more
cruell: for many of the adverse part, even such as lying
hid a good while were found out by those that were privie
unto them[10], hee by devising a new kinde of torture made
to confesse: namely by thrusting fire into the passage of
their secret parts: some also hee dismembred by cutting
off their hands. And this is for certaine knowne: that two
onely and no more, of the most notorious among them, to
wit, a Tribune of Senatours degree, and a Centurion, were
pardoned: who the sooner to shew that they were unguiltie,
had proved themselves to have beene effeminate Catamites,
and therfore could not possibly be of any reckoning, either
with Capitaine or Souldiours.

[1] Or earth. [2] Two most renowmed warriors of the Carthaginians, and
mortall enimies of the Romaines. [3] Of his owne name. [4] Who beeing
persecuted by Nero cut his owne maister veines. [5] The sonne in lawe of
Thrasea, even another Cato or Brutus and a man of most free speech in the
behalfe of the Common wealth. [6] For the father, Vespasian had slaine before.
[7] *Tractasset, i.* handled, al. *taxasset, i.* taxed or reproved. [8] Domitian.
[9] Of the Flavians and Vitellians. [10] *Dudum latentes, per conscios in-
vestigatos.*

TWELVE CÆSARS

11

Now, in this Crueltie of his hee was not onely excessive,
but also subtill and craftie; comming upon men when they
looked least for it. A Controller[1] of his owne, the very day
before he crucified him, hee called into his bed-chamber,
and made him to sit downe by him upon a pallet or beds
side: he dismissed him light-harted and merie: he deigned
him also a favour and remembrance from his own supper[2].
Unto Aretinus Clemens, a man of Consuls degree, one of
his familiar minions and bloodhounds to fetch in Booties,
when he purposed to condemne to death, he shewed the
same countenance, as before time, yea and more grace than
ordinary: untill at last, as hee went with him in the same
Licter[3], by occasion that hee espied the Informer against
him, 'How sayest thou,' quoth hee, 'Clemens, shall wee to
morrow heare this most errant knave and varlet, what hee
can say?' And because hee would with greater contempt
and disdaine abuse mens patience, hee never pronounced
any heavie and bloudie sentence, without some preamble
and preface of Clemencie: so that, there was not now, a
surer signe of some horrible end and Conclusion, than a
milde beginning and gentle exordium. Some that stoode
accused of Treason he inducted into the *Curia*[4]; and when
he had premised a Speech, That hee would make triall that
day, how deere hee was unto the Senate, hee soone effected
thus much thereby, that the parties should have their judgement, to suffer *More maiorum*[5]: and then, himselfe, affrighted
as it were with the rigorous cruelty of that punishment,
would intercede, in these words (for it shall not bee im-
pertinent to knowe the very same as hee delivered them)
'Permit my good LL. this to be obtained of your gracious
Piety (which I know I shall hardly obtaine) that yee would
doe so much favour unto these persons condemned, as that
they may choose what death they will die: for, by this yee

---

[1] *Actorem summarum.*   [2] A dish of meate, etc.   [3] *Simul gestanti.*
[4] Senate house.   [5] To have their necks fast locked in pillory, and so to
be beaten with rods to death.

shall spare your owne eyes, and all the world shall know, that I was present in the Senate.'

12

Having emptied his coffers with expences of buildings and Games exhibited to the people, as also with that Stipend[1] paied unto the Souldiours: over and above the former, hee assaied verily for easement of the charges belonging to the Camp, for to diminish the numbers and companies of Souldiours. But perceiving that heereby he was both in daunger of the Barbarians, and also never the lesse to seeke which way to be relieved from burdens: hee made no reckoning at all, but to raise booties, to rob and spoile he cared not how. The goods of quick and dead both, were every where seized upon: who the Accusers were, or what the matter was, it skilled not. Sufficient it was, if any deede or word whatsoever, were objected against one, to make it high treason against the Prince. Inheritances, were they never so farre off and belonging to the greatest straungers, were held confiscate and adjudged to the Emperours Coffers, in case but one would come forth and depose, that hee heard the party deceased say whiles hee lived, That Cæsar[a] was his heire. But, above all others the Jewes were most grievously plagued in the Exchequer[b]. Unto which were presented as many of them as either professed in Rome to live as Jewes, or else dissimuling their Nation, had not payed the Tributes imposed upon them. I remember, that my selfe being a very youth was in place when an aged Jew, fourescore and tenne yeeres olde, was by the Procuratour[2] in a most frequent Assembly searched, whether he were circumcised or no. From his very youth nothing civill and sociable hee was[3]: bolde of hart, audacious withall, and as well in words as deede beyond all measure excessive. Unto Cænis his fathers Concubine newly returned out of Istria, and offring to kisse his lips (as her manner was) hee put forth his hand. Taking it hainously that his

---

[1] *i.* of 3 *aurei.*   [2] Or Master of the Exchequer.   [3] But proud and scornfull.

TWELVE CÆSARS

brothers sonne in Law[1] had attending about him his Servitours also, clad in faire white, he cried out,

οὐκ ἀγαθὸν πολυκοιρανίη [2].

There is no good Plurality
In Lordship and in Sov'raigntie.

13

But when hee was mounted once to the Imperiall Seate, hee stucke not in the very Senate to make his boast, That he it was who had given unto his father and brother both, the Empire, and they had but delivered it up to him againe. Also when after Divorsement he brought home and remarried his wife, hee bashed not to give it out, that she was called to his sacred bed[3]. Moreover, upon the day when hee made a great Dinner unto the people[4], hee was well content and pleased to heare their acclamation throughout the Theater in these words,

Domino et Dominæ, fœliciter.
All happines to our Lord and Lady.

Likewise at the Solemnity of trying Maisteries in the Palatium, when all the people besought him with great consent and one accord, to restore Palfurius Sura[5] (one in times past degraded and thrust out of the Senate, but at that time crowned among the Oratours for his Eloquence) hee vouchsafed them no answere, but onely by voice of the publike crier commaunded them Silence. With semblable arrogancie, when as in the name[6] of his Procuratours he endited any formall Letters, thus hee began, Our Lord and God thus commaundeth. Whereupon afterwards this order was taken up, that neither in the writing or speech of any man[7] he should be otherwise called. No Statues suffred he to be erected for him in the Capitoll, but of gold and silver;

---

[1] Who married Titus his daughter Julia. [2] An Hemistichium out of Homer, *Iliad* 2, Ulisses words: as if he should say, I like not so many Cæsars. [3] *Pulvinar suum*, as if he had beene a God: for, their Gods and Goddesses they bestowed in certaine bed lofts called *Pulvinaria*. [4] During the solemne Games exhibited unto them. [5] To his Senatours place. [6] Or behalfe. [7] Common talke.

THE HISTORIE OF

and the same of a certaine weight, just [1]. As for two-fronted Jani and Arches with their foure Steedes, together with the Ensignes and Badges of Triumph, hee built them stately and so many in every quarter and Region of the Cittie, as that in one of the saide Arches there was this Mot in Greeke written, ἄρκει[a] *i*. It is enough. Hee tooke upon him seventeene Consulships, more than ever any man before him. Of which, those seven in the middle, hee bare continually one after another; and in manner all, in name and title onely: but none of them beyond the Kalends of May[2]; and most, to the Ides onely of Januarie[3]. Now, after his two triumphs[4], having assumed into his stile the addition of Germanicus, hee chaunged the denomination of the moneths September and October, calling them after his owne names Germanicus and Domitianus: for that in the one[5] hee entred upon his Empire, and was borne in the other[6].

14

In these courses that hee tooke, beeing both terrible and odious also unto all men, surprised he was in the end, and murdred by his friends[7] and freed men that were most inward with him; who together with his wife conspired his death. The last yeere and day of his life, the very houre also and what kinde of death he should die, he had long time before suspected. For when he was but a youth, the Chaldæan Astrologers had fore-tolde him all. His Father also one time at supper, when hee saw him forbeare to eate Mushromes, laughed him to scorne as ignorant of his owne destinie, for that hee did not feare the sword rather. And therefore beeing alwaies timorous and strucken into his pensive dumps upon the least suspitions presented, hee was beyond all measure troubled and disquieted: in so much as it is credibly reported, that no other cause moved him more, to dispense with that Edict which hee had proclaimed for the cutting downe and destroying of Vineyards, than cer-

---

[1] *Ponderis certi.* Sabellicus readeth *centeni, i.* of an hundred pounds, according to Statius Papinius of Domitians statue, *Sylv.* 5, *Da Capitolinis æternum sedibus aurum. Quo niteant sacri centeno pondere vultus Cæsaris.*
[2] Not above 4 moneths. [3] Not a fortnight full. [4] Over the Catti and Daci.
[5] September. [6] October. [7] Minions.

TWELVE CÆSARS

taine Pamphlets and Libels scattered abroad with these verses.

Κἄν με φάγῃς ἐπὶ ῥίζαν, ὅμως ἔτι καρποφορήσω,
ὅσσον ἐπισπεῖσαι καίσαρι θυομένῳ [1].

Eate me to roote ; yet fruit will I beare still and never misse,
Enough to poure on Cæsars head whiles sacrific'd he is.

In the same fearefulnesse hee refused a new honour and that which never was devised before, offred by the Senate unto him, (though otherwise most eager and greedie of all such things) whereby they decreed, That so often as hee was Consull, the Gentlemen of Rome, as it fell by lot to their turnes, should in their rich and gay coates and with militare Launces march before him among the Lictours and other Sergeants and Apparitours. When the time also of that daunger drew neere which he suspected, he became perplexed every day more than other: and therefore he garnished the walls of those galleries wherein hee was wont to rome himselfe and walke, with the stone Phengites ; by the images rebounding from the brightnesse whereof he might see before his face whatsoever was done behind his back. The most part of prisoners and persons in duresse, hee would not heare but being alone and in a secret place, taking holde first of their chaines in his owne hand. And because he would perswade his houshold servitours, that no man should be so hardy as to lay violent hand upon his owne Patrone to kill him, no though much good might ensue thereof, hee condemned Epaphroditus the Secretarie of Nero, for that it was thought, his Lord and Maister (after he was forlorne and forsaken of all) had his helping hand to dispatch him out of the world.

15

To conclude, his Unkles sonne Flavius Clemens [a] (a man for his lithernesse and negligence most contemptible) whose sonnes being yet very little ones, hee had openly ordained

[1] Alluding to the like verses of the Poet Evenus : which Ovide seemeth to expresse I *Fastorum* in Latine thus, *Rode caper vitem, tamen hic cum stabis ad aras, In tua quod spargi cornua possit, erit.*

FLAVIUS
DOMI-
TIANUS

THE HISTORIE OF

to bee his Successours: and abolishing their former names, commanded the one to be called Vespatian and the other Domitian, he killed sodainely, upon a slender and small suspition, even when he was scarce out of his Consulship. By which deede of his most of all, he hastened his own end and destruction. For 8 moneths space together, so many lightnings were seene and reported unto him, that he cryed out, 'Now let him[1] strike whom he will.' The Capitol was smitten and blasted therewith: the Temple also of the Flavian Linage: likewise his owne house in the Palatium, and verie bedchamber. Moreover, out of the base[2] of his triumphall Statue, the Title[3] being driven by force of a storme, fel down into the Sepulcher next adjoyning. That tree which being laid along, had risen up againe when Vespasian was yet a private person, fell sodainely then a seconde time. The Image of fortune at Preneste[4], which all the time of his Empire, when he recommended unto her the new yeere, was wont to give him an happy answere and alwaies the same, now in this last yeere, delivered one most wofull, and not without mention of blond. He dreamed, that Minerva[b], whom he worshipped superstitiously, departed out of her Chappell, and said, She could not protect him any longer, for that shee was by Jupiter disarmed. But with no one thing was hee so much disquieted, as with the answere of Ascletario the Astrologer, and the accident that chanced unto him thereupon. This Ascletario beeing enformed against, and not denying that he had delivered what by his art and learning he foresaw, he questioned with and asked, what his owne end should be; and when he made answer and affirmed, That his destinie was to be torne in peeces with dogs, and that shortly after, he caused him presently to be killed: but to reprove the rashnes and uncertaintie of his skill and profession, he commanded with all, that he should be buried with as great care as possibly might be. In the doing whereof accordingly, it fortuned that by a sodaine tempest, the corps being cast downe out of the funerall fire, the dogs tare and rent peecemeale, when it

---

[1] Jupiter or God.   [2] Or Pied stoole.   [3] Or Inscription.   [4] Where was an Oracle.

was but halfe burnt: and the same hapned to be reported unto him among other tales[1] and newes, of that day, as hee sat at supper, by Latinus the player and counterfeite jester, who as hee passed by, chaunced to see and marke so much.

16

The day before his death, when he had given commandement that certaine Mushromes set before him shold be kept against the morrow, he added moreover, 'If I may have use of them': and turning to those that were next him he said, The day following it would come to passe, that the Moone should embrue her selfe with bloud in the signe Aquarius, and some act be seene, whereof men should speake all the world over. But about midnight, so skared he was[2], that he started out of his bed. Hereuppon in the morning betimes he gave hearing unto the Soothsayer sent out of Germanie, who being asked his opinion about the lightning, had foretold a chang in the state: and him he condemned. And whiles he scratched verie harde at a wert in his forehead which was festered and growne to be sore, seeing bloud run out of it, 'Would God,' quoth he, 'this were all.' Then asked he what was a clocke, and insteede of the 5th houre[3] which he feared, word was brought for the nonce that it was the 6th. Being joious hereupon that the danger was nowe past, and hastening to cherish his body and make much of himselfe, Parthenius his principall Chamberlaine turned him an other way, sayinge there was one come who brought tidinges (I wot not what) of great consequence, and of a matter in no wise to be deferred. Voiding therfore all persons from him, he retired to his bedchamber, and there was he murdered.

17

As touching the manner how he was forlaide and of his death, thus much (in manner) hath beene divulged. Whiles

[1] Fabulus narrations to make Princes merry.   [2] He dreamt haply that Junius Rusticus whom hee had killed came upon him with a naked sword. Xiphilin.   [3] Of the clock.

THE HISTORIE OF

the conspiratours were in question with themselves and
doubtfull, when, and how, they should set upon him, that
is to say, whether he bathed or sat at supper, Stephen the
procuratour of Domitilla [1], and at the same time in trouble
for intercepting certaine monies, offered his advise and helping hand, who having for certaine dayes before bound up
and enwrapped his left arme (as if it had beene amisse)
with wool and swadling bandes, thereby to avert from himselfe all suspition, at the very houre interposed fraud and
made a lie. For, professing that hee would discover the
conspiracy, and in that regarde being admitted into the
chamber, as Domitian was reading of a bill which hee preferred unto him, and therewith stood amazed, hee stabbed
him beneth in the very share neere unto his privie parts.
When hee was thus wounded and beganne to struggle
and resist, Clodianus a Cornicularius [2] and Maximus a freed
man of Parthenius, and Saturius the Deane or Decurion
of the Chamberlaines with one out of his owne swordfencers
schoole, came in uppon him, gave him seven wounds, and
killed him outright. A youth and page of his, who stood
by (as his wonted manner was) because he had the charge
of his bedchamber Lares [a], and was present at this murder
committed, made this report moreover, that Domitian,
at the very first wound given, immediatly bad him reach
the dagger [3] that lay under his pillow, and to call in his
ministers and servitours: but at the beds head he found
nothing at al thereof save the haft onely: and as for the
doores besides, they were all fast shut: also, that Domitian
in this meane space, tooke hold of Stephen, bare him to the
ground and wrestled with him a longe time: that he one
while assaied to wrest his sword out of his hands, another
while (albeit his fingers were hurt and mangled) to plucke
out his eyes. Well, killed he was, the 14th day before
the Kalends of October [4], in the 45th yeere of his age,
and the 15th of his Empire. His dead bodie was caried
foorth upon the common bierre by the ordinary bearers:

[1] Whom Eusebius reporteth to have beene neipce by the sister of Flavius
Clemens and a Christian, therefore confined to the Iland Pontia.   [2] Certaine
souldiers were so tearmed.   [3] Or rapier.   [4] 17th of September.

254

TWELVE CÆSARS

and Phyllis his nource burned it in a funerall fire, within a country manour of his owne neere unto the Citie, situate upon the high way Latina. But the reliques thereof shee bestowed in the Temple of the Flavian family, and blended the same with the ashes of Julia the daughter of Titus, whom she had reared and brought up.

18

Of Stature he was tall, his countenance modest, and given much to rednes[a]: his eyes full and great, but his sight very dimme. Besides, faire he was and of comely presence especially in his youth: well shaped all his body throughout, excepting his feet: the toes wherof were of the shortest [1]. In processe of time, he became disfigured and blemished with baldnesse, with a fat grand-panch and sclender shanks: and yet they grew to be so leane upon occasion of a long sickenes. For his modesty and shame facednesse he so well perceived himselfe to be commended, that one time before the Senate he gave out these words, ' Hitherto certainly ye have liked wel of my minde and of my countenance.' With his bald head he was so much yrked, that hee tooke it as a reproach unto himself, if any man els were either in bord or good earnest twitted therewith: albeit in a certaine little booke, which he wrot unto a freind of his, concerning the nourishment and preservation of the haire of the head, he by way of consolation both to that friend and also to himselfe, inserted thus much.

> οὐχ ὁράᾳς οἷος κᾀγὼ καλός τε μέγαστε [2].
>
> See'st thou not yet how big and tall,
> How faire I am and comely with all?

' And yet,' quoth he, ' my destinie [3] and fortune wil be to have the same defect of haire: and with a stoute heart I endure, that the bush of my head waxeth olde in my fresh youth. And this would I have you to know, that nothing is more lovely, nothing more fraile and transitorie than beautie and favour.'

---

[1] *Restrictiores*, drawn inward.   [2] Homer *Iliad* 21. Lycaon the Sonne of Priamus unto Achilles.   [3] *Eadem me manent*, some read (*te*).

THE HISTORIE OF

19

Being impatient of all labour and paines taking, he was not lightly seene to walke in the Citie. In any expedition and march of the army seldome rod he on horsebacke, but was caried in a lictour[1]. No affection had hee to beare armes or weld weapons: but delighted he was especially to shoot arrows. Many men have seene him oftentimes, during his retiring abode at Alba, to kill with shot an hundred wild beasts of sundrie sorts at a time: and of very purpose to sticke some of them in the head; so, as that with two shoots hee would set his shafts in their fronts like a paire of hornes. Sometimes he would drive his arrows point blanke so just against the palme of a childes right hand, standing farre of and holding it foorth stretched open for a marke, as they should all directly passe through the voide spaces beetweene the fingers, and do him no harme at all.

20

All liberall studies in the beginning of his Empire he neglected: albeit hee tooke order to repaire the Libraries consumed with fire, to his exceeding great charges: making search from all parts for the copies of bookes lost, and sendinge as farre as to Alexandria[2ª], to write them out and correct them. But never gave he his minde to know histories; or to have any skill in verse, or to write ought, though necessitie so required. Except it were the commentaries and acts of Tiberius Cæsar hee never used to read any thing. For his Epistles, Orations and Edicts, hee employed the wits of other men to drawe and frame them. Howbeit, his ordinary speech was not unelegant: and otherwhiles you should have him come foorth even with notable sentences and Apophthegmes. As for example: 'Would God,' quoth he, 'I were as faire and well favoured, as Metius thinkes himselfe to be': and seeing ones head party coloured[3], with yellowish and white silver haires intermingled: hee said it was snow and mede mixed together[4].

[1] Upon mens shoulders.   [2] In Ægypt.   [3] Of two colours.   [4] A kind of delicate drinke among the Romains.

TWELVE CÆSARS

His saying it was, That the condition of Princes was most miserable, who could not bee credited as touching a conspiracie plainely detected unlesse they were slaine first.

21

Whensoever his leasure served, he solaced himselfe with dice play, even uppon the very worke daye, and in morning houres. Hee bathed by day time [1], and made his dinner so liberall to the full, that seldome for his supper he tooke any thing, unles it were a Matian Apple [2], and a smal supping or portion out of a narrow mouthed and great bellied glasse. He feasted often and that very plentifully, but his feasts were short and after a snatching manner: certes, hee never sat past sunne setting, nor admitted any reare bankets after supper. For, towards bedtime, hee did nothing, but in a secret chamber walke by himselfe alone.

22

To fleshly lust he was over much given. The ordinary use of Venus, as it were a kind of exercise, hee named Clinopale, as one would say, bed-wrestling. The report went, that himselfe used, with pinsers to depilate his concubines, and to swim among the commonest naughtie packes that were. His brothers daughter [3] offred first unto him in marriage whiles she was yet a maiden, when he had most resolutely refused, by reason he was entangled and overcome with the mariage of Domitia; not long after when she was bestowed upon another, of his owne accord he sollicited, and was naught with her, even verily whiles his brother Titus yet lived. Afterwards when she was bereft of father and husband both, hee loved her with most ardent affection, and that openly [4]: in so much, as that hee was the cause of her death, by forcing her to miscarie and cast away the untimely fruicte [5] wherewith she went.

---

[1] *De die.* [2] It tooke the name of one Matius who loved an hortyard well: like as *Appiana* and *Scaptiana mala* of Appius and Scaptius. [3] Julia. [4] As his wedded wife. [5] Conceived, as some say, by her former husband: others, by Domitian in her widowhead: and hereto accordeth Juvenal: *Quum tot abortivis, etc. Iulia vulvam solueret, et patruo similes effunderet offas.*

TWELVE CÆSARS

That he was killed the people tooke it indifferently : but
the souldiers, to the very heart : and forthwith went about
to canonize him a God, and to call him Divus[1]: ready
enough also to revenge his death; but they wanted heads
to lead them.   And yet within a whiles after they did it,
and calling most instantly and never giving over for the
authors of this murder[2] to be executed.   Contrariwise, the
Senate so much rejoiced, that beeing assembled in great
frequencie within the *Curia,* they could not rule themselves,
but strived a vie to rent and teare him now dead with the
most contumelious and bitterest kinds of acclamations[a] that
they could devise : commanding ladders to be brought in, his
skutcheons[3] and Images to be taken downe in their sight, and
even there in place to be throwen and dashed against the
hard floore : in the end that all titles wheresoever bearing
his name should be rased and scraped out, and his memoriall
abolished quite for ever.   Some few moneths before he was
murdered, there was a Crowe in the Capitoll spake these
wordes plainely, ἔσται πάντα καλῶς, *i.* All shall be well :
and there wanted not one, who interpreted this strang
Prodigie thus :

Nuper Tarpeio quæ sedit culmine cornix,
Est bene non potuit dicere, dixit Erit.
The Crow which lately sat on top of Tarpeie newes to tell,
Tis well when as she could not say, said yet, it will be well.

And reported it is that Domitian himselfe dreamed, howe
hee had a golden excrescence rising and bunching behind
his necke : and knew for certaine, that therby was portended
and foresignified unto the common wealth, an happier state
after him.   And so it fell out, I assure you shortly after :
such was the abstinent and moderate cariage of the Emperours next ensuing[b].

[1] A Saint or of sacred memorie.   [2] Petronius and Parthenius. Sext. Aurel.
[3] Coates of armes.

ANNOTATIONS

ANNOTATIONS UPON
CAIUS CÆSAR CALIGULA

1

^a CALLED by some, *Annales* or *Annariæ* : of others, *Comitiales*. By which provided it was, In what yeares of a mans age, he was capable of Questure, Preture, Consulate, or any other like Office of State : as also, it was limited, within what time betweene, one might eftsoones beare the same Office againe. Item, what the terme of everie Magistracie should be, etc. And albeit the auncient Romanes had no such lawes, but (as Cornelius Scipio at his petition of Ædileship made answere, when exception was taken against him for his young age) whomsoever the Quirites would charge to be a Magistrate, hee had yeares enough on his backe, yet afterwards, sundrie Statutes were enacted in that behalfe : although by vertue of speciall privileges, the same were not duly observed. By the Chronologie it appeareth, that he was but ninteene yeares old when he became Questor, like as Tiberius before him.

^b Which Tiberius envying his greatnesse, wrought, therby to expose him unto greater dangers.

3

^a Well might this unseasonable exercise puff up and fill his skin with crudities and foggie humors, but hurtfull unto his health it was, and brought upon him diseases, and namely, that called *Cardiacus*, of which, some say, he died. Let them looke to it therfore, who, because they would be fat, not only fall to bodily exercise out of time, even upon ful stomacks, but also every morning eate in their beds and sleepe upon it, yea and ordinarily take a nap at noone, so soone as their meat is out of their mouthes.

^b By this Attribute, Civill, in our Author, ye must understand, Courtesie, Affabilitie, and a part not exceeding that of private Citizens, without taking any state.

5

^a As if the Gods, whose Images were shrined within, were not to be honoured any longer as Gods, suffering so good a man as Germanicus was, to die. For, as in token of honour, the people used to adorne

TWELVE CÆSARS

the Statues and Images of famous persons with flowers and greene leaves, so, whom they did vilipend and despise, they were wont to cast stones at their Images and Statues.

b The Tutelarie Gods of the house which ordinarily stood within a closet, called thereupon *Lararium.*

c For, to what end should they reare children any more? since Germanicus, growen to so good proofe, sped no better, but was taken away by untimely death.

d In this place, the circumstance sheweth, that the King of Parthians is meant, how ever the Persian King and such mightie Monarches, having under their Dominion other pettie Kings as Tributaries or Homagers, be so called : like as Agamemnon also in Homere.

e Which at Rome betokened a generall mourning, occasioned upon some extraordinary calamitie, or feare of publicke daunger, even as with us, the shutting in of Shop-windowes, etc.

6

a About the mids of this moneth, began the feast *Saturnalia,* celebrated with good cheere, with revels, dances, gaming and all kinde of libertie.

9

a For, common souldiers wore a certaine studded shoe, named *Caliga.*

10

a Which was later than the ordinarie time, by reason of Tiberius his lingering. For usually these complements were performed at 47 yeares of age.

11

a In this habite and manner of attire, counterfeiting a woman, thereby to decline suspicion when he entered into other mens houses for to dishonour them and abuse their wives, whom our author termeth heere *Adulteria, pro adulteris,* as else where, *conjugia, pro conjugibus.*

b The fabulous Historie of Phæthon is well known, namely, how by misgovernment of the steeds which drew the Chariot of the Sunne his Father, he set the whole world on fire. By Phæthon therfore is meant, a combustion (as it were) and generall confusion of the Provinces, like as by the watersnake, the verie bane and poyson of the Roman State.

13

a To doe him the greater honour, they intertaine him upon the way (as the maner was) with Sacrifices, Torches, Tapers, and wax lights.

14

a An opinion there was deeply setled in mens heads, that the death of one man might be excused and redeemed, with the death of another.

ANNOTATIONS

^a The two hundred penie.

^b His halfe image downeward from the head to the waist, portrayed with a Shield or Scutchion: and the same was commonly set out with the largest. Hereupon, M. Tullius Cicero, when he saw such a demie personage representing his brother Quintus in the province that he governed (and a very litle man he was of stature) ' My brother,' quoth he, ' in his halfe part, is greater than in the whole.'

^b A festivall holiday solemnized by heardmen, in the honour of Pales their Goddesse and Patronesse. Upon which day, the foundation of Rome Citie was laid. This feast they kept, the 12 day before the Kalends of May, to wit, the 20 of Aprill.

18

^a Mænius, a riotous unthrift, when he had wasted his Patrimonie and sold his Capitall house in Rome, excepted in the sale, and reserved to himselfe and his beires, one Columne or Pillar, from which he projected and put forth into the street a jettie, and upon it built a gallerie: out of which he might behold the sword-fencers in the market place, whereunto he had a fayre prospect from the said Pillar. Whereupon all such galleries or buildings jetting out in the street, be called *Mænianæ*.

22

^a The end of one verse, and beginning of another, cited out of Homer in the second of his *Ilias*. The Poet ascribeth them unto sage Ulysses, in this sense :

> One [Soveraigne] Lord,
> One King let there be.

^b By exchaunging the ensignes and Ornaments of the Roman Soveraigne or Emperor, with the Regall Diadem, purple Robe and Scepter.

^c Phœnicopterus is a water foule haunting lakes and fennes, and the river Nilus, as Hesiodus writeth. The fethers be of colour read, or purple. Whereof it taketh the name : and the tongue is a most daintie and pleasant morsell. So said Apitius, *nepotum omnium altissimus gurges*. Of this Bird Martiall made an Epigram :

> *Dat mihi penna rubens nomen : sed lingua gulosis*
> *Nostra sæpit. Quid si garrula lingua fores.*

> My name I take of wings so red, but unto gluttons tast,
> My tongue right pleasing is : oh, what, if it could prate as fast.

^d Some take them for Bistards : Birds decked, no doubt, with most beautifull fethers : as may appeare by Tertullian against Marcion, in these words : *Una Tetraonis pennula, (taceo de pavo) sordidum artificem pronuntiabit tibi Creatorem ?*

261

TWELVE CÆSARS

e They are thought to be Hens of Guinny.

f By the description of Clitus, they be our Turkies.

g The Phesant called in old time Itis, (which was the sonne of Tereus and Progne, transformed, as Poets feigne, into this Bird) and afterwards Phasianus or Phasiana [*Avis*], tooke his name of Phasis a river and Citie in Colchis, according to this Epigram of Martials:

Argiva primum sum transportata Carina:
Ante mihi notum nil nisi Phasis erat.

In Argive ship transported first, I was to forraine land:
Fore time, nought else but Phasis towne, I knew, or Phasis strand.

23

a Philo reporteth this farre otherwise, and telleth a pitifull Narration: How, by commission from Caius, certaine Colonels and Centurians came to young Tiberius, commaunding him to kill himselfe: because, forsooth, unlawfull it was for any other to murder a Prince of the Imperiall bloud. The youth, who had never seene any man killed, and by reason of his tender yeares was nothing at all experienced in the world, requested first of them, who were come thus to him, for to strike off his head, which he held out unto them: but seeing his request would not be heard, he desired them yet, to instruct him, in what part of his bodie he should stab himselfe for the speediest death. And so by instructions from them he was his owne executioner.

25

a Romulus ravished the Sabine virgins: and Augustus by force tooke from Tiberius his wife Livia.

26

a *Selena*, in Greeke, signifieth the Moone. And well knowen it is, that as M. Antonius the Triumvir called himselfe Bacchus and Osiris, so Cleopatra his wife tooke pleasure to be named *Luna*, i. the Moone, and Isis. Whereupon they gave to their sonne Alexander begotten betweene them, the name of the sunne, and to their daughter Cleopatra the name of the Moone, or Selena, which is all one.

b The Consuls were reputed still (in outward shew) Soveraigne Magistrates, although indeed, the Cæsars caried all before them, and were absolute Monarches.

c Some read, *Tesseras decima citius*, i. Before the tenth houre, or foure of the clocke after noone, for so long continued the Stage-plaies ordinarily. At which time, the Emperours were wont to bestow their Tickets or Talies among the people, by vertue whereof they received such and such gifts.

d There be learned Criticks that expound this place farre otherwise, reading *Pegmares*, in steede of *Pegmatis*, and understanding thereby

262

ANNOTATIONS

such sword-fencers, whose good hap it had beene to escape with life, the fall from those Frames or Pageants called *Pegmata* or *Pegma*, which with certaine vices or Skrewes were set up, and let downe, upon which as on scaffolds, malefactors were brought forth, eyther to exhibit a shew unto the people, fighting one with another at sharpe, to the outrance, or to make them sport, by falling downe into a pit underneath, where eyther wild beasts were readie to devoure, or fire to consume them. A devise wrought by dissolving the joynts of the said *Pegmes* under them. And in this sense they interprete the rest that followeth, concerning *patres familias, i.* good honest Citizens householders.

27

ᵃ He had espied in the multitude of those prisoners and malefactors, two with bald heads, distant farre a sunder, and happily, as much as from the one end of the place unto the other: all those betweene, without respect of their cause, he commaunded to be put to death indifferently.

ᵇ An ordinarie thing it was at Rome, to sweare by the *Genius*, as also by the Fortune, the health, etc., of their Emperours. And what a devout oth this was, *per Genium, i.* the Dæmon, the spirit, or superintendent Angell of the Prince, which I take to be as much, as by his owne good selfe, appeareth by Tertullian, *Apologet.* cap. 28. *Citius apud vos per omnes deos, quam per Genium principis peieratur.*

ᶜ Seneca, lib. 2 *de Iræ*, cap. 33, reporteth the like example of Castor a right worshipful Gentleman of Rome, whose sonne, the same Caligula, upon verie envie that the young man was a proper and beautifull person, put to death in his fathers sight, and then invited the old man to supper, provoked him to carouse and be merie, which the good father was faine to endure and make semblance of contentment, for feare, least the Tyrant would have done as much by another sonne, whom he had living.

ᵈ *Catenis verberatum.* Among other chasticements of the bodie, there is reckoned *Vinculorum verberatio*, as Callistratus witnesseth, lib. 7 *de Pænis.* The ignorance whereof, hath made some to read, *in Catenis verberatum, i.* bound in chaines and then beaten, others, *habenis* for *catenis*: as if he had beene well lindged with lether thongs or halters ends, as slaves were wont to be served by the Lorarii.

28

ᵃ Albeit, the proper use of these *Graphia* was to cut or engrave letters onely, in tables of barke or soft wood: yet, because it was unlawfull to weare weapons in the Senate house, some, of a mischievous minde, made those writing stiles or Steeles so, as they might kill there-with, enacted therefore it was, that no man should carie about him such writing instruments of yron or steele, but of bone onely. And yet even these, as others also of reeds and quils, were made so keene and sharpe, that they were able to give a mortall wound.

TWELVE CÆSARS

29

^a For the manner of the Roman Emperours was, upon displeasure, to send Men and women away into some desert Isles, and there to confine them.

^b Ellebor, that groweth in the Isles Antycire, is of most effectuall operation. The roote is that, whereof is made our sneesing powder. It purgeth extreemely by vomit. Thereupon ariseth the Proverb, *Naviget Anticyram, i.* Let him sayle to Anticyra, applied to one that is melancholicke in the highest degree, and little better than mad. See Plinie, *Natural Hist.,* lib. 35, cap. 5.

30

^a Some conjecture verie well, that this Tetrinius was not surnamed Latro, being the addition appropriate to the noble Family of Rome, of the Portii, but a notorious theefe or robber, such as in Latin is called *Latro.* And of that sort commonly were they that performed before the people this bloudie fight with unrebated swords, without foiles. And no mervaile, if he termed all the Citizens there assembled *Tetrinios, i.* Theeves, considering he wished before, that he could cut of al their heads at one blow.

33

^a He suspected, that she had given him some love-drinks.

34

^a *Præter æquum.* How this can stand with his pride or malice, which our author hath propounded to exemplifie, I cannot see. In some copies we read, *præter eum, i.* beside him, that is to say, otherwise than he would have them, or approve. And one Critick or Judicious Lawier, Franc. Hottoman, as also Coracius, read, *præter Eccum,* as if hee should say, All Lawyers shall give none other answere but this. Behold him, meaning the Emperor Caius, therby referring the decision of all matters to his will and pleasure. Lastly, Torrentius concludeth the Period thus, *Ne quid respondere possint, i.* That they should give no answere at all. And for *præter æquum,* etc., he putteth *præterea, i.* Moreover, for a beginning of the next chapter.

35

^a Colosseros seemeth to be a word compounded of *Colossos* and *Eros.* The one importeth his talnesse, resembling the stately and Giantlike personages called Colossi, and the other, his lovely visage, representing Eros, even Love, or Cupid it selfe.

^b These fencers, called Threces or Thraces¹, thought to be the same that *Retiarii,* were lightly appointed for armour, and put to desperate fight, as having all parts of their bodies exposed to daunger, where-

---

¹ So thinks Sabellicus.

ANNOTATIONS

upon they were called also *Tunicati,* and were matched in opposition with the *Mirmillones,* as this verse of Ausonius implieth :

Quis mirmilloni componitur?[1] *æquimanus Thrax.*

Whereas the other named *Hoplomachi,* had for their defence, head peeces and targuets.   Senec. lib. 1, Epist. 7.

c The priest, called *Rex Nemorensis,* of a place where Diana Arcina was worshipped, within a temple beautified with a grove about it, by a barbarous custome of the Scithians, so long onely held his place, untill after one yeares revolution, some one stronger than himselfe, stepped unto him and overcame him in single fight, and so deposed him, like as, by the first institution, himselfe, foyling another in combat attained thereto.

37

a Seneca writeth, *Consolat. ad Helv.,* That it was ordinarie with him to consume at one supper ten millions of sesterces, and who studied himselfe, and laid his head to others, how he might at one supper make an even hand with the revenewes and tributes of all the provinces belonging to the state of Rome.

b Some read for [*de Cedris*] *Deceres,* after the forme of *Moneres,* meaning by *Deceres* a mightie gallie furnished with ten rankes of Oares, for such the Greeks call Δέκηρεις.

41

a *Dum multa commissa fierent.*   Which may be expounded otherwise thus, When as many things were forfaited and confiscate.

45

a Taking the name from *Exploratores,* a militarie terme, signifying the Avant-couriers and fore-riders, to discover the enemy, and to cleere the coasts.

51

a Yet Dion reporteth of him, that otherwhiles, when it thundred aloft, he would seeme to doe the like beneath with a thunder barrell, or such a kinde of devise : when it lightened, to make flashes with fireworks : and if a thunderbolt fell, to discharge likewise some stone out of an engine.

52

a Which ornaments belonged to Jupiter and Æsculapius.

b Resembling thereby Neptune, for it symbolizeth his power over waters in Sea, River, Lakes.

c The Ensigne of Mercury, betokening his Eloquence.

56

a So called, because they were exhibited in the Palatium.

[1] Or, *committitur.*

TWELVE CÆSARS

ᵃ Capitolium, although κατ' ἐξοχὴν, it was the stately mount or Castle of Rome, yet it became a generall name of all Citadels and strong Castles built for the defence of any Citie.

ᵇ Meaning the murder of Caius Julius Cæsar Dictator.

ᶜ Bearing the name of a notorious theefe, or Captayne rather of theeves, crucified for his desertes.

ANNOTATIONS UPON
TIBERIUS CLAUDIUS DRUSUS CÆSAR

1

ᵃ Like as in Rome, the gate called *Porta scelerata*, and the Streete *Vicus sceleratus* upon some semblable infortunate accidents.

2

ᵃ Wheras, by usuall custome such were brought into the Forum or common hall.

9

ᵃ By vertue of this Act, himselfe, his landes and goods were proscribed and exposed to open sale, in a Table hung up by an Edict from the masters of the Exchequer or Citie-Chamber. And if within the time appointed, he came not in, to satisfie the debt, nor any chapman or suretie to undertake it, he and his whole state fell by escheate as forfait and confiscate into the Princes hands.

17

ᵃ These Ilands are situate in the mouth of the River Rhodanus[1]: and they be so called of the order in which they lie.

21

ᵃ The name of this Fencer Palumbus, signifieth also in the Latin tongue a Stock-dove: which gave occasion unto him, to come out with this od jeast.

23

ᵃ Provided it was by the law Papiæ, That no woman under fiftie yeares of age should be maried to a man three-scor yeares old or upward: Item, That no man under three score yeares might wed a woman, fiftie yers old or above. Where, note: That these

· [1] Rhosne.

ANNOTATIONS

words [*à Tiberio*] as if he added the said Branch, seeme to have beene foysted in : considering that as it appeareth by Tacitus, the Emperour Tiberius went about to moderate the foresaid law, and not to make it more strict by annexing such a clause.

25

^a For feare of breaking up the pavements, if they rode in coach, wagon, chariot, or on horseback.

^b In divers Greeke and Latin writers, the names of Jewes and Christians were confounded : so as by Jewes they understood Christians.

^c *Orchestra* was that place in the fore-front of the Theater or Scaffolds, and neerest unto the Stage, wherein the Senators ordinarily sate, and sometime the Emperour himselfe.

^d *Popularia* were seats within the scaffolds and Theater, most remote from the Stage, wherein the common people were allowed to stand or sit. Betweene the said *Orchestra* and these *Popularia* were raunged the Knights or Gentlemen of Rome, and those rankes bare the name of *Equestria.*

^e So called, of the mountaine Eryx in Sicilie, where she was highly worshipped, and where she had a Temple.

28

^a As for Drusilla his wife, a Jew borne, she had beene maried indeed before to king Azyzus, as Josephus writeth : but as touching the other two Queens, whosoever they were, he was acquainted with them otherwise, and not in way of mariage, so farre as I can finde.

^b For everie man might not so doe, unlesse he had a Knights estate, which was foure hundred thousand *Sextarii*, or were free borne : neyther Libertines nor Mechanicall persons living by base trades and occupations were allowed.

29

^a Other writers, as Philostratus and Julianus, say moreover, That without his wife and freed men, he was χωφὸν πρόσωπον and δορυφόρημα τῆς βασιλείας, much like to a player in a dumbe shew, and the bare Image of a Kings Majestie, as Plutarch reporteth of Arridaus.

31

^a This disease, some Physicians name Καρδιαλγίαν, *i.* the heart-ach, or *Cardiacam passionem*, seated in the orifice of the stomach, which is called Καρδία. The paine whereof, Plinie affirmeth to be most intollerable, next unto the passion of the strangury.

32

^a *Flatum crepitumque ventris.* By *Flatum*, understand that riddance of wind downeward, *qui nares ferit, non aures.* Which in English commeth neere unto the Latin word, *Visio*, for that the verbe *Visire*,

267

TWELVE CÆSARS

TIBERIUS
CLAUDIUS
DRUSUS
CÆSAR

is the same that τὸ βοίσειν. As Cicero in his *Epistles* hath well, but covertly observed, out of the word *Divisio*, wherein he noteth *Quiddam Cacemphaton*. Which place some interpreters, for ignorance of the said verbe *Visio*, have expounded very absurdly.

33

ᵃ So sumptuous were these feastes, that *Pontificum Cœna*, and *Saliares Epulæ*, grew into a proverb, to expresse exceeding great bellie cheere, and most delicate fare.

34

ᵃ Seneca, lib. 1 *De Clementia* writeth, That Claudius caused more Paricides to be sowed within a leather male, etc., in five yeares space, than had beene ever before his daies.

ᵇ Whether they were hired thereto, or presuming of their owne strength, voluntarily entered upon such a combat, or forced to undergo that dangerous fight, or else exposed unto their greedie jawes for to be worried and devoured by them.

ᶜ This devise called heere *Automatum*, Horace by a Periphrasis, pretily expresseth thus, *Nervis alienis mobile lignum.*

35

ᵃ For with their *Graphia*, as hath beene noted before, they might do a mischiefe.

38

ᵃ *Iræ atque Iracundiæ. Ira* signifyeth the hote and momentarie passion of anger, soone enflamed and as soone quenched, and *Iracundia* seemeth to be taken heere, for the continuance of the said anger, and an inveterate setled wrath. Howsoever our Dictionaries would teach us the contrary. The one may be called Gall or Choler, the other Spleene or Melancholy.

ᵇ *Stultitiam neminem fingere*, or rather, *Stultitiam stultum neminem fingere, i.* That no foole counterfaits folly.

40

ᵃ It was an inconsiderate speech of an Emperor, and foolishly let fall, in the Senate especially, tending much to his discredit and dishonour: as if he sent to the Taverne for his wine, by the pot or bottle, and had not his own cellarage stored therewith.

ᵇ These words without all rime or reason were rife in his mouth, which unadvisedly he had taken up, and by use could not leave them.

41

ᵃ Some thinke, that he devised not new letters in the Alphabet, but new formes rather of the former: as namely to write for the Æolick digamma *F* the inverted character *ꟻ*, and for *œ* dipthong, *ai*.

268

ANNOTATIONS

43

ᵃ For, by report of Dion and Xiphilinus his stature farre exceeded the proportion of his years.

44

ᵃ And yet by circumstances it may be collected, that he caught his bane and died in the Palatium at Rome.

46

ᵃ These were, as it plainly appeareth, Questors, Ædiles, Tribunes, Prætors, Censors and Consuls. Of all these, some one or other died, excepting Censors, as Tacitus writeth, 12 *Annal.*

.

ANNOTATIONS UPON
NERO CLAUDIUS CÆSAR

5

ᵃ Tʜᴇsᴇ foure factions or crewes that ran with Chariots for the prise, were distinguished by foure colors of cloth, or liveries, and therupon called by their names, *Alba, i.* White, *Veneta,* watchet or light blew, *Præsina, i.* greene, and *Rosea, i.* Rose coloured or read. Unto which were added by Domitian *Aurata* and *Purpurea, i.* Gold coloured or yellow, and purple. The former foure Sidonius Apollinaris hath comprised in his Hendecasyllabes, thus :

> *Micant colores,*
> *Albus cum veneto, virens rubensque.*

> Then shine these crewes and make a gallant shew
> . In white, in blew, in greene and roset hew.

Proportionate they are unto the foure seasons of the yeare : white, to the Autumne or end of Sommer, Watchet to the winter, Greene to the spring, and Red to sommer, or as some would have it to the foure Elements.

ᵇ Physicians have observed three kinds of dropsie. The first is *Ascites,* wherein the belly doth swell with much water gathered betweene the inner skin or rine of the belly, and the cawle which lappeth the guts, and some wind withall, so named of ἀσκὸs in Greeke, *i.* A bottle, because in turning of the bodie to a side, the water is perceived to shog in the womb, like as liquor in a bottle halfe full, when it is shaken. The second, *Tympanites,* wherein the belly is hoven up with wind especially, and some water among. Whereby it will sound

269

TWELVE CÆSARS

like a taber or drum, if one tamper upon it, and thereof it was so
called. The third *Leucophlegmatias, anasarca, Hyposarca,* in Latin
Intercus, or *Aqua intercutem,* in the proper signification [1], when the
bodie all over is puffed up with water and wind running betweene the
fell and the flesh. And thereof as should seeme, died this Domitius.

6

ª To wit, the ninth day after he was borne, on which they used to
name their sonnes. And as this day was called *Nominalia,* so there
was a goddesse forsooth, president of this complement and ceremonies,
whom they named Nundina.

7

ª The manner was, during these solemnities in the Albane mount,
(where the chiefe magistrates were present) to leave for Provost of the
Citie, some principall young Gentleman of the Nobilitie, before whom
sitting judicially, causes of no great importance should be brought.

11

ª These youthfull sports *Iuvenalia,* or *Iuvenales ludi,* were first
instituted by this Nero, privately in houses or gardens, and orchards.
Wherein, of all degrees, ages and sexes they daunced and revelled.

12

ª The fabulous reports of Ladie Pasiphæ wife to King Minos, how
she was enamoured of a Bull, as also of Icarus the sonne of Dædalus,
who would needs attempt to flie in the ayre, be well enough knowen
to them that are but meanely seene in Poetrie.

ᵇ *Iuxca cubiculum eius decidit.* By *Cubiculum,* he meaneth heere, a
royall seat raised on high within that quarter of the Theater called
Orchestra, under a rich Tent or Canopie, where Emperors were wont
to sit when they beheld such solemnities. These Pavillions were
called in Greeke οὐρανισκοὶ κωνώπεα in some sort resembling bed-
chambers.

ᶜ So named because they that wrestled, ran, or otherwise exercised,
were naked, like as the place itselfe of such exercises thereupon tooke
the name Gymnasium.

16

ª Full and formall suppers, whereto men were invited, and at which
the guestes sate orderly marshalled according to their worth place,
and were called *cænæ rectæ,* and after this manner in other Princes
daies were their favorites feasted. In steed hereof came in *Sportulæ,*
i. allowances given unto them, eyther in money, or cates, in recompence of their ordinarie salutations and attendance.

ᵇ As there were sundrie factions or crewes favourizing this or that

[1] For Cornelius Celsus attributeth this name to all the kindes.

ANNOTATIONS

colour of the Chariotters, so were there likewise of Actours and players, whereupon many roiots, outrages, Fraies and murthers were committed.

17

ᵃ It should seeme, that for the pleading and triall of causes, such Tribunal seats, pues, benches and barrs, were erected at first, for the present occasion, and taken downe againe by certaine persons, who gathered therfore a rent of those that went to law.

18

ᵃ Divers Kings of Pontus were named Polemones as of Ægypt Ptolemæi, whereupon the realme Pontus, is by Vopiscus called Polemonius, like as the Alpes Cottiæ of Cottius.

• 19

ᵃ Many had attempted this beside him : but all their cost and labour came to nought : οὕτως χαλεπὸν ἀνθρώπῳ τὰ θεῖα βιάσασθαι.

20

ᵃ τῆς λανθανούσης μουσικῆς οὐδεὶς λόγος.
ᵇ In respect of a former fleet, that was wont to come before, and bring newes of the second laden with marchandise and under saile. Therefore those ships were called *naves Tabellariæ.*   Seneca.
ᶜ *Bombos,* resembling either the buzzing and humming noise of Bees, or the sound of trumpets.
ᵈ *Imbrices,* much after the manner of that rattling, which a sodaine shewre makes upon the tiles of an house, or the sound that crest tiles or gutter tiles may make.
ᵉ *Testas,* to expresse the crashing of potsheards or earthen pots, clattering one against another.
ᶠ *Insignes pinguissima coma.*   In which sense we read of *pingues togæ* and *Lacernæ.*   Yet some understand thereby λιπαροπλοκάμους, *i.* whose lokes and faix were so slicke and glib with sweet oyles, that they shone againe.

21

ᵃ For, so would he have it to be called.   And Thraseas Pætus was judicially convented, and deeply charged, because he had never offred sacrifice for that heavenly voice of his.   Tacit.
ᵇ Who was with child by her owne brother Macareus, whereupon her father Æolus caused the childe new borne to be cast before hungrie dogs : and sent a sword to his daughter to kill her selfe with.
ᶜ In revenge of his father Agamemnons death, by her murdered, whereupon he fell into a furious kinde of deepe melancholie.
ᵈ Who unwitting killed his owne father Laius, and as ignorantly wedded his owne mother Iocasta.

271

TWELVE CÆSARS

^e By putting on a garment next his skinne, envenomed with the poison of Nessus the Centaure, and so sent unto him as a token, from his wife Deianira.

24

^a It may be thought, that he then acted Œdipus or Creon or some other King, and therefore carried in his hand a regall staffe or Sceptre. Yet some interpret this of a Lawrel rod or braunch, such as Actors held in their hands while they sung.

^b For, at Olimpia, were Games also of Criers, striving who could cry lowdest, for the prize.

^c These were called *Hieronicæ*, as one would say, sacred victories, to witt at the solemne games in Greece, Nemea, Pythia, Istmia, and Olimpia.

25

^a Five thousand were there of these Gallants, as Xiphilinus writeth, ready to applaud him when he chaunted.

26

^a He meaneth eyther a peruke and cap of counterfait haire, Κόμας περιθέτους, Dioni thereby disguising himselfe : the same that in Caligula he termeth *Capillamentum*, or else some hood covering his head all save the eyes. Julius Capitolinus calleth it *Cucullionem*, wherewith the Emperour Verus played such parts by night, in imitation of Caligula and Nero.

^b *Quintana* was a Gate or Street rather in the Roman Campe, wherein was usually kept, *Forum rerum utensilium*, in resemblance whereof, he termed a certaine place in his house *Quintana*, in which he made sale of such wares and commodities, as he had gotten together by rifling and robbing.

^c It appeareth by Tacitus, that this was Julius Montanus, who, albeit he had not sitten in counsell as Senator, yet was *Laticlavius*, and wore the Senators Robe. Such Gentlemen were called *Iuvenes secundi ordinis*, in distinction of those of the Imperiall bloud, or otherwise neere allied unto the Emperour.

27

^a The manner was in old time to imploy the day in businesses, and therein to take no liberall meales, putting off the full refection, and cherishing of the bodie untill night. *Convivia de die*, argued Intemperance, much more then feasting from noone to midnight.

^b *Ambubaiarum*. These tooke their name (as most expositors have conjectured), *Quod circa Baias versarentur*. Yet some learned men of later time fetch the same from this Syriacke word *Anbubaiæ*, as if such were Syrian women, who being otherwise naughtie packes and callots, gat their living also by pla ng upon certaine instruments of musike, which they brought with them out of their native countrey.

272

ANNOTATIONS

^c *Copas imitantium.* Although *Copæ,* properly be such women as keepe victualling houses, readie not onely to entertaine, but also to invite and call in guestes, yet because these commonly are verie bold and unshamefaced, this terme goeth indifferently for strumpets and curtesans. For seldome shall a man see an impudent woman that is not withall incontinent, so inseparably is modestie joyned with Chastitie.

^d The corrupt text in this place hath given occasion of much obscuritie, and ministred matter enough for Criticks to worke upon, while some read *Mellita,* others *Myrtitrichila.* By which are ment certaine sweat junkets, as daintie wafers, etc.

^e This may be thought incredible, that banqueting conceits at one sitting should cost so much, and the aspersion of rose-water or other odoriferous liquors arise to more. Where is to be noted the observation of some, who for *ab Syrtio rosaria* read *aspersio rosaria,* that is to say, the artificiall besprinkling and aromatizing (as I may so say) of banqueting rowmes, out of spouts and pipes, conveying odoriferous waters and oyles, going under the name of *Rosaria.* Which spouts, if they were made of silver or gold, (as we read they were at the feast of Otho, when he gave Nero entertainment) might soone amount to that somme. To say nothing of the costly compound distilled waters, or extracts and oyles, themselves, drawn out of most pretious simples and spices.

28

^a Him he called, as other Authors write, Sabbina and Poppæa, after the name of his wife deceased.

29

^a In other writers he is named Pythagoras, so that it should seeme he caried two names.

30

^a A great Magician, whom he intertained thus royally, because he would have learned magicke of him. See Plinie.

^b Whereas Augustus when he played at this game, ventured no more, than for everie *Talus,* which were foure in all, a single denier. For it should seeme that the game of *Tali* heere mentioned, was *Pleistobolinda, i.* who could throw most with foure *Tali,* whether the same were cockall bones in deed, or made of gold, silver or Ivorie, with foure sides, everie one representing a chaunce, an *Ace* or unitie and *sise,* a *trey* and *quatre,* opposite, one unto the other. For they wanted *deux* and *cinque,* which the *Tessera Cubus,* or Die carying six faces, hath.

^c It is evident hereby, as also out of that verse of Juvenal,

Ut læti phaleris omnes et torquibus omnes,

that these *Phaleræ* were not Trappings and furniture belonging to

TWELVE CÆSARS

NERO
CLAUDIUS
CÆSAR

horses, but some other ornaments, wherewith footmen and horsemen both were trimly decked.

33

a In this verbe *Morari*, there is couched a double sense, which gives the grace unto this pleasant scoffe. For, being a meere Latin word, and having the first sillable by nature short, it signifieth, to stay or to make long abode: and taking it thus, Nero might be thought to imply thus much, that Claudius was now departed out of the companie of mortall men, and raunged among the heavenly wights. But take the same word, as Nero spake it, derived of μῶρος[1] in Greeke, which signifyeth, A foole, and hath the first syllable long,ʾit importeth, that Claudius played the foole no longer here in the world among men. Read the little pamphlet of Seneca entituled ἀποκολοκήντωσις, if ye would see Claudius depainted in his colours, and in a fooles coat: which he, as it may appeare, composed of purpose to gratifie Nero in that humour of his.

b The Greekes call this Καυστραν or τύβον. And the Romans in honour of their Princes, were wont to compasse the same all about with a wall of flint, or other durable stone, as marble.

34

a It may be it was in the same forme, that Justinus Martyr citeth out of *Orpheus* :

θύρας δ'ἐπίθεσθε βεβῆλος.
Fortes opponite profanis.

Which Virgil in some sort hath expressed thus :

Procul este profani.

And Claudian after him :

Gressus removete profani.

37

a The like example is reported by Vopiscus in *Aurelianus*, who tooke wonderfull delight in a mightie Eater [2], that in one day before his owne table, devoured a wild bore full and whole, an hundred loaves of bread, a wether mutton, and a pig.

38

a This Iambicke verse, as Dion writeth, was rife also in Tiberius Cæsars mouth.

b Albeit this word, *Insula*, beside the common signification of an Iland, is taken for an house standing entire by it selfe, a part from other, yet in this Author I observe that it is put els where for other

[1] *Moros.*   [2] Phagone.

274

ANNOTATIONS

houses also and tenements let out to tenants by the owners and Landlords, who are called *Domini Insularum*. And even in this acception, it may well goe in this place.

ᶜ This toure Horace describeth, *Carm.* lib. 3, Od. 19, in these words,

Molem propinquam nubibus arduis, etc.

39

ᵃ Which number ariseth to ten thousand a moneth. A mortalitie nothing comparable to that which as Eusebius reporteth, reigned at Rome in the daies of Vespasian, in which there died of the pestilence ten thousand a day, nor to that in Constantinople, when many daies, there were likewise ten thousand dead bodies caried forth. Procop. lib. 2, *de bello persico.*

ᵇ Such a rumor in deed ran rife, but untruly. Tacitus.

ᶜ Orestes to revenge his father Agamemnons death wrought by Clytemnestra his mother and Ægysthus the adulterer, murdered her.

ᵈ Alcmæon sonne of Amphiaraus and Eriphyle, killed her, bycause shee had contrived his fathers death.

ᵉ Æneas caried his old father Anchises upon his shoulders out of the fyre of Troy when it burned. Here is to be noted the duple sense of the verbe [*Sustulit*] in one and the same Latin verse : for in the former place, it signifieth to Kill, or make away, as Nero did his mother, in the later, to take up and cary, as Æneas did his father. This yeeldeth an elegant grace in Latin, and cannot so well be expressed in English.

ᶠ Apollo was surnamed *Pæan* of παίειν in Greek, which signifieth to strike, or of παύειν, to ease and allay paine, as being a God, that both sendeth diseases, and also cureth them. But commonly the Romaines terme him so, in this latter and better sense. He is styled likewise Hecatebeletes in Greek, which is as much, as shooting or wounding from afarr. In these abstruse significations and obscure termes therefore this Epigram implyeth thus much : That whiles Nero in the habit of Apollo plaieth upon the harpe. and would seeme to be a milde and gratious Prince : the Parthian King with bow and arrowes representing Apollo likewise, endaungered the Empire of Rome, and all, through the supine negligence of Nero geven to his Musick and other vanities excessively.

ᵍ This is ment by that huge house of Neroes building, and hath a reference to that desolate estate of Rome, when it was sacked and fyred by the French, after the imfortunate battaile of Allia, what time the Romaines were in consultation to abandon the Cittie and departe to Veii, there to inhabite.

ʰ It seemeth that Nero in his Poeme entituled *Troica*, had used to chaunt of Nauplius the father of Palamedes, who abid many calamities himselfe, and in revenge of his sonnes death, wrought much mischiefe to others. The Cynicke therefore, noteth Nero for his singing, as also for abusing his owne good parts in perpetrating all wickednesse, or else for mispending his treasure so dissolutely.

275

TWELVE CÆSARS

NERO
CLAUDIUS
CÆSAR

[1] Ἔρρωσο δὴ καὶ ὑγίαινε, οὔτε λέγειν οὔτε ἀκούειν, ἀγαθὸν, οὐ γὰρ προσίοντες ἄλλοις, οὔτε μέλλοντές τι πράττειν, ταῦτα λέγουσιν ἄνθρωποι, ἀλλὰ ἀπαλαττόμενοι ἀλλήλων, καὶ πρὸς ἄπνον τρεπόμενοι. Artemidor. lib. 1, cap. ult.

[k] By Orcus, or Pluto, taken for the God of Hell or the Grave, is understood death, in this place, readie to seize upon the Senatours, whose overthrow Nero had intended. Now, well knowne it is, that the manner was then, among the Romans, as at this day with us, to cary forth their dead with the feet forward.

40

[a] It should seeme, this answere was delivered in these words:

Ἐξηκοστὸν ἔτος τρισκαιδέκατόντε φυλάττου.

Of sixtieth yeare (I doe thee reed)
And thirteenth more, see thou take heed.

Whereby Apollo (for his oblique aunswers rightly of the Greeks termed Loxias) or the Divell himselfe, whether you will, playing with him in a two-fold and ambiguous construction, (as his manner was) deluded him. For whiles he rested secure, dreaming still of the 73 yeare, which he supposed was meant of his owne age, and which he was farre short of, he fell into the hands of Galba, a man indeede of those yeares.

45

[a] Rome was wont to be served of corne from Alexandrea in Ægypt, in the time of dearth especially, when Cicilie, otherwise reckoned *Horreum populi Romani*, i. the people of Romes Garner, was not able to furnish them. Now, when in steede of corne long expected, there arrived certaine saile from thence fraught with dust and sand for the sports of his gallants: no mervaile if all the discontentment and heart-burning of the people conceived against Cornmongers and such as made gaine by the scarcitie of graine, redounded upon Nero and his Courtiers.

[b] Νῦν γὰρ ἐστ' ἀγών. The end of some Trimetre or Senarie Iambicke verse in a Tragedie.

[c] Νῦν δεῖ ἐλαύνειν ἢ ἕλκειν, i. Now 'tis high time to drive or draw. In both which Empreses, by a most tart and bitter *Sarcasmus*, is taxed his excessive love of Charioting.

[d] The speech of the people, or of his mother, who could not reclayme him.

[e] As a Paricide or Killer of Parents, etc., whose judgement was to be sowed quicke within a lether budge, etc.

[f] There is not only an Homonyme in the word [*Gallos*] signifying the French Nation, and the crowing cocks, but an Amphibolie also in the sentence: whereby it may be understood, eyther that Nero with his chaunting, had awakened the French, who began now to revolt, as not

276

ANNOTATIONS

able any longer to endure his songs: or that the French awakened him, to bestirre himselfe and looke better about him: as if they were the Cockes indeed, to raise him out of his drowsie securitie.

ᵍ The ambiguitie of this word [Vindex], implieth both a private chastiser of servants for their faults, and also C. Julius Vindex, a revenger of publicke injuries, and a maintainer of the common libertie. Who now had taken Armes against Nero.

46

ᵃ *Auspicia*, albeit they properly do signifie presaging tokens delivered by birds: yet the sequence and circumstance of this passage, lead us rather to some other uncouth prodigies and straunge sightes.

ᵇ Nero was semblably distained, in another kinde: as having murdered his Father Claudius[1], his mother Agrippina, and his two wives Octavia and Poppæa.

47

ᵃ *A cælatura carminum Homeri.* Which if wee straine a little, may be Englished thus, for the workmanship and engraving upon them, out of Homers verses. Alluding to that standing massie cup of Nestors, described by Homer in the eleventh of his *Ilias*.

ᵇ An halfe verse out of Virgil, 12 *Æneid*. The words of Turnus unto his sister Juturna.

ᶜ Although there were divers *Præfecturæ* in Ægypt, called *Nomi*, as one would say, Shires or Divisions, as appeareth in Plinie, 5 lib. cap. 9. Yet by this place is to be understood the Presidencie over all Ægypt, which by the institution of Augustus, was ordinarily conferred upon some Gentlemen of Rome. By which, it appeareth, he would play at small game rather than sit out.

ANNOTATIONS UPON
SERVIUS SULPITIUS GALBA

3

ᵃ THE like narration is reported of Hipparche and Crates the Thebane, a Cynick Phylosopher.

6

ᵃ *Tessera data.* How ever this word [*Tessera*] in our Author hath other significations, to wit, of a watchword, a Signall, a Tally or Ticket, etc. Yet here verily, it seemeth to be put for a Precept or

---

[1] Who adopted him.

TWELVE CÆSARS

SERVIUS
SULPITIUS
GALBA

Commaundement, whether it were delivered by word of mouth unto those that stood next, or in writing, and so passed through the campe, it mattereth not.

^b It may appeare, that Gætulicus their former Generall, had allowed his Souldiers more libertie and pastime.

8

^a These were also called Tatii, by Tacitus, of Tatius King of the Sabines.

^b They tooke their name of Augustus : like as other orders afterwards, as Flaviana, etc., of the Emperours following.

10

^a In habit of a woman, and with winges, holding forth a garland in the right hand, and bearing in her left an Olive braunch : as is to be seene in many Antique coynes.

^b A truncke of a tree, or post erected : upon which hung the Armour and apparell of enemies slaine and despoiled.

14

^a During which time, were held the festivall daies of the *Saturnalia,* Newe yeares tide and others.

19

^a They used in olde time such curaces (in steed of brest plates) made of linnen webbs, folded eighteene times and more. For, so Nicetas Acominatus, lib. 1 *Rerum Isaaci Angeli* writeth : ἠριθμοῦντο δὲ εἰς ὀκτωκαίδεκα καὶ πωλείω ὑφαίματος συπτύγματα: which foulds being throughly steeped and soaked in viniger or Austere wine, with salt put thereto, and afterwardes well driven and wrought together in maner of Felt, became so stiffe, and an Armour of so good proofe, ὡς καὶ βέλους εἶσαι παντὸς στεγανώτερον, i. as that it would checke the dint of any dart or shot whatsoever.

^b As touching the Souldier thus reprooved by Galba, it was Julius Atticus, as Tacitus writeth, one of those who went under the name of *Spiculatores, i.* Bill-men : or *Speculatores* rather, as some would have it, employed in Espiall, executions, etc. as hath before beene noted. Heere also in the clause, *Dimota paganorum turba,* is to be understood the multitude of the people and common sort, who were not Souldiers. For so *Pagani* are taken, as in opposition to *Milites.*

20

^a These *Aurei* among the Romans were valued at one hundred *Sestertii* a peece, so as in round reckoning they may goe for our olde Edward Star-Reals, or fifteene shilling peeces. For, by exact computation, one of them ariseth to fifteene shillings, seven pence halfe penie, the fourth part just, of the Roman pound, (conteyning one

278

ANNOTATIONS

hundred Deniers or Atticke Drachmes) which maketh three pound, two shillings sixe pence starling.

b This place where Patrobius was executed, and into which they flung their heads, who by commaundement of the Cæsars were put to death, was called *Sestertius*. Plutarch.

ANNOTATIONS UPON
MARCUS SALVIUS OTHO

1

a NOT without the Rampyer and precinct of the Campe, where was the ordinarie place of execution : nor by the ministerie of a Centurion, who by order was deputed, to see Justice done : but in the verie face and most frequented quarter of the Campe called *Principia*, not farre from the Lord Generals Pavilion, and where the Principall Captaines quartered and lodged : wherein also, the maine Standard named the Ægle and other militarie ensignes of the bandes and cohorts were kept : even in his owne sight being Generall, whose manner was not to be present.

2

a This rude and grosse kinde of sport was thereupon called *Sagatio*, not unlike to that pastime with us in some place called the canvasing, and else where, the vanning of dogs.

3

a For, after that by commaundement of Nero, he and Poppæa, were in some sort put asunder, he sollicited her as being his owne wedded wife to keepe him companie, which, in regard of her marriage with Nero, was held Adulterie.

6

a A Columne erected in the upper end or head of the *Forum Romanum* : at which, all the principall high waies in Italy began, with directions therein engraven, to everie gate of the Citie, leading unto the said highwaies.

7

a Some read, for αὐλοῖς ἀσύλοῖς, to no good sense at all. But the former, accordeth well with Juvenal, *Satyr.* 11. Who to the same effect saith :

Buccæ
Noscenda est mensura tuæ,

279

TWELVE CÆSARS

and proverbially implyeth thus much, that he was not able to manage the Empire.

8

ᵃ *Germaniciani exercitus.* Which served in Campe, or as Garison Souldiers in Germanie, whether they were Romanes, Germanes or any other Auxiliaries from Associate Nations, it skilled not.

ᵇ The manner was, that who soever enterprised a warre-voyage should enter into the Chappell of Mars, where hung the sacred Scutcheons or Shields called *Ancilia,* and first stirre them, after that, shake the speare also of Mars, and say with all *Mars, Vigila, i.* Awake Mars. This had Otho done, but according to the religious ceremonie, not bestowed them quietly againe in their places.

12

ᵃ This bread was made of Beane and Rice flower, of the finest wheat also, a verie *Psilothrum* as the Physicians terme it, or a Depilatorie, to keepe haire from growing, especially being wet and soaked in some juyce or liquor appropriate therefore, as the bloud of bats, frogs, or the Tunie fish, etc. To this effeminacie of Otho, alludeth the Satyricall Poet Juvenal[1] in this verse :

Et pressum in faciem digitis extendere panem.

ANNOTATIONS UPON

AULUS VITELLIUS

1

ᵃ Tʜɪs Quintus Eulogius was the freed man of the said Quintus Vitellius.

2

ᵃ Some read *Sectionibus et Suturis* : expounding it thus, as if his sonne had been not a cobler, but a shoomaker indeed, occupied in cutting of new shoes and sowing them together.

ᵇ These kinde people, so double diligent about the feminine sexe, be fitly called good womens-men : and doting overmuch upon their wives, *Uxorii* in Latin, as one would say Bridegroomes still. Such an one Seneca makes report he knew, who could not endure to be without his wives company, one minute of an houre : and if upon necessitie he went abroad into the towne, yet would he take with him a stomacher of hers, and weare it ever next his heart, etc.

[1] *Satyra.*

ANNOTATIONS

^c No doubt the same was garnished with Gold, rich stones and pretious pearles. See Plin. lib. 9, cap. 35.

^d It may be gathered it was *Hemiplegia*, which we call the dead Palsey, taking the one side of the bodie, and most commonly ensuing upon an Apoplexie, if it were not the verie Apoplexie it selfe, (which is none other but an universall palsey) considering the quicke dispatch it made.

7

^a He meaneth the crew, or faction of chariotiers holding of the blew or watchet colour : which Vitellius and Galba both affected.

11

^a So called, of an infortunate battaile fought that day neere the river Allia : in which, the Romans were overthrowne by the French : who following the train of their victory, advanced their ensignes to Rome, forced the Citie, and put it to the sacke.

^b Some read *De Dominico, i.* out of Dominicus, for so it may seeme, was the booke of Neroes Canticles entituled, alluding to himselfe, who would be called *Rerum Dominus, i.* Lord of the world.

13

^a Cornelius Celsus findeth no fault with Asclepiades, who condemned vomiting, *Offensus eorum consuetudine, qui quotidie eiiciendo vorandi facultatem moliuntur, i.* as utterly disliking their manner, who by daily casting up their gorge, seeke to enable themselves for beastly gourdmandise. And to the same purpose he saith : *Istud luxuria causa fieri non oportere, i.* That this ought not to be put in use, for to maintaine riotous excesse. He admonisheth also, *Ne quis qui valere et senescere volet, hoc quotidianum faciat,* That no man who desireth to live long and in health would make it a daily practise. But Seneca reproveth such verie aptly in these words :

> *Edunt ut vomant, vomunt ut edant.*
> They eat, to vomit, and they vomit, to eat.

^b If Scarus were not the guilt head, a delicate fish no doubt it was in those daies, and better esteemed than the Acipenser, *i.* the Sturgion. It cheweth cud, and hath plaine teeth to grind withall, not indented like a combe or saw.

14

^a *Veraculis* or *vericulis,* or *divinaculis* : all to one sense, Such as will take upon them to tell fortunes, etc. Women of this profession Apuleius termeth *veratrices.*

^b *Bonum factum.* The usuall preface or preamble premised before Edicts and Proclamations, *Boni ominis causa.*

TWELVE CÆSARS

15

ᵃ By this ceremonie, he seemed to resigne up his Empyre.

16

ᵃ Making semblance thereby, that he was fled and gone, for, the manner was, at the Porters lodge doore, if no bodie were within, to tie up a mastive dog, for to give warning abroad if any man came. And not farre from the said lodge, such a dog, with a chaine, was usually painted upon the wall, with these words, in great letters :

Cave, Cave Canem, i. Beware, Beware the Dog.

18

ᵃ He meaneth that *Gallus Gallinaceus,* or dunghill cocke, that before had perched upon his head and shoulders, alluding to the French, who are likewise named *Galli.*

ANNOTATIONS UPON
FLAVIUS VESPASIANUS AUGUSTUS

1

ᵃ The fortieth part. Happily the fortieth penie of all bargaines of sales that were unlawfull.

2

ᵃ Which had a border or broade gard about it, embroidered with purple studdes like naile-heads, and therefore was called *Latas clavus*: and thereupon, Senators themselves, *Laticlavii.*

4

ᵃ In liew of φυλλοβολία : for, in token of love and affection they should have heaped upon him gay flowers, greene leaves and pleasant fruits.

ᵇ This, no doubt, had relation to the prophesie of the True Messias, and Saviour, Jesus Christ. The very words imply no lesse, according with these out of Holy Scripture : Ἐκ σοῦ ἐξελεύσεται ὁ ἡγούμενος, etc. Read Joseph. 6 book, chap. 31, of the destruction of Jerusalem.

5

ᵃ There is an hill of that name in Judæa. And because answers had beene given from thence, and nothing there was to be seene, neyther Image of a God, nor Temple, but a bare Altar, and the rever-

282

ANNOTATIONS

ence onely of the place, both Tacitus and Suetonius by the name of Carmelus, call that unknowen God unto them, who reigneth for ever.

[b] This sight, and the other following, betokened soveraigntie unto Vespasian, who warred then in the East countries, Judæa and Syria.

7

[a] This Basilides seemeth rather to have beene some Priest, or principall man of note, and not Libertus, i. his freed man, as some copies have. But who ever he was, to the setting forward of this dissignement of Vespasian, *Nomen et omen erat.*

10

[a] Out of the 35 Tribes of Rome, were chosen certaine Judges or Commissioners, named Centumvirs, to wit, out of every Tribe three, and albeit their number arose to an hundred and five, yet roundly they went for an hundred, and so were called. These I say, being ordained *Stelitibus judicandis,* determined private and civill matters betweene man and man, *de Testamentis, Stillicidiis,* and such like of no great moment. They put forth or erected a speare in the place where they sate in Jurisdiction: whereupon their court was named *Hasta Centumviralis.*

13

[a] Alluding to the name Cynicus. For these Philosophers tooke this denomination Cynicks, eyther of their dogged and currish demaund, or of a place where they taught and disputed, called *Cynosarges.*

16

[a] Which in Augustus Cæsars time amounted to twelve hundred thousand *Sestertii*: triple to the worth of a Roman Knight.

17

[a] This Colossus, Zenodorus a famous workeman, made before time for Nero.

18

[a] As namely, *Pueros Symphoniacos,* etc., Choristers or quiristers with most sweet breaths and pleasant voyces, etc.

[b] For, then had women their *Saturnalia,* like as the men in December. Those festivall holidaies were called *Matronalia,* in memoriall of Ladie Hersilia and other noble Dames, who in old time upon that day, interposed themselves as *Mediatrices,* betweene the Romans and Sabines, readie to strike a most bloodie battell.

19

[a] This is reprehended by Cornelius Celsus, lib. 2, cap. 14, in these words, *Neque audiendi sunt, qui numero finiunt, quoties aliquis perfricandus est: Illud enim ex viribus hominis colligendum est.*

283

TWELVE CÆSARS

20

^a To be caried between men in a chayre or seat called thereupon *Sella gestatoria*, or *Lectica*. Celsus reckoneth sundrie sorts of this Gestation, to wit, *Navi, Lectica, Scamno, Vehiculo*.

21

· ^a For, it was an ordinarie matter, in supper time, betweene the services and severall dishes, to cast the Dice or cockall bones, by fits.

^b *Prætextata verba*, by the figure Antiphrasis, are put for such words as beseemed not either the mouth or the eares of *Prætextati, i.* youths well borne, and of gentle bloud descended : who, in truth, should be modest and maidenlike : and in like manner, *prætextati mores*, signifie such behaviour.

^c Noting him for his ridiculous vanitie : which φλαῦρος in Greeke doth signifie.

^d Or, if ye read before, [*perductæ*] it must so stand in the Page of expenses, to this sense, laid out, for, or to Vespasian beloved : as if he had given her a reward for loving him, whereas she should have given unto him.

22

^a Some read, in steed of *Improbius irato, improbius nato*, that is to say, of no good making, but ill shaped to his height.

^b A peece of a verse in Homer, *Iliad 7*, spoken there of Ajax, advancing forward to fight with Hector, unto whom, or to whose long pike rather, he likeneth this gangrell.

^c Eyther of Fullers, Walkers, and Diers, who gathered and occupied much thereof about their clothes, or else, for the tubs that commonly stoode in od corners and noukes of the streets, to receive every mans water, that he made as he went.

23

^a At the foresaid Cutiliæ, which was a naturall bath in the Sabines country, of medicinable waters, howbeit exceeding cold. Plin. lib. 31, cap. 31.

284

ANNOTATIONS

ANNOTATIONS UPON
TITUS FLAVIUS VESPASIANUS
AUGUSTUS

1

ᵃ A PLACE in Rome so called of a building there, which stood upon
seven courses of Columnes or Pillars, arising all round and higher
every one than other, in manner of so many circles or girdles.

ᵇ He meaneth not a Physiognomer, who hath taken upon him by
inspection of eyes, forehead, face, etc., to tell ones nature and disposition : such an one as Zopyrus was, who noted Socrates for to
be by naturall inclination a wanton lover of women : but a fortune
teller, by looking on the forehead onely. Such as in these daies, by
the art of Palmestrie, for-sooth, can assure folke, how long they shall
live, and what not. If they do but see lines in the palmes of their
hands, or by feaxe in the forehead, will say, how many wives a man
shall have, etc. As vaine as those, who by counting the letters of the
husband and the wives name, will confidently pronounce, whether of
them shall burie the other.

3

ᵃ By titles in this place, and many others of Suetonius, are to be
understood inscriptions, testifying for what considerations such Statues
were erected. Such also were usually set up at publicke executions,
to shew the offences and causes why any suffered. A thing usuall
among the Romanes in their government, in what Province so ever,
as may appeare by that which stood upon the Crosse of our Saviour
Christ.

4

ᵃ That is to say a white band or ribband : such as the Royall Diademe at first was.

6

ᵃ Of these Baines, with what speede and celerity they were finished,
Martialis writeth thus :

Hic ubi miramur velocia munera, Thermas.

8

ᵃ Dooing them thus much credit in the eyes of the world, as to give
the allowance and approbation, or otherwise, of the weapons wherewith

285

TWELVE CÆSARS

they should fight. For, in this sense may Ornaments be taken : the
rather, because some copies have *Ferramenta*. Or this place may be
understood of other furniture, as well as armes, wherwith they should
come appointed into the listes.

9

ᵃ This hath beene observed in all ages, to fore-runne the death
of some Prince. Thus, before the end of Julius Cæsar, as Virgil
writeth,

> *Non alias lato occiderunt plura sereno*
> *Fulgura, etc.*

Horace likewise,

> —— *Per purum sonantes*
> *Egit equos volucremque currum.*

Our owne Chronicles[1] also exemplifie no lesse. To say nothing of
the fresh resemblance of that, which happened with us three yeares
since, in July.

10

ᵃ Some write, and Tzetzes by name, that hee was poysoned with
eating of Sea-hares.

ANNOTATIONS UPON
FLAVIUS DOMITIANUS

1

ᵃ THIS was some Satyricall Poeme, of which Juvenalis writeth thus :

> —— *Improbior satyram scribente Cinœdo,*

i. Nerone.

ᵇ A vestment of white linnen, after the manner of a Surplice : for
such priests thereupon were named *Linigeri*.

4

ᵃ *Toga Græcanica*. Which is spoken καταχρηστικῶς, *pro chlamyde,*
i. a cloake or loose cassocke. For *Toga* was *Romanorum*.

7

ᵃ Philostratus alledgeth another reason of this Edict, namely for

[1] A little before the death of king Henry the second.

286

ANNOTATIONS

that many seditious broyles and commotions were occasioned by drunkennesse.

ᵇ Or rather, as Casabonus expoundeth [*geminari castra*] that two legions should not encampe in one leaguer. For, the pollicie of warre found the same alwaies dangerous, in regard of mutinies, that by occasion thereof might arise. Souldiers, as Dion writeth, πρὸς τὴν ὄψιν τοῦ πλήθους σφῶν θρασύνονται, i. Seeing their owne numbers great, grew to be stout and malapert.

ᶜ For, before time, it was thought good Policy, that souldiers should lay up a portion of their donative, about the Ensignes within the campe, and not spend all their stocke, (which commonly they are given unto,) whereby they might be put in minde to fight more valiantly, and not to forsake their colours, so long as they had somewhat to save or loose.

8

ᵃ Namely, to be buried quicke under the ground, that is to say, to be let downe into some grot or vault, and there to be sterved to death.

10

ᵃ *Patrem-familias, i.* A good honest Citizen of Rome, such as came to behold the Games.

ᵇ Under these tyrannicall Emperours of Rome, that favorized, some this faction of Fencers and Chariot-riders, others that, it was high Treason and Impietie, for men to speake a word, not in open place onely and in the Theatre, but also at home in their houses, even in table talke, in commendation of the adverse faction, by way of comparison. Martial inviting a friend to his bourd, and promising that no mirth and free speech at meat should turne him to any daunger and displeasure, writeth thus unto him,

> *De Prasino conviva meus vomitoque loquatur :*
> *Noc facient quenquam pocula nostra reum.*

Now, it is to be understood, that Domitius affected the fensers called *Mirmillones,* against the others named *Thraces* or *Threces,* whom his brother Titus favoured.

ᶜ By Parmularius understand, him that speaks favourably in the behalfe of those fencers, named *Parmularii,* of the little bucklers, wherwith they were armed : otherwise called *Threces,* (as one would say Thracians, whose armature they had) in opposition of others which were the *Mirmillones,* who were otherwise appointed after the French fashion, and therefore tooke the name otherwhiles of *Galli,* and so is that verse of Horace to be expounded, *Thrax an Gallina Syro par ?* As touching blasphemie, no mervaile, if these Tyrants taking upon them to be Gods heere upon earth, held everie word derogatorie any waies unto their Majestie, high Treason and impietie.

ᵈ Domitian and other such monsterous Tyrants, as namely Caligula, envied all persons and things that were excellent. It behooved there-

TWELVE CÆSARS

fore Lamia to be silent, and to dissimule what he thought, as well as he might: although, for griefe of heart, happily, hee could not chuse but fetch a secret sigh to himselfe with a *Heu, i. Helas.*

12

ᵃ I observe a double acception of this word Cæsar, in this Historie penned by Suetonius. First, for a noble house in Rome whereof Julius Cæsar Dictator was descended. Whose line, eyther in bloud or by adoption, were called Cæsares. And in this sense it is truly said, that *Progenies Cæsarum in Nerone defecit, i.* that the race of the Cæsars was extinct in Nero. And in this sense the beires apparent of the Emperours in that line were named Cæsars. Secondly, for all the Soveraigne Emperours of Rome after Julius Cesar. So Galba and the rest, his successors were stiled Cesares.

ᵇ This exaction levied of the Jewes, which he calleth *Iudaicum fiscum,* was for the profession and exercise of the religion within Rome: who, as Xiphilinus witnesseth, were permitted before, by Vespasian his father to observe the rites and ceremonies of their owne religion, paying an yearely Tribute, to wit, a Didrachme. *i.* two Roman deniers, or fifteene pence with us. And so the Christians afterwardes for a time had the same Indulgence.

13

ᵃ In some copies are inserted these words, *Aream et Calvitiem,* to no sense, unlesse ye would have him thereby noted, for his baldenesse and fall of hayre, which some Physicians call *Area.*

15

ᵃ This Flavius Clemens is thought to have beene a Proselite, and convert to the Jewish Religion [1], by reason whereof, being somewhat mortified, and making conscience to do evill, he was reputed base minded, and as Suetonius saith, *contemptissimæ inertiæ.* Imputations charged by Paganes upon Christians, and the true servants of God, for their quiet cariage and modest behaviour.

ᵇ Whose sonne, I would not else, he would be thought, as who put one to death, because in his publike prayers he had not made mention of him, as the sonne of Minerva. Philostratus, lib. 7.

17

ᵃ Little Images, which Painims devoutly kept and worshipped, (as the Tutelare Gods of their bedchamber) within a certaine Closet called *Lararium.*

18

ᵃ It may be thought by the circumstance of this place, that this *Rubor vultus* in Domitian, was a tincture of vertue and modestie. But

---

[1] Or Christianity rather.

TWELVE CÆSARS

there was nothing lesse in him, so that it was rather an hypocriticall visard and maske, under which was couched a most fell and cruell nature, as being by the judgement of Tacitus more sanguinarie than Nero. For whereas Nero, *subtraxit oculos, iussitque scelera, non spectavit, sub Domitiano præcipua miseriarum pars erat videri et aspici, cum denotandis tot hominum palloribus, sufficeret sævus ille Domitiani vultus et rubor, quo se contra pudorem muniebat.* A flushing red therefore is not alwaies a signe of grace.

20

ª At Alexandria in Ægypt, was that famous Librarie of King Ptolemæus Philadelphus and the other Ptolomæes his progenitors and successors, conteyning to the number well neere of 700000 bookes. Aul. Gel. *Noct. Attic.* lib. 7, cap. 17.

23

ª Acclamations must be restrained heere to the worse sense, for all manner of Curses and Detestations, such as before were taken up by the people in this tune, *Tiberium in Tiberim,* and afterwards by the Senate, against Commodus, that wicked Emperor, in these termes, *Hosti patriæ honores detrahantur, paricida trahatur, hostis deorum, carnifex senatus unco trahatur, in spoliario ponatur, etc.*

ᵇ Nerva, Trajanus, Hadrianus, etc. Of whom Sextus Aurelius writeth thus : *Quid Nerva prudentius aut moderatius? Quid Traiano divinius? Quid præstantius Hadriano?*

THE HISTORIE OF

AN INDEX TO THE HISTORIE
AND MARGINALL GLOSSE[1]

[1 The Marginal Gloss of the original will be found in the footnotes of this edition.]

TWELVE CÆSARS

THE HISTORIE OF

292

TWELVE CÆSARS

293

294

TWELVE CÆSARS

THE HISTORIE OF

TWELVE CÆSARS

2 : PP

THE HISTORIE OF

TWELVE CÆSARS

TWELVE CÆSARS

THE HISTORIE OF

TWELVE CÆSARS

TWELVE CÆSARS

THE HISTORIE OF

AN INDEX TO THE ANNOTATIONS

306

TWELVE CÆSARS

TWELVE CÆSARS

TWELVE CÆSARS

INDEX TO THE ANNOTATIONS

FINIS

EDINBURGH

T. & A. CONSTABLE

Printers to Her Majesty

1899

Lightning Source UK Ltd.
Milton Keynes UK
UKHW020856110119
335396UK00013B/714/P

9 781330 373217